THE BALLAD OF THE LONE MEDIEVALIST

Before you start to read this book, take this moment to think about making a donation to punctum books, an independent non-profit press,

@ https://punctumbooks.com/support/

If you're reading the e-book, you can click on the image below to go directly to our donations site. Any amount, no matter the size, is appreciated and will help us to keep our ship of fools afloat. Contributions from dedicated readers will also help us to keep our commons open and to cultivate new work that can't find a welcoming port elsewhere. Our adventure is not possible without your support.
Vive la open-access.

Fig. 1. Hieronymus Bosch, *Ship of Fools* (1490–1500)

THE BALLAD OF THE LONE MEDIEVALIST. Copyright © 2018 by editors and authors. This work carries a Creative Commons BY-NC-SA 4.0 International license, which means that you are free to copy and redistribute the material in any medium or format, and you may also remix, transform and build upon the material, as long as you clearly attribute the work to the authors (but not in a way that suggests the authors or punctum books endorses you and your work), you do not use this work for commercial gain in any form whatsoever, and that for any remixing and transformation, you distribute your rebuild under the same license. http://creativecommons.org/licenses/by-nc-sa/4.0/

First published in 2018 by punctum books, Earth, Milky Way.
https://punctumbooks.com

ISBN-13: 978-1-947447-54-7 (print)
ISBN-13: 978-1-947447-55-4 (ePDF)

LCCN: 2018940292
Library of Congress Cataloging Data is available from the Library of Congress

Book design: Vincent W.J. van Gerven Oei

HIC SVNT MONSTRA

The Ballad of the Lone Medievalist

Edited by Kisha G. Tracy & John P. Sexton

Contents

Who Was That Masked Monk? *John P. Sexton and Kisha G. Tracy*	13
The Lone Medievalist: Casting the Net *Sarah Barott and Rachel Munson*	17

The Lone Medievalist as Teacher
Breaking Free of the Cloistered Classroom

Not So Lonesome Anymore: Bridging the Disciplines through Pedagogy *Peter Burkholder*	31
Keeping It Old-School on the New Faculty Majority *Geoffrey B. Elliott*	51
Interdisciplinary/Team Teaching and the Lone Medievalist *Natalie Grinnell*	65
And Gladly Wolde He Teche: The Medievalist and the History of the English Language Course *Robert Kellerman*	71
I Know! Let's Put on a Show! *Robert Stauffer*	79

Perpetual Invention and Performance-Based Research:
The Case of The Ballad of Robin Hood and the Potter 95
Carolyn Coulson

What's the Message?:
Building Community through Tolkien's *Beowulf* 109
Holly M. Wendt

Why Read *That*?: Selling the Middle Ages 119
Diane Cady

A Trip to England: Discovering the Ties between
Medievalism and Pop Culture 137
Danielle Girard, Sarah Huff, Justine Marsella, Alicia Protze, Abbie Rosen, Jacki Teague

The Lone Medievalist as Scholar:
Opus Clamantis in Deserto

From the Monk's Cell to the Professor's Office 145
Kisha G. Tracy

Embracing the Medievalist Margin 161
Alicia Spencer-Hall

The Medievalist's Soliloquy:
Struggles and Advice for Lone Medievalists 169
Tiffany A. Ziegler

Reflections of an Embarrassed Medievalist 177
Michael Elam

The Unicorn Learns Accountability 189
Misty Urban

How to Stop Being a Lonely Medievalist 199
M. Wendy Hennequin

Blended Medievalist Careers: Staying Optimistic While
Balancing Passion and Job Market Realities 205
Timothy R.W. Jordan and Aubri Anne McVey

A Study of the Unexpected:
The Advantages of Being the "Lone Medievalist" 221
Nikolas O. Hoel

Saga Thing and the Benefits of Podcasting the Medieval 227
Andrew M. Pfrenger

The Lone Medievalist at Work:
Or, How I Learned to Stop Worrying and Love the Job

Building Your Own Villa 249
Jane Chance

Twice Marginal and Twice Invisible:
On Being the Lone Medievalist Twice in One State 259
Michelle M. Sauer

Pushing Boundaries: Making the Medieval Relevant through
Public History and Engagement On and Off Campus 267
Amber Handy

Brought to You by Your Friendly Campus Medievalist 281
Lee Templeton

Down with Dante and Chaucer? Navigating a Great Books
Curriculum as a Medievalist 289
Sarah Harlan-Haughey

Of sondry folk: What I Learned After My First Year
as the Lone Medievalist on Campus 305
Ann M. Martinez

The Collaborative Medievalist 311
Courtney Rydel

Make Yourself At Home 319
John P. Sexton

This Eremitic Life

Notes from the North 341
Laura Saetveit Miles

Being a Medievalist in an A-medieval Country and in a
Region Overcrowded with Medievality: Two Stories
from Brasil and the Western Balkans 355
Ardian Muhaj

Is the Academic Medievalist Alone? 361
Kouky J. Fianu

A Philosopher's Approach to Being a Lone Medievalist 365
Pilar Herráiz Oliva

A Lone Medievalist on the Island 369
Christine E. Kozikowski

Contributors 373

INTRODUCTION

Who Was That Masked Monk?

John P. Sexton, Bridgewater State University
Kisha G. Tracy, Fitchburg State University

Hi. Are you a Lone Medievalist?

This volume is a sequel, of sorts, to an ongoing series of round tables at the International Congress on Medieval Studies held at Western Michigan University, beginning in 2015. The impetus for those sessions, and for this book, is the sense of isolation many medieval scholars feel in their professional lives. Often the only scholar of the period in their departments, their universities, or their surrounding area, medievalists can find it challenging to advocate for their work and field. The problem is only more pronounced for the medievalist in an adjunct teaching position or without an institutional position at all. When we work alone among colleagues, teach mostly (or entirely) outside our specializations, and compete with "more easily" understood or well-funded research, it is easy to feel disconnected from the larger discipline of medieval studies. Our scholarly production slows or ceases. Our language skills atrophy. Our knowledge ossifies. Soon, even attending a conference of fellow medievalists can feel isolating. Surrounded by scholars with greater institutional support, lower teaching loads, or more robust research agendas, we may feel alienated from the field we love — the work to which we've dedicated our careers.

The Lone Medievalist exists as a partial antidote to the problem of professional isolation. The nature of medieval studies has always been collaborative — paleographers, editors, translators, archeologists, preservationists, librarians, scholars, and students may all play a part in the creation of a single so-called "monograph." Yet our physical distance from one another (and the preferences of a professional system that privileges the individual scholar) tends to de-emphasize the work of the medieval collective. Our other duties, especially teaching and institutional service, have traditionally been even less connected to that collaborative spirit. Fortunately, the advent of the internet age, and with it, social media, digital reproductions, remote-conferencing, and long-distance collaboration have all improved the lot of the solitary scholar. Knowing and working with our fellows has never been easier, and with the right encouragement can result in remarkable new directions for the field of medieval studies as a whole.

Our organization builds on those new connective conduits. The goal of the Lone Medievalist sessions was and is to encourage far-flung and isolated medievalists of all stripes to share their knowledge, experiences, and strategies for successfully pursuing and sharing their work. We hope to build a platform for medievalists to provide support to one another. The Lone Medievalist isn't focused exclusively on scholarship, on teaching, on institutional life, or on the pursuit of new learning — it's focused on all of them. We privilege all aspects of the professional and intellectual life of medievalists.

Our experience in this new era is, we hope, surprisingly akin to the monastic vocation itself. The medieval monks, whose simple anonymity inspired the look of our organizational mascot and whose cloistered lives were a combination of eremitic and collective experience, knew that a supporting institution and like-minded colleagues provided the energy that made many things possible that would be exhausting, lonely, or even impossible for a single individual. Though our profession often requires that we work in disciplinary isolation, we are more connected than our predecessors could have imagined. In our work, and in our intellectual lives, we have the chance to build a new kind of cloister for ourselves — one that encompasses the entire world.

A Lone Medievalist need no longer be an isolated medievalist.

The idea for this volume grew out of our very first International Congress round table. It was clear then that Lone Medievalists had much to say and much to offer each other. We all have our own stories and our own strategies for managing our "lone" status. We thought that a collection of these stories would be useful and unique — if not also cathartic for the contributors and the readers — and thus this volume was born. We were pleased and surprised by the response to the original call for submissions. It seemed that the topic was of great interest to many, and both those who volunteered to contribute as well as others have expressed the desire to read about such experiences.

We were also pleased by the range of responses we received, the varying types of emphases that contributors identified in their contributions. In the end, these responses have naturally organized themselves into four sections.

The Lone Medievalist as Teacher: Breaking Free of the Cloistered Classroom

In this section, Lone Medievalists discuss how to approach the classroom, from turning students into colleagues to bringing the medieval into non-medieval courses. Medievalists are traditionally innovative teachers, and Lone Medievalists, perhaps by necessity, even more so.

The Lone Medievalist as Scholar: Opus Clamantis in Deserto

A challenge often faced by Lone Medievalists is how to find the time and the resources to maintain scholarship. While scholarship may not always follow the traditional paths that we became used to in graduate school, we can be creative in using our time and resources wisely — and maybe even forge new paths in the meantime.

The Lone Medievalist at Work: Or, How I Learned to Stop Worrying and Love the Job

The professional reality is that many of us are without colleagues who share our areas of expertise and interest. In most cases, a department will hire only a single medieval specialist — and may be hard-pressed to convince administrations or hiring committees to approve even that one. These essays provide suggestions and ideas for professional engagement, curriculum planning, and reappointment and tenure cases as the Lone Medievalist in a department or institution.

This Eremitic Life

Think being the only medievalist in your department is difficult? What about being the only one in a whole country? In this section, we get glimpses into the lives of Lone Medievalists on a global scale.

When we started organizing this collection, we were adamant that it would not be a forum simply for bewailing the state of medieval studies in small institutions. While we all recognize and acknowledge the challenges in being Lone Medievalists, these essays are deliberately crafted to offer strategies, camaraderie, advice, and alternatives. We hope readers find it forward-thinking and revitalizing as well as helpful to those of us in these positions.

The Lone Medievalist: Casting the Net

Sarah Barott & Rachel Munson, The Lone Medievalist Staff

When we first attended the International Congress for Medieval Studies in 2013, we had just begun to dip our toes into the expansive world of Medieval Studies. When we returned home we were so inspired that we both began extensively studying the Middle Ages and founded the Bemidji State University Medieval Club. Within months we had a solid community of medievalists and we felt at home. In 2015 at the 50th Annual International Congress for Medieval Studies, we attended the "Ballad of the Lone Medievalist" panel hosted by Dr. Kisha Tracy of Fitchburg State University and Dr. John Sexton of Bridgewater State University. We were astonished by how many medievalists felt alone at their universities. Didn't everyone have a colleague who studied medieval scholarship on their campus? The surprising answer was no. It was our understanding that the Lone Medievalist project, founded by Dr. Tracy and Dr. Sexton, began with the intent of creating a series of panels and publications to connect medievalists from around the world. We recognized the Lone Medievalist project's need for a more substantial community outside of the short amount of time allotted them at conferences. We thought a good basis would be to create a virtual community that emulated what we felt on our home campus.

Sarah then suggested an online hub which would allow medieval scholars to join together, share in discussion, trade syllabi, and connect for conferences. The next thing we knew we were having lunch with Dr. Tracy and Dr. Sexton and were exploring the idea further. We left our meeting with the go-ahead to get a website up and running for The Lone Medievalist.

The four of us began having weekly digital meetings to establish who was emailing whom, what projects we wanted to begin, and how we would create and edit our site. Before launching the website, a network of support was needed. We had compiled an extensive list of medievalist contacts and called upon all of them for help. One of the things that always fascinated us about the medieval conference system is the willingness to help burgeoning scholars.

Sarah Barott on Website Development

Our main goals for the website are collaboration, community, and scholarship. We wanted to create a resource for everyone to use and a way to get in touch with scholars from other schools. However, forming a community created a couple problems that we did not foresee.

The first large problem we ran into was deciding what tone to set for the website. We wanted to gear everything toward the Lone Medievalist, but we also wanted to make sure that we could get in touch with people from larger research universities to help recreate the collective that exists within these institutions at smaller universities. The website needed to be scholarly and have information readily-available, but also create the kind of engaging academic experience people have come to expect from their media. We wanted to include the jokes that no one else seemed to get and the open, helpful sense of comradery that we found at Kalamazoo. The Lone Medievalist Online has been designed to be informal and welcoming, but professional and scholarly.

Once we set the tone, we had to decide what type of website to use. After various suggestions ranging from a blog to a wiki, we settled on Wix. Wix.com is a program that helps the less-than tech savvy design websites. Wix is creator-friendly, easy to set-up and to maintain. There are applications available for purchase, but a problem with Wix is that it's difficult to get people to *use* said applications. For instance our discussion board "Mutt" takes people away from the website and forces them to register on a different page. We feel that this has deterred many people from using our discussion board, which is unfortunate because we envisioned it being such a wonderful tool.

Another app that caused a problem on the site was the syllabi drop box. We designed this area of the site for scholars to place any syllabi they felt comfortable sharing. The first app that we used on Wix was not helpful, in that it would only show one syllabi at a time. We wanted a whole bank of syllabi for people to draw from, not just one highlighted syllabus. We thought about creating a Dropbox, but decided to use Google Drive instead. This has been incredibly helpful because, when people send syllabi to the Lone Medievalist, we can click once and share it on the site. So far we've received syllabi from a diverse group of scholars. Now that this issue has been fixed, the Google Drive works well for its purposes.

Many discussions revolved around what type of content to add to the site. Because the site is run by a small group of volunteers (five to be exact), we rely on suggestions from others. So far getting people involved on the actual website has been difficult. Our social media stream, an area on our homepage that publishes our Facebook and Twitter feeds, has almost taken the place of a chat room. Initially, we had hoped that the site would provide a sense of community that took place directly at thelonemedievalist.com and not exclusively on social media. As things stand, The Lone Medievalist Online seems to be working as more of a newsletter and announcements of what we do.

One feature we were excited about was the Google Map application. We placed a comment bar next to the Google Map in hopes that our viewers (currently 188[1]) would place unique and unexpected resources on the map. We wanted larger libraries,

---

1   As of July 2016.

museums, high schools, or smaller colleges looking for steady lecture streams, language camps, etc. The Lone Medievalist must look for out-of-the-box places to get to a physical community that can help keep skills in English, History, Archaeology, and the Arts honed. We are worried that the red dots might become an overwhelming sea, therefore we are exploring the use of another map system, but for now the map works wonderfully.

Our syllabi drop box, book review section, and other content-driven areas of the site caused a bit of discussion concerning how open we wanted the site to be. While the goal of The Lone Medievalist Online is to be open to the public we felt that much of the response areas, syllabi content, and book reviews warranted an amount of privacy and user control. We considered privacy settings to protect intellectual property as much as possible. In our digital age of online harassment, we also felt it necessary to know who was logging onto the site and to retain the right to block them from the site if necessary (Wix does provide this ability). As a result, members of the website are asked to log in with an email address and password. We debated for a while on the necessity of having guidelines on an academic site, as we didn't want to impede anyone's discussion. In the end we decided that an open community like ours must have guidelines to follow. We have done our best to encourage discussion while still maintaining standards. We have not seen any problems like this occur, but feel that being prepared never hurts.

We currently have 188 site members, people who have created accounts and now have access to the full expanse of the website. This number is much lower than our social interactions on Facebook and Twitter, which hasn't troubled us too much. It is much easier to "like" a page on Facebook and checking Facebook for updates has been integrated into daily life. We know that it will take time before the same can be said for The Lone Medievalist website, but we hope to obtain the same sense of automatically checking for new content at least once a month.

Rachel Munson on Social Media

Social media sites are intricate webs that allow for successful marketing campaigns, public outreach, personal and business-based promotions, and act as resources for connections and memes. I began creating the Lone Medievalist social media outlets on August 6, 2015 by creating a Twitter account, a Facebook page, and a Pinterest profile. In my experience, Twitter and Facebook are the social media outlets on which we can obtain maximum impact. The Pinterest page acts primarily as storage for medieval content, such as pictures, articles, etc.

Facebook has become a major marketing resource. People of nearly any age, businesses both large and small, public figures (such as Chaucer), and even cats have Facebook. It works as a useful tool for starting and sustaining community. Within the first day of being live on Facebook, we had 146 followers. Within the first week, 264 followers. Within the first month, 312 followers. As of July 21st, 2016, a little less than a year old, we gathered 585 followers and are averaging a total reach of 4,665 Facebook users a week.[2]

The Lone Medievalist Online's launch occurred on August 10, 2015,[3] and we intentionally published the site after the establishment of our social media outlets and the commencement of an intense social media campaign to gain momentum for the project. I created a total of twenty postable graphics to engage and excite our followers in the four days leading to the website's reveal. Creating a graphic for followers to interact with visually

---

[2] Total reach is defined as all those who have seen our posts. Typically on Facebook, a single activity will tell you how many people have clicked "like" on said activity and how many people the post has reached. Followers and non-followers can see our posts and Facebook is set up by its managers to show posts to various users.

[3] Due to the anticipation and build of the launch, August analytics demonstrate a strong outlier peak, hence the sharp decrease between August and September on the above graph. As the project ages more accurate numbers will be attained.

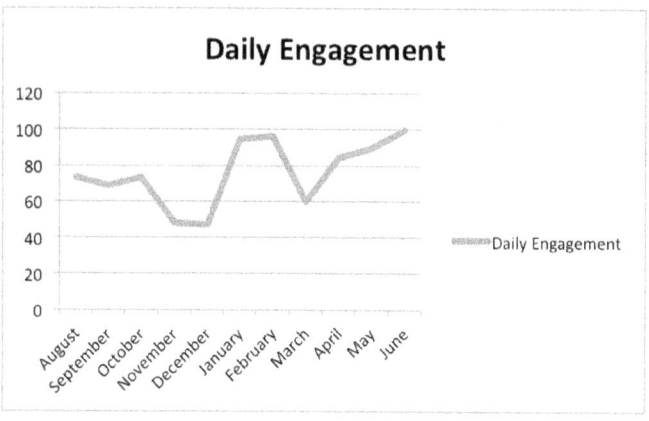

is one of the best tools that social media managers can use to increase engagement.

Collecting analytical data is vital in creating a clear and succinct plan for the future. Since our Facebook birth, The Lone Medievalist has averaged two "likes" every day, a daily engagement[4] of seventy-eight users, a daily organic reach[5] of 930, and 57,975 organic impressions[6] per 28-day cycle.

A benefit to our Lone Medievalist team has been having a very interactive co-founder who is able to access and share content. Dr. Tracy has been pivotal in the development and engagement of our social media outlets and followers.

There was a time when Twitter and Facebook battled for user attention, but over the past few years it has become clear that using both outlets is the recipe for a successful marketing campaign. Twitter, with its high-paced atmosphere, allows for more

---

4 Facebook engagement is based on those who interact with our page, whether is be a physical click or a story generated from our content.

5 Organic reach is measured by how many Facebook users have visited our Page, or saw our Page or one of its posts in their news feed or ticker. This includes those who have "liked" our Page and those who have yet to like our Page.

6 Organic impressions represents the number of times our posted content was seen in a Facebook News Feed or ticker.

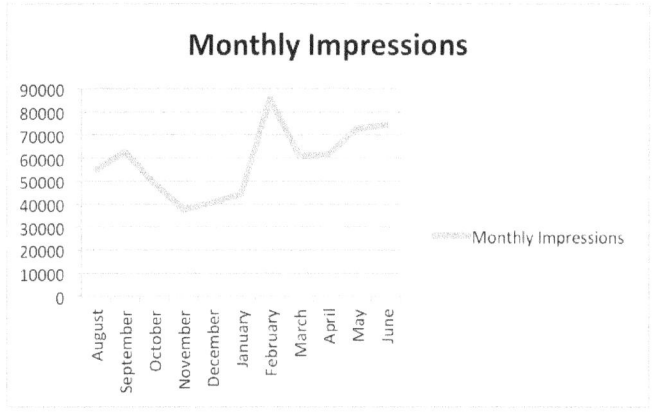

frequent and repetitive content posts. In the world of Facebook, with the strict EdgeRank algorithm,[7] it is possible to drown content, meaning that posts get buried and not seen, thus making the post's value nearly moot. On Twitter, a user must constantly post in order to *not* get lost amongst all the content that Twitter users are posting. Since our Twitter page was launched on August 7, 2015, we have made 941 Tweets, gathered 530 followers, and have followed 420 other Twitter users. Our Twitter handle[8] is @LoneMedievalist, and, although we have had mild success with our hash-tagging efforts, there is still a lot of engagement work to be done on Twitter.

Moving forward it is my goal to track Twitter analytical data more thoroughly and accurately. It remains true that gathering analytical data is extremely important and having a strong team of co-workers to assist in the actual content posts allows me more time to focus on the metrics of what works and what doesn't for any given social media campaign and outlet. My goal for the future of @LoneMedievalist on Twitter is to maintain

---

7 The EdgeRank Algorithm is a strict formula set in place with the creators of Facebook to monitor any given post's organic reach and impressions.
8 An identifying hashtag, a word or phrase that is associated with a specific Twitter page or topic.

and gather more metrics to assist in the development of future marketing plans for this project. Overall, analytics prove that we have been averaging a 17.37% increase in engagement from month to month demonstrating the success of our campaign. This is impressive for being less than a year old.

A challenge that we have confronted is engaging both men and women equally. Being a team of three women (Sarah Barott, Dr. Tracy, and myself) and one man (Dr. Sexton), many of our social media posts have a distinctly feminine voice. This is not a bad thing, and we do not mean to say that genders cannot intersect but we fear that we are missing a potential audience. On Facebook, 61% of our current[9] followers are women, and 37% are men. According to a study conducted by Monica Anderson with the Pew Research Center study in 2015, a heavier female presence on Facebook is not uncommon, sitting at about 77% in relation to 66% male counterparts.[10] However, Sarah and I have brainstormed heavily on how to attract and engage more men with our page. We are still working on building our male audience. We have also discussed how to engage a wider spectrum of age groups. Our age demographic primarily lies between the ages of 25 and 44 years old. 38.6% of our female followers and 23.2% of our male followers fall within this age range. Yes, this is a wide age range and is an entirely acceptable and appreciated age group, but the more the merrier. Our next largest age group are those who fall between 45 and 54 years old. 17.06% of our total followers fall within that age spectrum. This is not a significant deviation from Facebook demographics which conveys an 82% usage rate from 18 to 29 year olds, 79% of 30 to 49 year olds, and 64% of 50 to 64 year olds,[11] however consistent outreach to varying demographics is the best marketing strategy we can employ.

---

9 As of June 2016.

10 Monica Anderson, "Men catch up with women on overall social media use," *Pew Research Center* (August 2015), http://pewrsr.ch/1KS03ST.

11 Maeve Duggan, "The Demographics of Social Media Users," *Pew Research Center* (August 2015), http://www.pewinternet.org/2015/08/19/the-demographics-of-social-media-users/.

When Sarah and I joined this project in May of 2015, we had a clear understanding that this was to be a global campaign to unite Lone Medievalists within a cohesive and communicative hub. This understanding was only strengthened with our social media presence as, though the majority of our followers live within the United States (65.469%), 33.149% of our followers live elsewhere. We engage with Lone Medievalists from the United Kingdom, France, The Bahamas, Vietnam, Brazil, etc. We cross language barriers and interact with those who speak Portuguese, Italian, German, etc. Our efforts in the world of social media is truly crossing borders and connecting medievalists in ways that it never has before.

Another challenge that we've faced recently is a discussion on what type of information we want to post to our social media feed. We want the site to portray professionalism and scholarship, but it is important in an online setting to include pop/modern culture. Thus, it is important to provide our followers will a variety of information that covers a wide range of topics and appeal. We want to be as comfortable posting from Buzzfeed as we are from scholarly publications. Sometimes a little humor, such as the existence of cookie cutters in the shape of a castle or a cat sitting on a gargoyle, can go a long way—especially in the world of social media.[12] Sometimes communities need the lighthearted side of life, along with the heavier scholarly life. Our ability to post a spectrum of content has worked wonders in gaining followers and engagement.

Creating a heavy online presence in the world of Medieval Studies is something that has not *really* been done before. Yes, there are organizations that infiltrate and promote cross-cultural and cross-border interactions, but creating an arena that is both informal and professional is something that has not yet been seen. We have received and addressed comments about this issue, and, when we have been asked why we post comics, middlebrow, or trendy articles to our social media pages and

---

12 The picture we posted of a cat sitting on a gargoyle from the National Trust had an organic reach of 937 people and gathered 50 likes.

website, the simple answer is this: we recognize the importance of upholding the standards of scholarship and professionalism, but in an online setting that is meant to foster a familial community essence, not everything is 100% formal. We wanted to create a community that could operate like a family: with laughter, discussion, formalities, and informalities. This, we believe, is the basis of a well-built community that will last and welcome medievalists of all ages and experience. Further, if we want to create a community that mimics that of a campus environment, we must also invoke the humor and kindness that drew us to the field in the first place.

The Future

Sarah traveled to the Southeastern Medieval Association (SEMA) conference, during which The Lone Medievalist held an informal dinner to ask for feedback, comments, or suggestions that might aid in our success. The dinner went extremely well, and we gleaned a great deal of useful information. One suggestion that we have decided to implement is a book review resource on the site. We do have an informal book review section of the site, but the new book review area will be geared towards Lone Medievalists who need books that deal in generalities for less specific areas of study. The trick to executing this new page successfully will be getting actual reviews from participants.

One of the main problems that has come up repeatedly when we speak to Lone Medievalists is how to integrate medieval topics into English survey classes. Many people don't have the time to search for a student-level book that is not hyper-focused. We want to start assigning books to undergraduates to foster young writers in professionalism and have them shortly offer a review of the book, commenting on how helpful it was and what it entails that might work for more generalized courses. With the book review site we would like to post ideas and specific syllabi for which this approach has worked: for example, integrating the medieval into composition classes if possible. This would give Lone Medievalists a source for finding books to buy for the library, their classes, or themselves without being forced to research extensively. The added benefit of helping professionalize graduate students would make this project a worthwhile endeavor.

Simplicity is vital in our endeavor. Understanding the busy and crowded lives that Lone Medievalists live, we want to create as many simple resources as possible on our site. A concern that we have heard (and experienced) a multitude of times is the loss of language skills due to busy schedules. One area of the site we would like to establish is a language page, on which people could start correspondence in Old English, Old Norse, or Latin, etc. It would contain links, fun language challenges (such as a book club that reads *Alice in Wonderland* in Old English together), or just a place to discuss a problems with translation. Again, the chat room forum has been suggested for this area, but a more structured approach seems like a good idea as well. Our goal is to make pursuing skills and passions as easy as possible in the busy lives of medievalists.

Another future idea we are looking into is a guide to help create a medieval club on any campus as a means to provide Lone Medievalists a way to reach out to students. This guide would be easily printable and have a list of ideas that would work on any given campus. We recognize that every campus is unique and that the guide may not apply to every campus, but we would strive to make it as general as possible.

Another area that we intend to expand upon in the future is travel funding. Many Lone Medievalists struggle with finding funding for trips to conferences, research, and other related costs. Our end goal for this section of The Lone Medievalist Online would be a page of easily accessible grants for smaller schools. When a Lone Medievalist is asked to teach a heavy load, he/she doesn't always have time to hunt down research grants. At this point, The Lone Medievalist would step in and create a network so they wouldn't have to do so.

Further, the site is designed to assist in the social components of scholarship. We do have the conference connection page for medievalists to connect at conferences and assist them in finding rides, scheduling dinners, etc. However, the area we want to work on is identifying other Lone Medievalists at conferences. In the (admittedly few) conferences we have attended, we've always been with a small group but interacted with many people who came by themselves. If we could publicize where we are going to be at any given time during a conference, or if a Lone Medievalist wanted to ask a question about what hotels to check out, where everyone will be eating dinner, and other pertinent information from our site, we could eliminate the feeling of being alone at conferences. It's hard to be in a place where everyone else seems to know someone. This application/announcement/social media presence would give the Lone Medievalist a chance to meet others who are also visiting a new city by themselves. We are currently working on an identifying tool to be worn or displayed at conferences for Lone Medievalists; at the International Congress in 2016, we handed out stickers with our logo to help Lone Medievalists find each other. This is also when Twitter becomes an essential component of the medievalist's life. We are very rarely away from their cell phones or wireless devices, Facebook, or Twitter. At conferences, Tweeting is on the rise. We plan to Tweet at any and all of our upcoming conferences.

We have big plans for the future of The Lone Medievalist Online. More importantly, we feel we have struck a nerve and have expanded upon the need discovered by Dr. Tracy and Dr. Sexton for a cohesive community of Lone Medievalists. In our ever-changing world of technology and social interactions, there is infinite opportunity for growth and expansion for medieval academia. Digital humanities provide tools that are proving to be increasingly helpful in the world of medieval scholarship, bridging geographical gaps by acting as vehicles for sharing content, ideas, and passions.

The Lone Medievalist as Teacher

Breaking Free of the Cloistered Classroom

Not So Lonesome Anymore: Bridging the Disciplines through Pedagogy

Peter Burkholder, Fairleigh Dickinson University

It's perhaps inevitable for medievalists to feel a bit isolated. The very terms "medieval" and "Middle Ages" hardly conjure up positive images among the general public and even our non-brethren academics, resulting in such negative stereotypes towards the field that meaningful discourse can end before it even begins. When not surrounded by kindred specialists, it's tempting to empathize with pre-millennial Irish monks sailing out bravely into the North Atlantic, pretending the professional solitude is precisely what we seek, even if it isn't.

Those who study the Middle Ages could be forgiven for feeling that their situation is unique, that no one else could possibly understand the seclusion which comes with studying societies long ago and far away, with trying to appreciate mindsets and worldviews of people who often thought in fundamentally different, even perplexing ways. What else to do but don our emotional armor and carry on as academic outliers?

This is all a romantic notion, but probably an unnecessary one. As a medievalist, I'll be the first to testify that fellow academics often can't appreciate the nature of what I study and all the attendant problems that crop up as a consequence of investigating a distant and foreign past. But some perspective is needed. Looking at the makeup of my own department — not a history department, but an interdisciplinary social sciences and humanities one, as is so often the case at smaller liberal arts colleges — it becomes apparent that the faculty mostly consist of one-off specialists like me. There are multiple political scientists, but their training and research foci diverge significantly, a pattern holding true for the sociologists and criminologists as well. While I'm the sole premodernist, my fellow historians' interests are scattered across time and space, meaning they too, face obstacles to connecting not only with their history colleagues, but with the other social scientists. Our one anthropologist and solitary geographer can make valid claims to being the most isolated members of the department. Suddenly my predicament seems not so daunting in comparison with the latter two and is probably on par with the remaining departmental cohort. Maybe we're all plying the metaphorical waters of the North Atlantic, but at least we're doing so as a small, if dispersed, squadron.

Is academic isolation something that affects only my department? Hardly. My colleagues over in biology, to take but one example, find themselves in a similar predicament. Although they all fall under the same disciplinary rubric, their specialties range from cell biology to genetics to evolution to ecotoxicology. Like my own department, the biologists attest that there's precious little overlap between their research fields. Scientists they all may be, but their common bonds get increasingly fragile as we expand their academic horizon to include such related fields as chemistry, physics and computer science. Our squadron of isolation might be growing into a bona fide fleet.

And yet, many of us *do* manage to communicate with each other — and it's not just social niceties or the usual faculty banter. Nor is it only the historians talking substantively with other historians, but the biologists with the psychologists, the mathematicians with the writing faculty. Such interdisciplinary discourse might appear improbable on the face of it, until we remember the activity in which we all partake, and to which we probably devote more time and energy than any other professional requirement, namely: teaching.[1]

In 2009 I founded the Faculty Teaching Development Committee on my campus, and it's met at least once a month during the academic year ever since. Instructors from across the spectrum of disciplines gather to talk about pedagogical scholarship, to host teaching- and learning-related presentations, to observe fellow instructors for non-evaluative purposes, and to view and discuss documentaries on issues in higher education. A parallel group on research development (of which I was a member) struggled to last for a single year, ultimately folding due to lack of participation. Why the different fates of these two groups?

A Personal Trajectory towards Teaching & Learning

A little personal reflection is perhaps instructive at this juncture. Besides the fact that my undergraduate training was not in history (I double-majored in mathematics and French), the impression I get is that my own graduate school experience was fairly typical. Attending two different research-oriented, large public institutions, I was primarily trained for historical research. Teaching was performed first as a teaching assistant, then as an instructor of my own courses as I neared degree completion. Pedagogical development was spotty, unsystematic and obviously of secondary import. After finishing the doctorate, I inevitably taught my medium-size, public university students the same way I'd done while a graduate student, thereby mim-

---

[1] On relative time spent by historians on teaching vs. other professional responsibilities, see Robert Townsend, "Gender and Success in Academia: More from the Historians' Career Paths Survey," *Perspectives on History* 51, no. 1 (January 2013): esp. Fig. 3: Average Number of Hours per Week Spent on Academic and Personal Activities, http://www.historians.org/perspectives/issues/2013/1301/Historians-Career-Path-Survey-Gender-and-Success.cfm. On faculty in general, see Jeffrey Milem et al., "Faculty Time Allocation: A Study of Change over Twenty Years," *Journal of Higher Education* 71, no. 4 (2000): 454–75.

icking the instruction I'd witnessed while an undergraduate and teaching assistant.

None of this is to say that the instruction I'd observed or received was of poor quality, though in hindsight, some probably was. But like the vast majority of other history PhDs who are lucky enough to land full-time positions, I found myself the lone specialist at an institution (not my current one) whose prime directive was not research but teaching (in fact, we didn't even offer a history major). Much criticism has been directed toward the current model of graduate education for precisely this reason — that it's incommensurate with the actual work in which most of its alumni will engage.[2] In the field of history, only a small minority (perhaps 25%) of PhDs will end up at research-intensive institutions.[3] In my case, the signs of a mismatch appeared early. To take but one example, students had no idea how to read primary sources — documents which I knew were important and felt compelled to assign, but which I rarely even got to, given the "coverage" approach (an issue discussed below) I took to my courses. Despite generally positive student ratings, I knew I had a teaching problem, but I couldn't put my finger on precisely what it was, let alone how to fix it.

I was quite fortunate that, in my third year on the job, my campus formed a scholarship of teaching and learning (SoTL) cohort as part of a system-wide initiative in public higher education. I successfully applied to the program and was exposed for the first time to pedagogical literature. One of the first ar-

---

[2] Spanning 14 years' worth of debate on this matter, see Denise Magner, "Critics Urge Overhaul of Ph.D. Training, but Disagree Sharply on How to Do So," *The Chronicle of Higher Education* (28 April 2000), http://chronicle.com/article/Critics-Urge-Overhaul-of-PhD/27472; and Leonard Cassuto, "How Should Graduate School Change?" *The Chronicle of Higher Education* (13 January 2014), http://chronicle.com/article/How-Should-Graduate-School/143945/. For more in-depth coverage, see Leonard Cassuto, *The Graduate School Mess: What Caused It and How We Can Fix It* (Cambridge: Harvard University Press, 2015).

[3] James Grossman, "To Be a Historian Is to Be a Teacher: Integrating History Education into Graduate Training," *Perspectives on History* 53, no. 8 (2015): 9–10.

ticles I read, by SoTL pioneer Randy Bass of Georgetown University, was nothing short of an epiphany: teaching problems aren't "bad things"; rather, just like in our traditional research, such problems represent opportunities to explore, grapple with, improve upon and share.[4] I was naively astonished that other academics — and not just historians — struggled with the same issues I did, and I was likewise astonished at the volume of scholarship pertaining to matters of teaching and learning. This was a new but exciting field to me, one which transgressed disciplinary boundaries, so that my isolation as a medievalist was no longer a liability. I became a mentor to new initiates to the SoTL program; I collaborated with instructors across a wide range of disciplines; I received a year-long teaching fellowship; I met Randy Bass, and even traveled to Georgetown to do some work with his Visible Knowledge Project; I actively experimented with new (though not always successful) approaches to teaching the past; and I began sharing my experiences at conferences and in publications.

Those first five years were critical, as I'd been at a crossroads without even knowing it. It would've been easy — maybe even typical — to blame my early teaching problems on the students, to continue instructing them in the same flawed ways, to pour my efforts into the research for which I'd been specifically trained while in graduate school. Maybe that would've brought even greater professional success, depending on how one measures it. But my chosen path positioned me well for when I moved to my present position at a small liberal arts college contained within a larger private university. Classes are small, allowing me to work closely with students in ways I couldn't at my previous institutions. My knowledge of pedagogy and professional development also permitted me to establish the teaching development committee described previously, thus overlaying a SoTL framework onto a college where it previously hadn't existed, and replicating the process of bringing together colleagues

---

4 Randy Bass, "The Scholarship of Teaching: What's the Problem?" *Inventio* 1, no. 1 (1999), https://my.vanderbilt.edu/sotl/files/2013/08/Bass-Problem1.pdf.

from across the disciplines. Looking back, it's hard to imagine I made a bad career choice by devoting so much time and energy to teaching and learning pursuits.

Teaching & Learning Issues as Shared Experience

Teaching has been described as an act of isolation.[5] On the one hand, the term is ironic: by definition, teaching involves interacting with those being taught. But there's validity in the phrase as well, insofar as we tend to spend very little time actually observing what our fellow academics do as teachers. There's the obligatory teaching observation for annual review and promotion purposes, and we tend to collectively gripe about flagrant student behavior and administrative shortcomings. Yet, substantive, evidence-based pedagogical discourse requires a serious commitment. Even at self-identified "teaching first" institutions, faculty performing risk-reward calculations may conclude that the surest path to professional success lies not in pedagogy, but in traditional research.[6] Matters of teaching and learning thus get shunted to secondary positions of importance, leaving us much the poorer for it: there is more overlap in our classroom challenges than we may realize, so that teaching constitutes a *lingua franca* for academics who might otherwise have difficulty communicating across their disciplinary divides.[7] The

---

5 See for instance Jeffrey Mirel and Simona Goldin, "Alone in the Classroom: Why Teachers Are Too Isolated," *The Atlantic* (17 April 2012), http://www.theatlantic.com/national/archive/2012/04/alone-in-the-classroom-why-teachers-are-too-isolated/255976/.

6 Faculty views on this matter are distilled in Richard Arum and Josipa Roksa, *Academically Adrift: Limited Learning on College Campuses* (Chicago: University of Chicago Press, 2011), 5–13; on historians' views in particular, see Townsend, "What Makes a Successful Academic Career in History?" *Perspectives on History* 50, no. 9 (December 2012): esp. Fig. 3: Perceived Value of Particular Activities for Promotion and Tenure at Institution, by Carnegie Type, http://www.historians.org/perspectives/issues/2012/1212/What-Makes-a-Successful-Academic.cfm.

7 In this vein, see Peter Burkholder, "Transcending Disciplinary Boundaries: Conversations about Student Research Projects," *Faculty Focus* (23 June 2014), http://www.facultyfocus.com/articles/teaching-and-learning/

research development committee, mentioned earlier, folded for lack of establishing these intersections.

What common issues do medievalists and other academics face? How do these issues transcend the field of medieval history and allow for productive conversations with those outside of our subject area? When it comes to how faculty teach their disciplines, the overlaps are potentially many. One might think that an undergraduate survey course on medieval history would have little in common with, say, a calculus or political science or pharmacy course. But that's only if we remain locked in our disciplinary silos, thinking of our classes as collections of course-specific material where the students' job is to master content. The latter is what leads to an incoherent, balkanized undergraduate curriculum where there are no obvious connections between classes, where integrated learning happens only by happy accidents. Making matters worse, experts and non-experts arrange and connect knowledge in fundamentally different ways. While a professional historian can readily appreciate how a communications, writing or math course could benefit those enrolled in history classes (and vice versa), students tend to view such offerings as discrete units to satisfy graduation requirements and with no obvious overlap or mutually supporting attributes.[8] Such a tendency is further reinforced if those other courses emphasize gaining knowledge over the development of higher-order modes of understanding.

Do medievalists aspire to instill not just content, but more sophisticated ways of thinking in their charges? I've never met one who doesn't make that claim, but good intentions don't necessarily yield desired results — much as I learned in my first two years of full-time employment. There's been precious little ac-

---

transcending-disciplinary-boundaries-conversations-student-research-projects/; and "Backward Design, Forward Progress," *Faculty Focus* (16 May 2016), http://www.facultyfocus.com/articles/instructional-design/backward-design-forward-progress/.

8 See Susan Ambrose et al., *How Learning Works: 7 Research-Based Principles for Smart Teaching* (San Francisco: Jossey-Bass, 2010), ch. 2: "How Does the Way Students Organize Knowledge Affect Their Learning?"

tual research done on how college-level historians in general, and medievalists in particular, actually design and teach their classes. But what little there is suggests that what's called the "coverage model" predominates. That is, the past is an agreed-upon story, an assembly of people, places and events, and a quality history course dutifully "covers" this material.[9] The disturbing logical corollary: a "better" course delivers even more content. The threat of inundating students with a tidal wave of factual material looms large, especially in medieval courses which routinely treat hundreds of years' worth of history. Content does matter, but it can become tyrannical, crowding out the higher-order thinking skills faculty identify as crucial to a college education.[10]

Even if a general story of the Middle Ages could be agreed upon — and I have grave doubts about that prospect — medievalists inevitably would have to pare down that content as a matter of practicality; lone medievalists may feel especially apprehensive about the selection process.[11] After all, their courses may be the students' only exposure to the Middle Ages, so culling anything may seem like sacrilege. But this constitutes a false choice and a misapprehension. First, the "problem" of cutting

---

9 Joel Sipress and David Voelker, "From Learning History to Doing History: Beyond the Coverage Model," in *Exploring Signature Pedagogies*, eds. Regan Gurung et al., 19–35 (Sterling: Stylus, 2009); Lendol Calder, "Uncoverage: Toward a Signature Pedagogy for the History Survey," *Journal of American History* 92 (2006): 1358–70.

10 Opinions on the role of content are overviewed in Burkholder, "A Content Means to a Critical Thinking End: Group Quizzing in History Surveys," *The History Teacher* 47, no. 4 (2014): 551–78, at 552–55. Faculty's expressed views on the importance of higher-order learning (e.g., critical thinking) as opposed to content mastery are found in Arum and Roksa, *Academically Adrift,* 35–36. But the authors demonstrate that college education falls well short of achieving those goals; ibid., 73–77.

11 The inherent problem of selecting topics and chronologies for the Middle Ages is touched on in Joel Rosenthal, "Teaching the Medieval Survey: All of Europe!!" *Studies in Medieval and Renaissance Teaching* 23, no. 1 (2016): 135–46. Rosenthal addresses real issues pertaining to subject matter selection, but he also inadvertently highlights the problem of beginning course design with content as opposed to learning goals.

content is an issue only if content mastery is the primary learning goal of the course — and as indicated above, most medievalists, and faculty in general, would reject that premise, even if their course designs and teaching practices say otherwise. More likely, it is the habits of mind of historians in general, and medievalists in particular, that we seek to introduce to, and develop in, our students. The history of the Middle Ages serves as a necessary and vital context in this pursuit, but knowledge of the medieval period is a means to a higher and transferable cognitive end, not an end unto itself.[12]

Second, the solitary premodernist can find solace in the fact that teachers in *all* disciplines face the same impossibility of covering it all, and thus that selective treatment of material is an inevitability and a skill going beyond the confines of medieval history. It's easy enough to appreciate how related disciplines in the humanities and social sciences necessarily choose what topics to cover and which texts to use. It's also understandable that success in some courses (e.g., calculus) is predicated on a certain degree of mastery in a prerequisite (e.g., algebra). But even the sciences share with medievalists the pedagogical conundrum of content choice and selecting from methods for introducing, explaining and working with basic course material. Rather than viewing our classes primarily as vehicles for content delivery, Grant Wiggins and Jay McTighe argue persuasively for "backward design," that is, building our courses around desired learning goals and assessment from the outset. Only when the latter issues are identified and agreed upon is content marshalled to serve those needs, instead of the reverse.[13]

---

12 On the need to actively use content, not just cover it, see Maryellen Weimer, "Diversifying the Role Course Content Plays," *Faculty Focus* (24 September 2014), http://www.facultyfocus.com/articles/teaching-professor-blog/course-content-can-fulfill-multiple-roles/.

13 Grant Wiggins and Jay McTighe, *Understanding by Design,* exp. 2nd edn. (Upper Saddle River: Pearson, 2005); and Burkholder, "Backward Design."

Cryptic Texts & Multiple Histories

In his useful though idiosyncratic study of the habits and practices of the country's best college teachers, Ken Bain introduces the idea of the "expectation failure." This is a situation where students are confronted with the fact that their extant modes of understanding won't serve them in a new context, and ideally this permeates the college landscape. (The ubiquitous notion that medieval seafarers thought the earth was flat is a simple example of this type of learning impediment.) Such failures are not a bad thing; on the contrary, they're essential to pushing students into new, more sophisticated ways of thinking.[14] What constitutes a substantive expectation failure in history courses, medieval or otherwise? There are several candidates, but I'll limit myself to just two here: first, the productive reading of primary sources, which requires metatextual analysis and empathy; and second, grappling with and evaluating the ever-changing past, as manifested in historiography. Both of these tend to receive minimal attention in K-12 education (with Advanced Placement courses being a notable exception). In fact, a broad survey of the general public's pre-college experiences with academic history exposes an emphasis on dry and seemingly useless content. Most students thus arrive in college history classrooms with a simplified view of the past, one which is static and generally agreed upon, and their perceived job is to absorb and reproduce as much information about that past as possible.[15] Hitting stu-

---

14 Ken Bain, *What the Best College Teachers Do* (Cambridge: Harvard University Press, 2004), 28. The reader might find the related idea of "learning bottlenecks" useful in this context; see Arlene Díaz et al., "The History Learning Project: A Department 'Decodes' Its Students," *The Journal of American History* 94, no. 4 (2008): 1211–24.

15 Roy Rosenzweig and David Thelen, *The Presence of the Past: Popular Uses of History in American Life* (New York: Columbia University Press, 1998), 31, 109–14. Survey results indicating this default view of history is still alive and well among students are in Elizabeth Belanger, "Bridging the Understanding Gap: An Approach to Teaching First-Year Students How to 'Do' History," *The History Teacher* 49, no. 1 (2015): 35–62, at 38–39.

dents with expectation failures is one way to shake them out of such complacency.

Students' reading and understanding of primary texts has been studied extensively by Stanford University's Sam Wineburg, and his findings have had a tremendous impact on history education. In particular, Wineburg has examined how expert historians and their non-expert students read primary sources, and the differences are striking. Before even reading a primary source (or any text, for that matter), experts employ a "sourcing heuristic" in order to locate the reading in time and place, and to determine whether the author is credible and consistent with other sources. Once this is established, the experts don't read the document but interrogate it, analyzing it not so much for information as for evidence. They understand that what's not written but implied is probably even more important than what's stated explicitly, and they constantly check the document against itself for consistency and bias. Non-experts, on the other hand, view a text as a text as a text. They read it in linear fashion for information which is assumed to be true and limited to what's written on the page. Perhaps Wineburg's most astounding finding is that professional historians will read primary texts on a far more sophisticated level than students, regardless of whether the latter have more knowledge of and training in the historical context of the document. In other words, a practicing medievalist will likely outperform a college student with a concentration in U.S. history when it comes to interpreting documents from colonial America. The takeaway is that training, experience and habits of mind are far more important to this basic historical skill than possessing a repertoire of content knowledge.[16]

Getting students to read primary sources productively is a difficult task, but perhaps especially so in medieval history

---

16 Sam Wineburg, *Historical Thinking and Other Unnatural Acts* (Philadelphia: Temple University Press, 2001), ch. 3: "On the Reading of Historical Texts." See also Peter Burkholder, "Why You Read Like an Expert—And Why Your Students Probably Don't," *Faculty Focus* (17 November 2014), http://www.facultyfocus.com/articles/teaching-and-learning/read-like-expert-students-probably-dont/.

courses. Students come to these courses with deep temporal and geographical chasms separating them from the subject matter and with a host of biases, usually negative on the whole. (If you doubt the latter, ask your students to write a preconceptions essay at the start of the semester for your next medieval course. Their views will be instructive.) These non-experts must be broken out of a reflexive urge to judge — and even mock or outright reject — the actors under consideration, thus requiring a concomitant need for historical empathy. Wineburg notes that premodern courses are particularly useful for developing this latter capacity, as the setting is too distant, too alien for the application of present-day understandings and values.[17]

A recent reading of Abbo of St. Germain's *Bella Parisiacae Urbis* drove this point home well: the class couldn't understand why an account ostensibly about a ninth-century Viking attack on Paris would get sidetracked on a bevy of miracle stories and the impossibility of a long-dead saint engaging in actual combat. Only by carefully sourcing the text and seeking to understand the author's mindset could we get beyond judging the account for not telling us precisely what we — sitting in a distant, twenty-first-century classroom in suburban northern New Jersey — wanted to know. In the end, none of us, myself included, could pretend to fully comprehend Abbo's worldview and modes of storytelling. Nonetheless, we had come to appreciate not only the events surrounding the siege of Paris, but the medieval values and attitudes of a person who actually lived through it — with all the attendant problems that arise from a biased, eyewitness source.[18] Ultimately, many students need to confront the fact that not every text can be read the same, and that — despite their literacy, and however painful it is to admit it — they don't know how to read primary sources very well.

---

17 Wineburg, *Historical Thinking*, 6–7.
18 The account used in class was Anthony Adams and A.G. Rigg, "A Verse Translation of Abbo of St. Germain's *Bella Parisiacae Urbis*," *The Journal of Medieval Latin* 14 (2004): 1–68. A more recent translation is *Viking Attacks on Paris: The* Bella Parisiacae Urbis *of Abbo of Saint-Germain-des-Prés*, ed., trans. & intro. Nirmal Dass (Paris: Peeters Publishers, 2007).

This constitutes a metacognitive challenge to students, especially weaker and more inexperienced ones, whose educational self-assessments tend to be highly inaccurate.[19] While some of these difficulties of literary criticism are specific to the medieval era, many of them are not, thus lending their applicability to other settings.

Like primary source analysis, historiography represents another essential "expectation failure" to an understanding of the past. *When and why did Rome fall? (Or perhaps it didn't really "fall" at all!) Why did the Crusades take place? How literate were medieval populations? Did the mounted knight "dominate" the military landscape?* To students nourished on an unchanging, omniscient story of events as told through textbooks — a story with little hint of doubt or disagreement among practitioners — the notion that historians are uncertain of much and argue about nearly everything is both novel and unsettling. From their everyday lives, even novices can readily appreciate that the stories we tell about the past will vary, sometimes considerably so. It need not be that one story is "correct" to the exclusion of all others, though that may be the case in some simple instances. Yet, prodding students to apply such personal knowledge to an understanding of broader history is a challenge, one which, when things go wrong, can come down to direct questions to the professor about which interpretation is right and which isn't.

---

19 This matter is discussed in John Girash, "Metacognition and Instruction," in *Applying Science of Learning in Education*, eds. Victor Benassi et al., 152–68 (s.l.: Society for the Teaching of Psychology, 2014), 155–56; and Stephen Chew, "Helping Students Get the Most Out of Studying," in *Applying Science of Learning*, 215–23, at 218. On undergraduate history students' metacognitive awareness, see Peter Burkholder, "Metacognitive Roadblocks: How Students' Perceived Knowledge and Abilities May Hinder Performance in Undergraduate History Courses," *American Historical Association Tuning Project Report* (May 2015). On high school graduates' tenuous reading abilities, see Laura Moser, "More Students Are Graduating High School Than Ever Before. But Can They Read?" *Slate* (22 October 2015), http://www.slate.com/blogs/schooled/2015/10/22/high_school_graduation_rates_are_rising_and_students_achievement_seems_to.html.

I know of no surefire or easy path to teaching an appreciation for historiographical debate, but I do know that exposing students to such ambiguity is essential to their transformation from history students to budding historians. I would further argue that an ability to weigh the relative merits of evidence-based scholarship is a skill which must be taught explicitly, repeatedly, and even to the exclusion of some precious content. Nor can an introduction to historiography (or primary source analysis, for that matter) wait until an upper-division methods or capstone course: developing these skills takes a tremendous amount of time, effort, failure, and readjustment. Using the first year or two of an undergraduate curriculum primarily to instill basic content is to kick the can down the road — and it's unlikely the foundational material will even be retained unless actively used for some more ambitious purpose. Finally, one can readily grasp how this is a teaching and learning problem extending beyond medieval history, or even the entire history subject area, for that matter. How is the teaching of professional debate and ambiguity handled in other fields? What constitutes reliable evidence and methods of interpretation? What forms of assessment best measure a student's mastery of such difficult material? Are some topics or methods more conducive to teaching these skills than others? Basic teaching questions like these are helpful for starting discussions and forging collaborations between medievalists and non-medievalists alike, and thus serve as a pathway out of disciplinary isolation, if one chooses to take it.

Knowing vs. Understanding as Common Pedagogical Ground

The possibilities for such cross-pollination between fields were driven home to me during a teaching development session with chemistry faculty. Discussing the role of factual material within the context of cognitive psychologist Daniel Willingham's excellent book, *Why Don't Students Like School?*, we stumbled into the matter of the history curriculum at my institution. History majors, I explained, have course requirements, including prerequisites for some courses as well as intermediate- and advanced-level obligations. But mostly, within their major, these students are free to choose from classes in U.S., African, Asian, Latin American, Middle Eastern, European, and world history offerings delving into myriad topics spread over various time periods. In addition, non-majors can — indeed, are encouraged to — slot in to many of these classes without prior training. The chemists, drawing on their experiences in the sciences where accumulated knowledge is viewed as essential, couldn't understand how this was possible. "How could a person take a course on the Middle Ages without first taking one in ancient history?," they objected. "How could a student possibly understand a class on post-World War II America without a solid grounding in what came before?"

I initially tried to explain that success in a history course isn't so much a matter of knowing lots of previous history, although that can certainly help; rather, it's more a function of higher-order thinking skills such as analyzing, evaluating, synthesizing and explaining — skills that can develop elsewhere and are transferable from one course setting to another. This predictably went nowhere. So, rather than continuing to address their protests directly, I turned the tables. "The periodic table of elements is fundamental content for any chemistry course, right?," I asked. Of course, they agreed. "You're all chemistry professors. How many of you have the periodic table memorized?" Well, none of them — but the information on that table is easily retrieved, obviating the need to commit it to memory. The key, they insisted, isn't *knowing* the table top-to-bottom, but *understanding how it works.* Thus, what an outsider views as essential knowledge may not be so essential after all (*quod erat demonstrandum*). More importantly, despite the distance separating our fields of expertise, we concurred that cultivating habits of mind, as opposed to imparting raw information, was an educational goal in both of our disciplines.

The above anecdote necessarily suggests that there are common teaching and learning issues between historians, regardless of the subfield of study. This isn't to suggest that medieval history courses are somehow interchangeable with their non-medieval counterparts. But there are threads of pedagogical continuity binding medievalists with faculty in other areas of historical expertise, thereby offering even the "lone medievalist" some camaraderie with his or her institutional peers. My creation of an archive-based research assignment is a case in point: students investigate Gilded Age documents from the family estate now serving as our college campus, but they do so by employing the medievalist's methods of diplomatics. Only by consulting with my Americanist colleagues and reference librarians was the project even possible.[20] The American Historical Association's "Tuning Project," which I joined in early 2015, is predicated on teaching and learning overlaps between the subfields of history and constitutes an extra-institutional opportunity for solitary medievalists to collaborate with fellow historians.[21] Such work is critical to establishing a desired learning arc throughout not only an individual course, but an entire curriculum. It requires recognizing both the common and unique elements of our craft, collaborating with colleagues, and wrestling with the very nature of what we seek to do as history educators.

Strength in Collaborative Numbers

Delving into fundamental problems of teaching and learning is not without risks. First, there are the perceptions of colleagues to contend with. While in my own case I've mostly found support for pedagogical inquiry, traditionalists might object to "wasting time" on such issues, especially if these efforts are seen as detrimental to performing the "real work" of subject-area research. Faculty are sensitive to this bias against teaching development even at self-proclaimed "teaching first" institutions, where the surest path to tenure and promotion is perceived to

---

20 The project is described and evaluated in Peter Burkholder, "Getting Medieval on American History Research: A Method to Help Students Think Historically," *The History Teacher* 43, no. 4 (2010): 545–62.

21 See the Tuning Project website at http://www.historians.org/teaching-and-learning/current-projects/tuning.

be discipline-specific publications and grants/awards.[22] Having a core group of colleagues who are sympathetic towards pedagogical exploration can help ensure that teaching and learning investigations are not in vain from a professional standpoint.

Second, students might not like the types of instruction and course design that emerge from teaching development and learner-centered curricula. It's not for nothing that Wineburg calls "historical thinking" an "unnatural act": the close reading of primary sources for agendas and implicit evidence is something most students have not been trained to do, nor have they been confronted with multiple interpretations of the past. Moreover, these are not quick and easy skills to obtain. They take a great investment of time and effort (learning specialists cite the "ten-year rule" as the necessary minimum to develop true expertise), and failures along the way are practically guaranteed.[23] Getting students to make the necessary investment in new forms of learning, to develop novel skillsets, to realize their understanding of the past has possibly been simplistic and inadequate — all but the most serious and motivated might reflexively reject these premises, and demand a return to a simpler, more familiar "absorb and replicate" style of learning. There is growing evidence and consensus that active learning techniques yield better results than passive ones.[24] But we also know from cognitive science that, as strange as it sounds, the brain is designed *not* to think — and when thinking does occur, it's hard work.[25] Professors who push their students into intellectual zones of discomfort may find themselves punished at the end of the semester with poor student evaluations which are com-

---

22 See note 6 above.
23 On the so-called ten-year rule, see Daniel Willingham, *Why Don't Students Like School?* (San Francisco: Jossey-Bass, 2009), 139–40.
24 Scott Freeman et al., "Active Learning Increases Student Performance in Science, Engineering, and Mathematics," PNAS 111, no. 23 (2014): 8410–15; Maryellen Weimer, "More Evidence that Active Learning Trumps Lecturing," *Faculty Focus* (3 June 2015), http://www.facultyfocus.com/articles/teaching-professor-blog/more-evidence-that-active-learning-trumps-lecturing/.
25 Willingham, *Why Don't Students Like School*, 4–9.

monly misinterpreted and, for better or for worse, often carry enormous weight in faculty reviews.[26] Thus, medievalists and others who opt for more challenging but ultimately more rewarding learning environments face potential trouble on both flanks: dissatisfied students and skeptical faculty/administrators. Formal teaching development programs are essential to legitimizing the more ambitious learner-centered approaches and providing cover to those faculty who choose to take risks in the classroom.

One would think that investing a great deal of time in pedagogical literature and research would bring definitive answers to fundamental teaching and learning questions. I've been closely involved in such work for over a dozen years now, and indeed I've found closure on a handful of issues. My efforts and successes have been recognized with multiple awards at the institutional and national levels. But as with the research in our disciplines, recognitions don't buy answers: an attempt to solve one problem usually begets several new ones, with the latter often being even more intractable and vexing than the original inquiry. I'm reminded of the futility of chasing a rainbow; yet, it's the very act of chasing, not arriving, which ultimately matters in our research and professional development pursuits — and it's both pleasant and advantageous to share the journey with colleagues, be they medievalists or not.

So, in the end, even as the sole premodernist in my department and one of only two medievalists in my entire college, I'm

---

26 On student resistance, see Maryellen Weimer, *Learner-Centered Teaching: Five Key Changes to Practice* (San Francisco: Jossey-Bass, 2002), ch. 7: "Responding to Resistance"; and Shannon Seidel and Kimberly Tanner, "'What if students revolt?' — Considering Student Resistance: Origins, Options, and Opportunities for Investigation," *Cell Biology Education — Life Sciences Education* 12 (2013): 586–95. On the misuse of student evaluations, G.A. Boysen et al., "The (Mis)interpretation of Teaching Evaluations by College Faculty and Administrators," *Assessment & Evaluation in Higher Education* 39, no. 6 (2014), 641–56. A discussion of teaching evaluations goes beyond the purview of this chapter, but readers should note that there's no shortage of studies showing a lack of correlation between evaluation scores and actual student learning.

not so lonely. Just as Latin served as the common tongue among the educated in the medieval West, the language of teaching is a convenient and valuable bridge spanning not only the history subfields, but disparate and seemingly unrelated disciplines. And that's a good thing: If I remember right, many of those isolated monks who sailed into the North Atlantic didn't fare so well when the Norse came along. *Ex pluribus fortitudo!*

Keeping It Old-School on the New Faculty Majority

Geoffrey B. Elliott

I have the good fortune to teach in an English department at a Big 12 school. While it is not as well-funded as, say, the mechanical engineering department or any of the departments in the business school, it does have a fair bit of resources available. Tenured and tenure-track faculty members are eligible for travel support, research grants, sabbaticals, and college- and university-wide awards that carry substantial stipends. Training programs and continuing education opportunities are widely available, as well, and the building in which the department is housed is one of the oldest on campus, constructed in a fine style and solid enough to withstand tornadoes and earthquakes.

Adding my voice to the *Ballad* may be a bit of an oddity, as I am not the only medievalist in the department. There is one other, a tenured associate professor who specializes in Old English. I am the only member of the department who specializes in Middle English, however, and the only one among the many contingent faculty in the department who specializes in medieval literature of any sort. While I am privileged among the academic precariat — I have office space in which to meet with students, a desk and computer with which to do at least some of the work involved in my position, an annual contract that lends itself to renewal, and some health care benefits — I am nonetheless in a position that typically has me teach so-called service courses. In my time in my current position, I have only once been assigned to teach a class that explicitly includes my area of expertise: a sophomore-level survey of British literature, spanning its beginnings through 1800. In such a course, I could give no more than a few weeks to my general area of expertise and even less to my specialty of Malory and his transmission.

In the courses more commonly assigned to me — the commonplaces of first-year composition and general introductory literature, as well as technical writing — I have even less formal opportunity to do so. While a survey of early British literature *has* to include Middle English works and can easily include specific authors of note, composition programs increasingly push against the use of literature as a teaching vehicle, general literature surveys tend to work with much more recent writings, and technical writing focuses so tightly on the purportedly practical that anything other than sober workplace writing is looked at askance. That such classes, both in my current department and at many other institutions, prescribe standard textbooks and, in no small number of cases, assignment sequences serves to restrict them further. Those who teach such classes, most commonly adjunct and other contingent faculty, commonly operate under conditions that preclude them from spending much time away from the work of teaching them.[1] Thus, those of us who are medievalists within English departments and similar institutional groups find ourselves pressed for how we can remain immersed in our chosen fields amid the demands of earning our too-often too-small paychecks.

Some ways of pushing back against that pressing occurred to me more or less by chance as I taught in another position. As a full-time instructor at a technical school in midtown Manhattan, I worked with students whose academic and socio-cultural backgrounds do not register as conducive to the liberal arts

---

1 Janet Ruth Heller, "Contingent Faculty and the Evaluation Process," CCC 64, no. 1 (2012): A8–12, at A8.

educational tradition in the United States. Many of them, immigrants or the children of immigrants and dramatically underserved by their educational experiences in the United States and elsewhere in the world, struggled with conversational modern English, let alone the arcane convolutions of historical Englishes seemingly far removed from their experiences. In trying to reach them, to connect with them so that we could move forward in the classroom together, my own limitations became evident. I did not — and, I regret to add, still do not — have much access to their backgrounds; I worked around the situation by embracing more fully the passion I have for my own educational foundations, almost retreating into the past to address the present. To my early surprise and continuing pleasure, it worked. My doing such things as integrating Anglo-Saxon-style riddles into first-year composition classes, tracing receptions of the medieval in later literatures in general literature surveys, and presenting research and edited materials in medieval practices to technical writing classes has helped both to ensure student success — making keeping a job and its too-necessary paychecks more likely — and to keep me engaged with, if not abreast of, my chosen field of study. I add my voice to the *Ballad* with the hope that such strains may be taken up by others who will sing them better than I.

First-Year Composition

Like many others who teach off the tenure track in English departments, I am often assigned to teach first-year composition. This has been true everywhere I have taught at the college level, from my graduate school through working in New York City and into my present position. As I write this, in fact, I am assigned nothing but first-year composition classes, and while the assignment has certain benefits — I only have one prep this term, and I have fewer than 75 students across all four sections, so that I only have so much grading to do at a time — it does see me operate under a fairly strict programmatic doctrine. Major assignments for the course are centrally predetermined in terms of weight in the course, genre of composition, and page length/word count. The same was true of similar assignments at other institutions where I have worked; the kinds and sizes of papers I was expected to cover were set before I even received my teaching assignments each term.

Amid the programmatic standards, however, there has been a certain percentage of the grade left to the instructor's discretion. My first-year composition classes have seen some of that discretionary grading assigned to student professionalism. Since first-year composition can serve as microcosm for college as a whole,[2] and since many students at the kinds of schools where I have taught are first-generation college students, having an explicit set of expectations for behavior in the new and unfamiliar environment serves well; it helps to clarify matters generally unfamiliar to many students.[3] More of the discretionary grading, however, is devoted to homework assignments and quizzes. For the former, I ask students to bring in early versions of their papers for peer and more formal review, practices that some students report appreciating greatly.

The quizzes I assign my students often work with riddles, either adapted from such texts as the Exeter Book or written to follow the models of those riddles. With the adaptations, I translate or take a translation of some of the shorter riddles, make small adjustments to the modern English texts to account for cultural changes, and embed proofreading errors of the sort I have noticed frequently in the papers students had recently submitted to me. These typically involve comma usage deviating from the style manual from which my class operates — generally either MLA or what is laid out in the prescribed textbook. Students are asked to proofread the riddle, offer an answer, and explain from the details of the text why the answer they provide is correct; only the proofreading and the argumentation are as-

---

2   Timothy L. Carens, "Serpents in the Garden: English Professors in Contemporary Film and Television," *College English* 73, no. 1 (2012): 9–27, at 10.
3   Gerald Graff, "Our Undemocratic Curriculum," *Profession* (2007): 128–35, at 128–30.

sessed. They thus simultaneously receive practice in reviewing texts for mechanical correctness and arguing varying interpretations from textual evidence — both goals common to writing courses and expectations about writing courses other instructors, in English and in other disciplines, often have.

Two examples can usefully illustrate the process. Riddle 50,[4] for instance, I cast for my current (as I write this) students as "By two dumb things is a warrior brightly extracted brought into the world in wonder for the use of lords. For the hurt of the other foe bears it against foe. Strong though it is it is easily bound and obeys well serving quietly if people tend it duly and feed it fairly. It offers them comfort and happiness in life but it rewards with destruction those who let it grow proud [*sic*]. Say what it is." The answer given to the original riddle is "fire," and while only a few of those enrolled in my classes got the answer "right," many of them did well on the tasks of proofreading and of explaining the validity of the answers they *did* provide. One convincingly argued that the riddle, as presented, refers to a Chihuahua, demonstrating not only a welcome willingness to engage odd interpretations, but also a sense of play appropriate to the riddles themselves and a burgeoning ability to offer and substantiate an opinion about a text based on it and attestable experience. Meanwhile, I got to practice my admittedly rusty skills at translation and adaptation, as well as finding easily accessible sources of data from which to conduct future research (since I am not on the tenure track, I have to consider that I may have to relocate, and an online research apparatus makes relocating easier). Each suggests itself to me as a good thing.

I did something similar with Riddle 61.[5] The students in my classes as I write this received it as "I have often been trapped in a closet. On occasion I have been taken out and delivered to an-

---

[4] "Riddle 50," *Online Corpus of Old English Poetry*, http://aspr.oepoetry.ca/a3.22.50.html. The translation, which is admittedly loose and adjusted to suit the purpose to which I put it, is mine.

[5] "Riddle 61," *Online Corpus of Old English Poetry*, http://aspr.oepoetry.ca/a3.34.1.html. The translation, which is admittedly loose and adjusted to suit the purpose to which I put it, is mine.

other as bidden and that other would poke his head inside me. From below with me upturned he would join with me in a tight fit. If his strength kept up some sort of hairy thing was bound to fill me [*sic*]. Say what I am." To be sure, the text is changed from its original — for which the answer is given as "ornamented shirt" or "helmet." Many students came up with an answer much like that, noting that some kind of shirt or hat is what the text describes. One who stands out explained the answer by way of a story, making a narrative to account for the answer; for the student, the riddle describes a turtleneck whose owner has grown heavier between winters and struggles therefore to wear something that had fit easily before. Again, the students were afforded the opportunity not only to proofread, but also to argue from textual evidence and even to exercise their creative repertoire, and I was able to work on translation and adaptation. Classroom and program purposes are served no less than my own interests; everybody wins.

The results are anecdotal, certainly, but it is an anecdote of which I have seen versions for some years. The student examples noted are not the first to make such comments and move in such directions. I have occasionally received some questions from other faculty and program administrators about the practice; how it connects to outcome statements does not always present itself clearly. But many of my colleagues, as well as members of the hiring committee that brought me into my current position, have expressed interest in or appreciation of the technique, commenting favorably on it. Many of my students also report enjoying the riddle exercises — helpful for the evaluations upon which so much work off the tenure track depends — and they report benefiting from them. My own observations suggest that, after a few attempts, student performance on the riddles — and on their other writing assignments — increases sharply. For me, for my classes, it has been effective, and it has been a way to keep myself in practice on something related to what I do in a class that typically is *not*.

General Introduction to Literature

As noted above, I have been afforded the opportunity to teach in my area of study at my current institution. It has been some time since I have gotten to do so, however; I am far more likely to be assigned to teach a general literature class than one in *any* specific area. I, and those in positions similar to mine, are likely to be given classes that try to "cover the breadth" of literature in three genres: prose fiction, poetry, and drama. They seem always to display a presentist bias; many operate under programmatic standards for textbook selection, and many common textbooks struggle to go even so far back as Shakespeare (although the *Norton Introduction to Literature,* a fairly standard textbook, manages to include Aesop, Sophocles and Petrarch — but nothing from older forms of English appears in its table of contents[6]). They seem, too, to be full of students who know they are in the class because they *have* to be in it and *hate* to be in it because of the obligation. Incorporating the medieval into a present-biased class replete with unwilling students is something of a challenge, but it is hardly insuperable.

Two methods of doing so suggest themselves to me. The first stems from a practice I began in my first-year composition classes and have transferred to other classes I have taught: composing assignments alongside students. That is, I write responses to the assignments I give my students — or something close to them. To expand on the idea: my literature classes typically follow one of two assignment sequences. In the first, students are asked to draft a conference-length paper in stages: beginning abstract, annotated bibliography, exploratory essay (four to five pages, something like 1,400 to 1,750 words, exclusive of bibliography), and conference paper. This is in addition to quizzes, out-of-class online discussions, and an institution-mandated in-class final exam. The topic is usually assigned as something in the standard textbook but not covered by the assigned reading

---

6 Kelly Mays, ed., *The Norton Introduction to Literature,* 11th edn. (New York: Norton, 2013), v–xxix.

list. In the other, students are asked to draft several shorter papers, one on a work in each of the major genres covered. Again, topics are usually assigned as items in the standard textbook but *not* covered by the assigned reading list.

In either case, I write papers alongside the students, drafting an abstract or an annotated bibliography as they are asked to do, composing short papers or conference papers alongside them — but mine focus on my own needs, rather than addressing the materials assigned to the students. I frame the divergence as allowing me to produce models for the students that do not entail me doing their work for them — and they do so, helping the students to see the form of the work I want from them while allowing them the freedom necessary to conduct that work for themselves. Students tend to express their appreciation. I recently conducted an anonymous survey of my classes through a Google Form, and results note that many value having examples of work to follow and want more of them to be developed. When I have asked past classes about the examples, albeit less formally, I have received similar replies. It also allows me to generate essays for my own purposes, whether for professional development and service activities (writing samples are helpful in academic and professional portfolios, and some societies ask for short essays from members) or for my own conference work at Kalamazoo and elsewhere. The practice also registers well with administrators, as modeling desired behavior is an excellent pedagogical practice, and students appreciate both the explicit models and the implied sympathy of them.

A second method of incorporating the medieval into a general introduction to literature class is somewhat more time-intensive and complicated than drafting examples for students that happen to coincide with already-standing research projects. The approach is to frame the course as a whole in terms of source or reception studies, centering course discussion and assignments on the identification of medieval figures and tropes in the later literatures on which prescribed texts for such classes focus. It can work in conjunction with the first method to good effect, with the instructor drafting a paper making use of the technique as a model for students to follow in their own work. The practice does conduce more to *medievalism* than to the *medieval*, as such, since it looks at presentation and interpretation of the medieval rather than at the medieval itself. Even so, it requires a deep understanding of the medieval to carry out well, and guiding students to the development of such understanding does much to help reinforce an instructor's own knowledge of medieval and related materials.

Deploying the source/reception studies approach requires substantial narrowing of the medieval, traces of which are to be sought in the later literatures treated in the usual literature survey. As traditionally defined, the medieval in English covers a thousand years and several languages; constraints of program-standard textbooks and syllabi will not permit more than a brief synopsis of the whole, and administrators are not like to approve of deviating from the "regular" course by such a large degree. Such constraints *will* permit narrower attention to a specific period, work, or restricted body of literature, however, if it is presented as a frame for inquiry. For example, Arthurian legend exerts significant influence on the later literatures of the English-speaking world, including those works most likely to be treated in a general literature survey, or in the genre fiction that students are far more likely to read willingly and in the other media they consume. Assigning students to read selected passages from major Arthurian works such as Malory and *Sir Gawain and the Green Knight* (in a reputable translation, given the course) could be presented as background readings to help them carry out explications of the texts assigned in the class. How the assigned texts correspond to and deviate from the patterns asserted in the Arthurian literature could be used either to explicate how the medieval is reinterpreted by the postmedieval or to investigate specifics of how the prevailing concepts change over time. Either is a legitimate exercise in a general literature survey, amenable to the purposes to which such courses tend to be put. Both help the medievalists among the contingent faculty often assigned to teach such classes to work within their fields while addressing the work they must do for their paychecks.

Technical Writing

Contingent faculty are perhaps less likely to be assigned technical writing classes than they are to be assigned first-year writing classes or literature surveys. Often an upper-division class or a class taken during the last semester of a two-year program, technical writing is usually required of students in engineering and medical fields, meeting programmatic and institutional accreditation requirements and ostensibly helping students in those fields learn how to address those *outside* their fields in writing in professional contexts. For example, several of the accreditation standards descriptions provided on the Accreditation Board for Engineering and Technology (ABET) website speak to the need to prepare students to do such things as "assist in the creation of an effective project plan"[7] or "explain basic concepts in management, business, public policy, and leadership; and explain the importance of professional licensure."[8] Technical writing classes address those needs. They are commonly assigned to full-time faculty brought in as specialists in that area, but "commonly" still leaves much room for contingent faculty and non-specialist faculty to be assigned to teach sections of the course. They often do so under supervision and narrow prescription of policies and procedures meant to ensure equivalency among sections of the course taught within each term and from term to term.

When I have been one of the contingent, non-specialist faculty assigned to teach technical writing, I have worked within typically narrow strictures. At my current institution, technical writing is an upper-division class taught across a number of sections, and it is considered a component of the professional writing program offered at the undergraduate and graduate levels. Most sections are taught by graduate students in rhetoric and composition, many of whom specialize in technical and profes-

---

7 "Criteria for Accrediting Computing Programs, 2015–2016," *ABET*, http://www.abet.org/accreditation/accreditation-criteria/criteria-for-accrediting-computing-programs-2015–2016/.
8 Ibid.

sional writing; the remainder are taught by full-time contract faculty — visiting assistant professors. Major assignments are determined by program dictates, much as, and for much the same reasons as, are those in first-year composition. Their genres and requirements are standardized across the many sections of the course taught each term, ostensibly to ensure equivalence across the sections, with some discretionary grading allocated for homework assignments and in-class exercises.

As I teach the course, I work to provide models for my students to follow no less than I do for my first-year and literature students, although the nature of the research I do and the assignments the students face makes it more of a challenge for me to *draft* those examples. What I tend to do instead is to use the need to *find* examples for my students to review (both as models to follow and as exercises in critique and interpretation of technical writing so that they are made more familiar with both reading and writing technical documents) to stimulate my own journal reading. It is easy to let such reading slip aside, after all, against the demands of a more-than-full teaching load, but integrating those teaching demands with ongoing professional reading helps with keeping current — and it tends to help administrative assessments of teaching practices in that it connects the work the students do to practical examples.

Several examples of useful models for technical writing appear in the pages of the October 2014 issue of *Speculum*. One is James A. Palmer's "Piety and Social Distinction in Late Medieval Roman Peacemaking,"[9] which explicates one of the variations away from medieval peacemaking deployed by Romans across the fourteenth century and discusses its purposes and effects. As a longer piece, it is one that does well to be made available to students in advance of the class meeting where it is discussed. Making it available to students allows them to review relevant textual and paratextual features of the document, including the declension of headings and deployment of cited materials and

---

9 James A. Palmer, "Piety and Social Distinction in Late Medieval Roman Peacekeeping," *Speculum* 89, no. 4 (2014): 974–1004.

addenda — all of which factor into principles of composition and document design on which technical writing focuses. It also allows them to read the text in detail, looking at concerns of diction and phrasing as deployed for an educated, intelligent audience composed of many non-specialists; *Speculum* is an explicitly interdisciplinary journal, its articles written and read by scholars in languages and literatures, history, architecture, music, and other fields. They cannot assume they are being read only by those in their own fields, and so they are forced to write more accessibly than they otherwise might — something which the students in technical writing classes are being trained to do. As the students find models of the things they are asked to do in their papers in the text, the medievalist instructor is given an opportunity to read the article, remaining abreast of scholarship in the midst of teaching a class outside his or her specialty.

Another article from the same issue of the journal that would work well with a technical writing class is Rachel Koopmans's "Early Sixteenth-Century Stained Glass at St. Michael-le-Belfrey and the Commemorations of Thomas Becket in Late Medieval York."[10] As with the Palmer example, the length suggests that the piece be made available to students in advance of classroom discussion. Also like the Palmer piece, the Koopmans article allows students to see effective declension of headings, incorporation of addenda, and tailoring of diction to discuss detailed and complex concepts to those who, although educated and intelligent, are not specialists in the relevant field, exemplifying many properties of the best technical writing. The Koopmans piece also makes substantial use of visuals to bolster its argument, and the technical writing courses I have taught have been asked to emphasize the incorporation of visual data such as photographs, sketches, and tables — each of which Koopmans deploys to good effect in her article. The Koopmans piece thus presents itself as offering all of what Palmer's does, and more, with concomitantly

---

10 Rachel Koopmans, "Early Sixteenth-Century Stained Glass at St. Michael-le-Belfrey and the Commemorations of Thomas Becket in Late Medieval York," *Speculum* 89, no. 4 (2014): 1040–1100.

superior effects for student learning and administrative appreciation, along with at least the same level of benefit to the medievalist instructor of a technical writing class.

There is a temptation to use actual medieval examples of technical writing as examples in the class as they appear to be more direct applications of the medieval to the course. Chaucer's *Treatise on the Astrolabe* is easily described as a piece of technical writing, for example, "an elementary textbook meant of a young child" in which "Chaucer's propositions are for a ten-year-old"[11] — clearly a discussion meant for a non-specialist audience, such as technical writing classes often teach students to address. Problems with such an idea arise quickly, however. The language barrier, even to as accessible a Middle English as Chaucer's, is difficult to negotiate for those outside of relevant fields. Similarly, access to useful editions of such texts, while eased in part through electronic means, is still not certain. On a more pragmatic level, program and department administrators, themselves not likely to be medievalists, may well react adversely to the presentation of texts in medieval languages to those who are not specializing in the study thereof. Struggling against such concerns may well be worth doing — for those whose positions are secure. For those who, like me, are members of the new faculty majority, holding contingent positions, such a struggle is likely to be counterproductive. Better, then, to rely on scholarship in modern English when teaching a technical writing class than to try to bring in the medieval itself, but even such a measure helps.

Conclusion

There are other classes medievalists among the expanding precariat may be asked to teach, and they will require other methods for incorporating strains of the medieval into the harmonies

---

[11] John Reidy, introduction to *A Treatise on the Astrolabe,* in *The Riverside Chaucer,* 3rd edn., ed. Larry D. Benson (Boston: Houghton Mifflin Company, 1987), 661.

they promote. Even in the kinds of classes discussed above, there may be differences of circumstance that prevent the teaching practices detailed above from working well. But perhaps even in such cases, they may offer some suggestion about how those among the new faculty majority can do something to keep their classes embedded in the old-school work they have studied.

Interdisciplinary/Team Teaching and the Lone Medievalist

Natalie Grinnell, Wofford College

Being the only medievalist on one's campus can be lonely, not because one's colleagues are unwelcoming or uncollegial, but because the language of our intellectual passion is missing from campus. It's not merely that those around us are not reading the same journals or attending the same conferences that we enjoy, but that their very definition of *medieval* is likely to be far removed from what we actually study, given medievalism's powerful influence on the portrayal of the Middle Ages in contemporary literature, film, and pop culture. Moreover, when it comes to the humanities, current political forces, with their emphases on the practicality of a college degree, are far more likely to promote the study of modern languages, politics, and religion than their medieval cousins, reaching across cultures geographically, but less often temporally. As a result, the lone medievalist may come to feel isolated, and even unappreciated, regardless of his or her actual rank or relationships with fellow faculty.

One solution to this isolation is to reach out through team-teaching, particularly interdisciplinary team teaching. Over the last few decades, studies have consistently shown that creative, energetic interdisciplinary team-teaching can produce improved student learning outcomes, as well as a positive introduction to the values of a liberal arts education.[1] Moreover, the connections formed through interdisciplinary team-teaching can be brought to bear on our own research, as medieval studies itself constantly embraces new theoretical approaches from a wide range of disciplines.[2]

Non-medievalists may find this claim dubious, presuming that most of a medievalist's expertise is not only archaic, but also esoteric. What, one might wonder, has a medievalist to contribute to a biology or accounting course? Of course, the answer partially lies in the nature of a medievalist's education. Regardless of our specific discipline, the alterity of the Middle Ages demands that medievalists spend time learning about its material and philosophical landscape, its economics as well as its religions, and its iconography as well as its languages. To explore even a small part of our field requires us to push past disciplinary boundaries or risk making gross errors in plausibility and fact. Evidence may be found most dramatically in the "What Every Medievalist Should Know" lists originally constructed by James W. Marchand in the 1990s and distributed on the Medieval Texts – Philology Codicology and Technology listserv (MEDTEXTL)[3]. Marchand describes these lists as "meant for the beginning-to-semi-advanced graduate student,"[4] and they are a bibliography for beginning medievalists encompassing music, science, rhetoric, art, literature, history…well, it is an enor-

---

1 See, for example, Rebecca S. Anderson and Bruce W. Speck, "'Oh, What a Difference a Team Makes': Why Team Teaching Makes a Difference," *Teaching and Teacher Education* 14, no. 7 (1998): 671–86 and Nels C. Pearson and Ashley Byun McKay, "Emergent Properties: Interdisciplinary Team Teaching in Literature and Biology," *Currents in Teaching and Learning* 2, no. 2 (2010): 79–88.

2 See, for example, the importance of environmental studies in producing the ecocritical approaches to medieval studies in the work of Jeffrey Jerome Cohen, Lisa J. Kiser, or Lesley Kordecki.

3 James W. Marchand, "What Every Medievalist Should Know," *The ORB: On-line Reference Book for Medieval Studies,* http://www.the-orb.net/wemsk/wemskmenu.html.

4 James W. Marchand, "Introduction: *The ORB: On-line Reference Book for Medieval Studies,* http://www.the-orb.net/wemsk/wemskintro.html.

mous list, added to over the years by other listserv participants. Marchand himself was a German professor, but that is a fact that would be impossible to deduce from the list itself. To one who studies the Middle Ages, a single discipline is never enough.

As a result, then, of the interdisciplinary nature of medieval studies, the lone medievalist is well prepared to make intellectual connections with scholars throughout a college or university. As the lone medievalist at Wofford College[5], a small, private liberal arts college in Spartanburg, South Carolina, I have found ample opportunity to collaborate with my colleagues across campus, specifically through two important programs at the college: the interim term and the interdisciplinary learning communities.

Wofford operates on a calendar consisting of two thirteen-week semesters interrupted by a four-week session each January referred to as *interim*. Created in the 1960s, Wofford's interim "permits and encourages teachers and students to explore the new and untried, and in doing so to run risks that could not be justified in the semesters,"[6] and is therefore a perfect venue for a medievalist to create team-taught courses with non-medievalists. In January 2000, I had my first experience with such a course. Jameica Hill, from the Department of Chemistry, and I team-taught an interim course titled, Weird Science: A History of Science and Pseudoscience, in which we explored scientific theories from the ancient world through the nineteenth century. Topics included Ancient Egyptian astronomy, Babylonian mathematics, Islamic alchemy and astronomy from the Middle Ages, and eventually eugenics, spiritualism and telekinesis. Of course, to make sense of these bodies of knowledge, we addressed not only technological innovation, but also economics, religion, and politics. The students in this class, as in most interim courses, came from many different majors and included both first-year students and juniors and seniors. They were enthusiastic and

---

5 I should note that Caroline A. Mark, formerly Caroline A. Cunningham, of the Department of Modern Languages at Wofford, was also trained as a medievalist; however, she currently defines herself as generalist.
6 "Interim Program Description," *Wofford College,* http://www.wofford.edu/interim/description.aspx.

refreshingly willing to suspend what they thought they knew about the universe and imagine it defined by ideas and cultures with which they had little familiarity. As a younger professor and someone new to Wofford, I found this class invaluable to my growing understanding both of our student population and of the challenges and skills of my colleagues in the sciences. Moreover, as we explained and illustrated long-supplanted ideas about the cosmos, we were reminded of just how compelling some of them could be.

Over the past fifteen years, I have continued to team-teach the interim course when I get the chance. I have taught a course on the works and influence of J.R.R. Tolkien with a psychology professor and a course on puppetry with a post-colonialist. I've taken groups of students on a cultural tour of Ireland with an expert in modern literature and a trip to Prague with a history professor and expert on the Cold War. Each of these experiences has allowed me not only to offer my expertise on medieval culture and literature to my students and colleagues, but it has stretched my own intellectual horizons, prodding me to think about the structure of the medieval romance in relation to theories of narrative from neuroscience or about what eco-feminist theory can reveal about the landscape of Avalon. Moreover, I've been able to make connections outside of Wofford, not only on our European trips, but among the arts community in Spartanburg, when, for example, I helped teach a course in pottery designed by one of our neuroscientists, who went on leave, and team-taught with local artist Ann Gleason at Spartanburg's Chapman Cultural Center. It is difficult to underestimate the value of these connections, particularly at a small college: the more I know about what my colleagues do, on and off-campus, the more effectively we can advocate for one another, support one another, and assist one another in both teaching and research.

Not long after I received tenure at Wofford, we began a program to encourage the creation of learning communities during the regular semesters. Under this program, two courses would be linked by a common theme, and students would take both courses as a block. Given the difficulties of scheduling, it wasn't possible for me to participate with my 300-level courses, but in the spring of 2011, Dr. Charlotte Knotts-Zides, a professor of mathematics, and I linked her course in first-year mathematics with my English 102 course in writing about fiction to create a learning community titled Math, Murder and Mystery. The courses combined practice in quantitative reasoning and the art of deduction with literary analysis and research skills. On first glance, it may not appear that my training as a medievalist contributed to the success of this project. On the contrary, however, my previous study of Chaucer, Boethius, and Jean de Meun is what prepared me to consider the connections between aesthetics and science and, specifically, between literature and mathematics. And watching our students struggle with and overcome their fear of mathematics, as well as Dr. Knotts-Zides's patience in nudging them forward, inspired me to create more carefully scaffolded assignments. Just as she encourages students to practice simple and then more complex problems, using repetition and reinforcement to gain the skills demanded by her discipline, I've created a set of four interlocking exercises for learning citation methods that precede the first paper assignment in my current 102 classes, an approach that has not only improved my students' skills, but has reduced their anxiety in learning them.

Not everyone is comfortable with the idea of opening one's course to a second professor; it necessarily requires the surrender of some autonomy in the classroom, and I myself highly value that autonomy, since it speaks of respect and confidence in the skill and dedication of faculty to the art of teaching. Nevertheless, each of my experiences team-teaching at Wofford has been of long-term benefit, both for my students and for me. Unfortunately, there are forces in academia that discourage this kind of experimentation. Campuses with rising enrollments but fewer faculty hires find it difficult to justify the supposed inefficiency of assigning two professors to a single course, as Wofford has done for many interim classes, and we may find it a serious logistical challenge to link two courses and persuade students of the benefits of signing up for both. Moreover, in a time of budget constraints, money or course release for course development may be difficult to find, and many faculty may consider team-teaching an ethically dubious practice if it increases the number of adjunct appointments on campus. And the assessment movement, which was just beginning when I was hired at Wofford, can, if handled badly, turn creative pedagogical experimentation into a nightmarish stream of paperwork.

Nevertheless, team-teaching, particularly interdisciplinary team-teaching, has allowed me in particular to connect with colleagues from disparate fields of study, improve my own teaching, and explore intellectual realms that I might avoid if I had a medieval studies program on campus to encourage a more narrow and demanding concentration on my own speciality. I have not become a generalist at Wofford; I still teach and conduct research in my own field, but I think my understanding of academia as a whole is both broadened and deepened by stretching outside of that field when I have the opportunity.

And Gladly Wolde He Teche: The Medievalist and the History of the English Language Course

Robert Kellerman, University of Maine at Augusta

When I was hired on the tenure track by University of Maine at Augusta, a small branch of Maine's public university system, there were no courses in medieval or Renaissance literature at all other than the ubiquitous Shakespeare course that was taught by the British literature specialist. The job advertisement for my position simply stated that the English program sought a candidate to teach "composition and literature," with no particular specialization attached to the position. On being hired, I was thus in the enviable position of proposing and creating the courses in my field that I then taught; in essence, I filled a position that I subsequently designed to my own specifications. I am extremely grateful that my colleagues were enthusiastic about having the curriculum augmented with courses in early English literature.

Because I teach in a small program, this meant that I was the "lone medievalist" at my school, not to mention the lone Renaissance scholar — a state of affairs that I expect is common for those of us teaching in smaller schools. (Though the other specialist in British literature very happily and enthusiastically teaches Shakespeare, her specialization is actually nineteenth-century literature.) This casting of a very wide net is reflected in job advertisements for positions at smaller schools, which often call for a candidate to teach "pre-eighteenth-century literature," assuming her or his ability to teach *all* of it: Old English, Middle English, sixteenth- and seventeenth-century literature. This expectation goes against the grain of the kind of narrow specialization under which graduate schools organize their curricula.

Because my dissertation actually covered literature from the fourteenth through the seventeenth century — a fairly wide range, given the kind of period specialization that doctoral programs often demand — I was in a solid position to develop and teach a wide range of classes for my school, and I suspect many of us are. I am grateful for the opportunity to teach in the fields of both medieval and Renaissance literature, though I also must acknowledge that the state of Maine can be a lonely place for anybody on a faculty in a small school where nobody else really teaches in these fields. This is not true only for me, but for my many colleagues, all of whom go regularly to conferences, maintain professional relationships with other scholars, and seek out those who, as it were, speak the same academic "language."

That said, one course that has definitely helped my program and my own scholarly interests is one that I did not anticipate when I began at UMA: our history of the English language course. When the English faculty revised its curriculum six years ago — which consisted of dropping courses that had not been taught for years, adding others that had been developed and were now taught regularly, and revising the program requirements to align with the new curriculum that resulted — we considered dropping an introduction to linguistics course. It had been taught by a long-retired colleague, and for some reason the course itself had never been dropped from the catalog listings, even though it had not been taught for about fifteen years. In graduate school, I took a linguistics course similar to it, but as an undergraduate I had taken a history of the English language course. This seemed to me to be a more appropriate course at the undergraduate level in that it more closely aligned with literature and the texts that students read in their undergraduate program. So I proposed that, instead of dropping the course, I retool it into a history of the English language course and teach it once to see how it would run. If it proved popular, then we would consider making it a permanent course.

A medievalist is a logical choice to teach such a course, even if she or he isn't trained specifically in linguistics (as I wasn't), because obviously work in medieval literature demands the study of the historical periods of the English language. I have not formally studied Old English since graduate school, so that my reading skills are very rusty, though I have taught *Beowulf* and shorter related Old English texts in translation regularly in our English literature survey courses. But those graduate seminars in Old English gave me enough grounding in the grammar and vocabulary of the language that I can reasonably discuss how Old English works and its place in the development of English. My Middle English is quite strong, as I expect it is for most medievalists, if only because it is likely that we took a Chaucer seminar at some point in our careers — and, of course, Middle English is considerably easier than Old English. In addition, working in Renaissance literature has given me a strong grounding in much of the later course content of the history of the language course.

It hasn't provided context for all of the course content, though, and this is where I have found that I am extremely grateful for the opportunity to teach this course. For my textbook, I have used the classic *History of the English Language* by Baugh and Cable (Prentice-Hall, now in its fifth edition)[1] on the recommendation of a former colleague who is a linguist and who primarily teaches linguistics. Baugh and Cable's text has several advantages: its coverage is comprehensive, they write in an academic but accessible style, and most important, they cover American English well. Many history of the language textbooks are written for the British market, and they naturally cover Brit-

---

1   Albert C. Baugh and Thomas Cable, *A History of the English Language,* 6th edn. (London: Routledge, 2013).

ish English more thoroughly, in particular the many dialects spoken in Britain today. Baugh and Cable's American orientation is a plus for American students. I augment this textbook with R.L. Trask's *Language: The Basics* (Routledge, in its second edition)[2] in order to give students an introduction to the basics of linguistics, now that we no longer have a linguistics course, and the materials about how language works — grammatically, culturally, and socially — give students a wider view of a skill that they have mastered and take for granted.

Teaching from these texts has grounded me in the developments of the language in the eighteenth century and beyond, which has informed my teaching of the entire two-course survey of English literature, which I now teach regularly. It has also grounded me far better in the developments of American English and world "Englishes," and the field of linguistics has become a secondary field of academic interest for me because of this course.

Teaching such a course in a small department has further advantages. The course naturally and logically gives me the opportunity to promote my own courses in early English literature. I have found that students are fascinated by Old and Middle English, as we were when we were undergraduates. Thus they are interested in taking courses in which they get to actually read the material that looks so odd on the page, even if they read it in translation. This is especially true if one discusses the culture of Anglo-Saxon, medieval, and Renaissance England, which of course one does in order to demonstrate how language both shapes and is shaped by its culture. Promoting my own courses is frankly opportunistic, and I admit this freely. My experience is that a course titled "medieval literature" does not necessarily sell as well as courses on media and film, popular culture, gender studies — courses that are, to put to use the phrasing of some of my colleagues, sexier on paper than my courses. Students actually *love* medieval literature, once they're in the medieval literature class. The challenge is to get them there in the first place.

---

2   R.L. Trask, *Language: The Basics,* 2nd edn. (London: Routledge, 1995).

I have also found that the course is a good place to promote our university's language courses as well, which endears me to my colleague who teaches French, our only traditional foreign language offering. (Our other offering is American Sign Language.) Our school has a minimal foreign language requirement for English majors of one year, or two courses, but the history of the language course underscores why language study matters in all sorts of ways. When students enter into the French courses and the history of the language course — often simultaneously — they find it worthwhile to go on to take the second- and third-year advanced language courses because they realize that language study is actually interesting and useful and that it connects them better to their *own* first language. As both my French professor colleague and I say, "If you want to really understand your native language, learn another one." In a small, modestly endowed school such as ours, filling both lower- and upper-level courses really matters. Often they do not run if we cannot fill them with a minimum number of students because there is no money to underwrite them. Promoting other courses in any course one teaches is a smart move in itself, as it helps students understand how courses in the program and among other programs are interrelated.

I was concerned initially about the popularity of this course, but filling it has not been an issue. In fact, much to everybody's surprise, it has *never* been an issue. I am sure that at least initially it was not the course itself that attracted students. (After all, until I created the course, we had never had a course with this subject matter.) It's more likely that, the first time we offered the course, it was offered at a good time that worked with our students' work schedules. Our student body is largely non-traditional and all of them commute to campus, so scheduling seriously matters. The course was scheduled for the late afternoon, a time frame that I advocate for many of my upper-level courses because it allows working adults to attend. Since that first offering, I have also made the course available online and will teach it in the upcoming fall semester on compressed video — essentially a live class with students in different locations, using video conference technology to connect us all. This allows the course to reach the widest audience possible; since my school was the campus originally charged in the University of Maine System with distance education, this kind of flexibility in course delivery is key.

Because our English program is relatively small, I knew that the language course would have a sizeable number of non-majors in the class. That didn't surprise me. What *did* surprise me was how popular the course was. I got strong student evaluations that first time, and the course has been filled or nearly so every time I have offered it. And now, since the course has been around for six years, the word on the academic street is that it's well worth taking. I would like to say that this is all the result of my teaching, but I don't think that this is the case, though of course I *do* hope it's a factor. I do think that a much greater factor is the nature of the subject matter. As I point out the in first class meeting every time I teach this course, everybody in the course is *already* an expert linguist. That is, every student has mastered her or his mother tongue, so that the linguistic expertise with which one comes into the course is already in place. Furthermore, many students have already studied a language, often in high school, so that they have some knowledge of how languages work already. And in Maine, with its strong French Québécois heritage, many students come from bilingual families, even if French is no longer normally spoken (which tends to be the case). Few courses can build on a student knowledge base that can be best described as "expert," but history of the English language is one of them that can. Much of the course, in fact, teaches students things that they already instinctively knew but had no idea that they knew; for example, when we read Trask's chapter about language acquisition in infants and how the human mind seems to be hard-wired for language acquisition, my students who are parents with toddlers are happily stunned to realize that their two-year-olds are daily picking up the vocabulary and grammar of their mother tongue to the point that they too will be experts by the time they are five or six. Likewise, students are delighted to discover that irregular verbs have plagued English speakers and writers for centuries, and that all of the rules of grammar that they learned in high school are actually opinions about how the language *ought* to function and not necessarily how it *does* function. This course gives students the ability and opportunity to explore and analyze their own language to a highly sophisticated level.

The course material is fascinating in itself, though students don't necessarily sign up for the course thinking that this will be the case. As an undergraduate I remember Baugh and Cable's text as being somewhat dry; for example, their discussion of strong and weak verb forms in Old English is technical and somewhat difficult for students to grasp entirely. But the course lends itself to endless discussions about how language is intensely *political*. Given that it is so inextricably tied to personal identity and, by extension, cultural and national identities, it can't help but be. Students, however, are often unaware of this or have not fully acknowledged language's ties to identity politics. But this issue comes to the fore as the course continues, as we discuss the British Empire, the American century and its rise as a world power, and the rise of English itself as the leading world language in its many permutations. The advantage of playing up the political nature of English, or indeed any language, in this course is that it connects the course to other fields and courses that students are taking. Students often comment on the issues that they are studying in other courses, from world history, when we discuss the geopolitics of world Englishes, to computer science, when we discuss programming languages and how the computer industry borrows familiar words and coins new ones for its own use. Making the disciplines of English, language, and literature relevant is not a challenge for those of us who have dedicated our professional lives to them, but it is not always immediately apparent to students why language is relevant. This course makes it very clear why it is.

Since we started offering the course, its popularity and its relevance to the English program and other programs in the university have led the English faculty to make it a requirement for English majors. While this gives the course a certain legitimacy and a built-in student audience, we nevertheless have a small English program, so that the course even now must draw students from all disciplines. Even so, offering this course has tacitly given more legitimacy to the fields of medieval and Renaissance studies at my institution and has helped strengthen interest in the courses that I offer in those fields. I have no illusions that medieval and Renaissance literature are absolutely central to the English program at my school. But my school has given me the opportunity to explore a closely-related field that draws on my expertise in early English literature and culture that *has* proven itself central enough to the program to be a requirement. In a time in higher education when English programs are often expected to justify themselves — and medievalists are further expected to justify themselves *within* the English program — a course with proven relevance that serves a wide audience and is popular is not a bad thing to offer.

I Know! Let's Put on a Show!

Robert Stauffer, Dominican College

Perhaps one of the earliest narrative tropes I encountered was the one where a group of kids try to save the orphanage, or their parents' homes, or the school by putting on a show. I still have a clear image of a five- or six-year-old Spanky, dressed as a Roman soldier, reciting Mark Antony's speech from Shakespeare's *Julius Caesar*, while trying to dodge spitballs from his friends and the domineering of his overprotective mother. By bringing down the house (quite literally, of course) he was able to win the prize so the young girl with stage fright could buy a new dress.[1] The trope was made famous in Rodgers and Hart's musical comedy, *Babes in Arms*, starring Mickey Rooney and Judy Garland, and the two actors made quite a few movies featuring this plot device. I guess having had this story line run through my head so many times as a kid, it sank in and resurfaces every now and again as something I would like to try. So when I encountered trouble getting students and colleagues interested in the work featured in my dissertation, the old trope naturally sprang to mind.

---

1   This is from Season 13 of what is now known as *The Little Rascals*, an episode called "Beginner's Luck," which was aired on February 23, 1935, according to TV.com. This was probably also my first encounter with Shakespeare.

At the MLA meeting in Seattle in January of 2012, I ran into one of my mentors from Arizona State, Curtis Perry, who is now at the University of Illinois in Champagne. He had recruited me to be one of his teaching assistants for Renaissance literature years before, but I had heard the siren song of medieval literature and had left him to pursue some earlier works. I was finally on the job market full time after having received my PhD the previous spring, and had been diligently hammering away at job applications while working as an adjunct at St. Francis College in Brooklyn, but had not received any callbacks. I was beginning to grow worried that my six years as a PhD candidate had been for nothing. When I opened up to him about my concerns, he sat me down and asked me to give him my pitch. I spent the next five minutes telling him about the exciting time I had had as a student tracking down materials on a late-thirteenth, early fourteenth century French mystic named Marguerite Porete, who had been tried and executed in 1310; about how her book had been translated — even after her execution for heresy — into Latin, English, and Italian; about the conference I had attended in Paris on the anniversary of her death; on the connections I had made between her book, *The Mirror of Simple Souls,* and other works that might lend clues as to why it had been translated into English sometime during the following century. He listened patiently and when the five minutes were up, he held up his hand, and said in mock-interviewese, "Thank you for your interest, but we will be going in another direction to fill this position." I was heartbroken.

He told me that everything I'd been discussing was immensely interesting — to a scholar — but as a department head trying to fill a position, none of this would be of interest. "Rob, most colleges need a guy who can teach *Beowulf* and Chaucer and who can fill in a little with Shakespeare. Marguerite Porete, while she sounds interesting, is useless for a department in a typical liberal arts college." He told me to reconstruct my cover letter to emphasize the basics, to show that I had experience teaching the usual authors. I did so, and the very next application I sent out landed me my current position.[2]

I should have realized then and there that the life of a medievalist in a general educational college system was going to be hard, at least as far as bringing in my research. After only a few weeks at my new job, I began to notice that mentions of even Beowulf and Chaucer, let alone Marguerite and her *Mirror,* brought on that glassy-eyed look when I spoke to many colleagues. My school mostly caters to good students who are looking for an education that will help land them a good job, so medieval literature is a tough sell to even the brightest of students. Luckily, as part of our general education classes, the students are required to take at least one medieval course, and while art and history are my main competition, literature seems the most accessible to most of my students. I have a rotation of three classes that cover interesting, but fairly standard, materials: *Sir Gawain and the Green Knight* and Chrétien de Troyes's *Perceval* are among the most exotic. Don't get me wrong, I do enjoy teaching these works, but there's no real room for the work I spent more than six years contemplating and so I spend most of my time thinking about anything but Marguerite Porete and her book.

The coordinator of the English department at Dominican College, Ellen Dolgin, has been very kind and spends a lot of time trying to include my topics of interest in the classes she assigns me. She has also encouraged my conference attendance. One of the very first opportunities she had to get me onto a panel she was hosting at the local Northeast MLA in Harrisburg was about Joan of Arc, and after hearing me go on about my own heretic, she invited me to write a paper for her panel. I immediately proposed a comparison of the two—how one was still condemned, but the other had managed to rehabilitate

---

2 I am probably remembering this a little more harshly and Curtis is more direct and high-handed in my memory than he ever has been to me in real life. But the truth is that he gave me an insight into the harsh truth of the industry, an insight that was only proven by the success I had using it.

herself all the way to sainthood — but she seemed disappointed. Her own work on Joan, as seen mostly through the lens of the twentieth century, and her study of the theater give her a very different perspective on this medieval woman and so my proposal may not have been exactly what she had bargained for.[3] "I don't think my audience will be interested in Marguerite Porete — she's too obscure."[4] And perhaps she was right. The paper ended up as a look at how other authors saw Joan, particularly Shakespeare, who is well known, and Christine de Pizan, who at least was a little better known than my Marguerite.

Another opportunity to bring Marguerite's *Mirror* to a wider audience arrived while I was having lunch with several of the organizers for the following Northeast MLA meeting during that conference. As this was the first of the smaller conference to which I had been, I was surprised about the fact that there were very few (if any) panels that were multilingual. As an English professor, I felt like I missed two-thirds of the conference, because the various papers presented in other languages were part of panels only relevant to those languages. Since the next conference was going to be in Canada, I felt as though at least one French and English panel should be scheduled. When I mentioned this to the 2015 president, she asked me if I had an idea for one. Without missing a beat, I suggested a reading of Marguerite Porete's *Mirror* in the various languages for which we have manuscripts: Latin, Middle English, Old and Middle French, and Italian.[5] I was told to get on it right away.

I was inspired by two events that occurred during my studies. The first of my inspirations was Benjamin Bagby's haunting per-

---

3 Ellen Ecker Dolgin, *Modernizing Joan of Arc: Conceptions, Costumes, and Canonization* (Jefferson: McFarland & Company, 2008).

4 Again, this quote is from the memory of a sensitive junior academic responding to the fact that his chosen dissertation subject is pretty much an unknown.

5 There are three Middle English manuscripts, two Italian ones, and five Latin, to go with the Middle French version: Chantilly, Musée Condé, MS F XIV 26 (ancien 986), which has been used to make most of the modern translations in English. An Old French fragment exists in Valenciennes, Bibliothèque municipale ms. 239.

formance of *Beowulf* in Anglo-Saxon. Back in April 2003, while I was still studying for my master's, Bagby brought his performance to Angel Orensanz Center for the Arts in the Lower East Side of Manhattan, and my wife and I went to see him spin out the first 852 lines of this medieval classic with only a wooden harp to accompany him. Though they did provide a translation in supertitles, we could feel the power of the words through his performance. The presence of the performer right there in front of me hearkened back to the way medieval *scops* must have played before kings. Just as the actors in a live performance of a play can interact with the audience, Bagby was able to reach out into the audience and bring the story to life.[6] *Beowulf* had never felt so real to me before. Bagby's performance inspired me to teach it in my high school classroom to great response from the students. Though I did not have the means to show them Bagby's marvelous performance at the time, I was able to bring a little of his enthusiasm and drama to my own readings. Though I was neither as accomplished a performer nor did I perform it in Old English as Bagby had, the memory of his performance greatly influenced my own, and the students were able to see this ancient poem with which they had been struggling as a living, emotional work.

The second inspiration came from my PhD days at Arizona State. A friend of mine—Jeremy Eisenberg—and I decided to take Chaucer's challenge and translate a little piece of Chrétien de Troyes's *Lancelot* in octosyllabic rhyming couplets. I was the guy creating the trot from the Old French and he was the poet trying to make it sound good. We each critiqued each other's work until it was in pretty interesting shape; we created about 800 lines of poetry and an introduction explaining our process that was later published in the University of Wisconsin: Fox Valley journal.[7] We chose the "Knight of the Ford," in which the un-

---

6 A DVD of his performance was released in 2005, which can be found on his website BagbyBeowulf.com.
7 Jeremy Eisenberg and Robert Stauffer. "The Knight of the Ford: A Scene from *Lancelot, the Knight of the Cart* by Chrétien de Troyes," *Fox Cry Review* 34, September (2008): 20–29.

named Lancelot, entranced by thoughts of Guenevere, stumbles into a ford protected by a knight. They fight until the unnamed ford knight surrenders and is handed over to an inexplicably present young lady. The piece worked well as a dialogue, which we discovered in the creation of the poem and we got the idea to actually perform the piece during a graduate conference. We were also invited in to a class on performance to present it again. Something magical happened in both performances: a piece of literature, often overlooked, took on new life in performance. We were able to express the humor of the piece, and a few of the hidden meanings we had taken and incorporated into our work, in a way that we could not do in a lecture. By letting the audience experience the poem in performance rather than in explanation, we reached more of them in a way that they would certainly remember.

I have never been one for performing in front of a crowd, even in teaching. Sure, I sing in the shower and in my car when I'm driving alone, but I would never consider doing this in a public forum, even one with a captive audience. But during these two performances something awoke in me that recognized the importance of performance as a connection between the student and the work. I saw how performance brought the piece to life and challenged the starkness of the words on the page. Thanks to Jeremy's interest in the process, we discovered that we were not the only ones to notice this; it became apparent that performance was a way to get some of these medieval works back into the public eye.

I began to think of ways to bring such performance to the classroom and how this could work well for Marguerite's *Mirror*. The performance idea seemed to work well with relatively known works like *Beowulf* and Chrétien's *Lancelot*, but could it work with something as obscure as the *Mirror*? Toronto's NeMLA meeting would provide the opportunity to find out.

I contacted several of the people I had met at both the International Congress for Medieval Studies in Kalamazoo over the years and the conference in Paris in 2010 in honor of the seven hundredth anniversary of Marguerite Porete's death and asked if any of them might be able to attend the conference in Toronto the following spring.[8] Sadly, no one else was going and I was beginning to despair of pulling this off. Then I got the idea to ask several people if they wouldn't mind recording themselves reading various passages.

Marguerite's *Mirror* is written in the form of a play with three main characters: Love (ostensibly God), Reason, and the Soul. In the Chantilly manuscript, the text of the book appears with the names of the characters at the beginning of each passage, just like any other play would be formatted. There are several other characters who appear here and there with names like Truth or Holy Church the Little or The Height of the Intellect of Love. The Soul and Love spend the better part of the *Mirror* trying to explain to Reason why an individual soul would want to surrender herself to become one with God, while Reason keeps asking more and more questions. Love is very generous to Reason throughout the text and always tries to make Reason understand that asking questions is exactly what keeps her separate from God. By accepting nothingness — noughting — the Soul has become one with God and no longer has to worry about being separated from her. All three of the main characters are females, which probably also helped in the condemnation of the text in 1310.

The play is a long one — more than sixty thousand words in length in the Chantilly manuscript — so there have been a lot of questions about whether the book was meant to be read aloud. Barbara Newman has suggested that the play may have been read aloud as part of the *puys* of Northern France in the late thirteenth and early fourteenth centuries.[9] Its public nature

---

8   The 2010 conference was coordinated by three Marguerite Porete scholars, and a volume of essays followed: Sean L. Field, Robert E. Lerner, and Sylvain Piron, *Marguerite Porete et le* Miroir des simples âmes: *Perspectives historiques, philosophiques et littéraires* (Paris: Librarie Philosophique J. Vrin, 2013).

9   See Barbara Newman, *Medieval Crossover: Reading the Secular against the Sacred* (Notre Dame: University of Notre Dame Press, 2013), esp. chap. 3, "Conversion: The Literary Tradition of Marguerite Porete," 111–66.

may in fact be what roused the Church's anger at both the text and its author. Clearly, though, there was far-reaching interest in the text within the Church. The Middle English and Latin texts travel with approbations from three sources, one of which has been identified as Godfrey of Fontaines, a master of theology at the University of Paris at the end of the thirteenth century, who suggested that while this text should not be made available to all people, it was a worthy text that deserved some study. But it is quite possible that even he would have been uncomfortable having it shouted out on the street corners of France or having it performed in a public theater.

My idea was to have each of the primary parts — Love, Reason, and the Soul — read in the various languages of the extant manuscripts. I thought it best that Love be read in the Middle French of the Chantilly manuscript, Reason in Latin, and the Soul in Middle English, and I knew just the people for the parts.

Zan Kocher has long been associated with the *Mirror,* having studied it and written about it for more than thirty years. His book, *The Allegories of Love in Marguerite Porete,* is a mainstay of studies about the *Mirror* and connects the *Mirror* to several secular romances that also would have been subject to performance. He was one of the first people to tell me of the discovery by Geneviève Hasenohr of a new manuscript of a fragment of the *Mirror* discovered and brought to light among American scholars by Sean Field and Robert Lerner.[10] I had the great good fortune to travel with Zan to Valenciennes to see the new manuscript during the conference in 2010 and learned so much about both texts from him through the years since. I knew he would be perfect as the character Love right away and was pleased when he accepted my request to do the readings on camera.

Marleen Cré gave me my first insights into the three Middle English manuscripts — particularly the British Library MS

---

10 Geneviève Hasenohr, "La tradition du *Miroir des simples âmes* au xve siècle: de Marguerite Porete (†1310) à Marguerite de Navarre," *Comptes rendus des séances de l'Académie des Inscriptions et Belles-Lettres* 4 (1999): 1347–66; and Robert E. Lerner, "New Light on *The Mirror of Simple Souls,*" *Speculum* 85, no. 1 (2010): 91–116.

Additional 37790 — in her magnificent book *Vernacular Mysticism in the Charterhouse*. I met her at the Paris conference and was astounded by the wealth of information she had about the *Mirror* and other books like it that had found their way from France to England. I knew that her reading of the Middle English would be wonderful and again was pleased to find her amenable to the task. Justine Trombley, a graduate student when I met her at Kalamazoo, has done wonderful work with the Latin manuscripts. Though I had no idea at the time what an actress she was, I knew that her love of the Latin would make her a perfect candidate for the role of Reason.

Though the idea had come to me more than a year before the performance date, I had not thought it all through until January of 2015. I was still hopeful I could get people to come to the conference to do the reading there, so when I finally gave in, there was only about two months left before the conference. My instructions to my readers scattered all over the world — Zan on the west coast of the United States, Justine in Scotland, and Marleen in Antwerp — were few. My plan was to have them each film themselves for three or four different readings and then I would splice them all together here in New York and cart the finished product with me to Toronto. Of course, I had never done anything like this before and knew very little about the various obstacles to getting this right.

Though I suggested simple ideas about dress and location for the filming, I was really afraid of scaring off my actors and so let them make the final decisions on wardrobe and placement. Zan explained to me how he took the little direction I gave him to create his role: "[Love] speaks with confoundingly high authority. She not only personifies human love for God but also turns out to be a face of God himself. Also Love is masculine in medieval Latin, but feminine in Old and Middle French. Medieval paintings personify her as a robed, perfectly regal-looking lady with long wavy hair. I turned out to be a luddite baritone with sideburns. Maybe wearing a bathrobe would compensate? Lacking a video camera or operator, I perched an aging laptop on pieces of furniture while reading aloud. As a first ill-fated attempt to appear spiritual, I tried to align my head in front of round household objects that might remotely resemble a halo. This proved impossible, as the camera angles made them skew to the sides. Then I stacked dictionaries under the laptop, to gaze upward at the lens in another desperate bid to look spiritual. More light was needed: a construction job spotlight with a metal mesh frying-pan cover balanced on top to diffuse its glare. Reading to the laptop, I remembered what professors had told me in graduate school: nobody knows exactly how medieval French sounded."

Marleen writes: "I thoroughly enjoyed this chance to give voice to the beautiful, theologically challenging, poetic, intensely human text that Marguerite Porete's *Mirror* is. It was fun to speak the lines of the soul in Middle English. I had wanted to film with the apple trees in bloom in the background, but that didn't work. I was filming against the light, but it was interesting to try and select a setting that would fit the soul (Latin Reason sitting in an office with books, and French Amour against a white curtain). It was amusing that some audience members noticed my glasses (decidedly un-medieval) — I hope they also noticed the beauty of the Middle English translator's diction in his re-voicing of Marguerite's text." While the concept of Marleen's glasses could easily have been understood in the Middle Ages, the style was definitely twenty-first century, and yet that seemed to make the reading all the more relevant to the audience. They also loved the setting she chose. During the last passage, Marleen's dog barked, as if on cue, and the audience was drawn in to her performance all the more. Even though the language was unclear to the audience, the reality of the emotion and power behind the words were evident.

Choosing the passages we would read proved challenging as well.[11] There is a lot of talk, as you might imagine, in a spiritual

---

11 I used the Guarnieri/Verdeyen text (Marguerite Porete, *Speculum simplicium animarum/ Le mirouer des simples âmes*, eds. Romana Guarnieri and Paul Verdeyen [Turnhout: Brepols, 1986]) for the Middle French and Latin, and the Doiron edition (Marilyn Doiron, ed., "*The Mirror of Simple Souls*:

text like the *Mirror,* and the question was how we would engage the audience in the text. The opening passage to the book is a good one, as Marguerite uses it to explain why she is writing this book and the main ideas of the work. She tells us a story, using a scene from the popular romance *The Romance of Alexander,* and explains how she, like Candace from the romance, fell in love with a king she had never seen, and draws a picture of him — Candace with a painting, Marguerite with her book — so that she may feel closer to him. Love tells the story and the Soul makes the connection between the heroine of *Alexander* and herself: a nice simple passage with which to begin.

Chapter 11 of the Chantilly *Mirror* is a wonderful little question and answer session among the three primary characters. They get to interact a lot. Love laughs at many of Reason's questions, not in a mocking way, but in a loving head-shaking way a teacher might have for a student who is still struggling to get past her own prejudices against the difficulties of a text. This one would prove the most difficult as the interactions would need to be cut together neatly so as to make the dialogue sound alive. Zan wrote of this process: "Marguerite Porete had crafted the mystical conversations so tightly that in the video it seemed as though the characters were talking to one another, even though we recorded our lines separately in different locations."

We included the Valenciennes fragments, which amounts to much of what Chantilly records in chapters 77 and 78, because we wanted to include the older French. Zan did a wonderful job reading this section and one could really hear the difference in the language.

But chapters 85 through 88 are where the action is. This was actually the very first sequence I knew I wanted to incorporate into the video. During the conversation, Love and the Soul explain how the Soul, by the gift of noughting, has become one with God and therefore needs to answer to no one, not even God. The union being complete, the Soul is now lost in God and

---

A Middle English Translation," *Archivio italiano per la storia della pietà* 5 [1968]: 241–355) for the Middle English.

simply is God. Reason can no longer bear the strain and cries out: "Ah God! … How dare one say this? I dare not listen to it. I am fainting truly, Lady Soul, in hearing you; my heart is failing. I have no more life," and promptly dies. The Soul immediately responds: "Alas! Why did it take so long, this death!"[12] Justine's acting really came through for us here as she sputtered the lines in Latin and then passed out stage right. The audience really reacted well — first in astonishment, as they only heard her Latin words, and then with bouts of laughter as they realized that Reason's questioning was over.

Justine writes of her performance: "Performing the *Mirror* was in a sense very surreal, because as a medievalist your time is always spent reading sources, and not really thinking about how it might sound out loud, and when you do hear it read out, it brings a depth and immediacy to it that one wouldn't normally think about. In terms of the *Mirror* specifically, it made me think of Marguerite herself reading out loud to listeners, and the later audiences who surely must have read it aloud to others at some point. I think that brought home to me just how much more 'shocking' some of her statements may have seemed when uttered aloud, rather than just being happened upon while looking contemplatively at a page."

This last section also was important because it included lines for three new characters: Courtesy, Truth, and Nobility of the Unity of the Soul. One day while I was describing the project to a few colleagues at Dominican College, one of them — Giovanna Czander — suggested that I have those parts read in Italian, the one language I had not yet used from among the extant manuscripts, and then volunteered to read them for me. And this is the whole point of the project: here was someone who was not intimately familiar with the works of Marguerite Porete volunteering to just read the works. Giovanna is the Religious Studies professor at Dominican College and we have discussed

---

12 This modern English translation used here is taken from Ellen Babinsky's 1993 translation of the *Mirror* (Marguerite Porete, *The Mirror of Simple Souls* [New York: Paulist Press, 1993], 163).

our studies quite a bit around the office. Giovanna describes her experience this way: "Preparing to do a dramatized reading of an excerpt from Marguerite Porete's *Mirror* gave me a surprising insight on her work. I had not realized until then how the text lends itself to being read aloud and even performed. I could almost see the characters as I read the text and imagine the possible interpretations. I had fun doing this and I realize that this playful dimension is also part of the fact that the text may have actually been a 'play.'" Her reading, as it involved three separate characters, required her to come up with three "costumes": a candle for Truth, a wreath for Courtesy, and a hat for the Nobility of the Unity of the Soul. While her costumes were simple, her reading was well performed and our audience enjoyed the subtleties of the various characters. I was moved by her reading, as it finally gave me an opportunity to bring the reading of this marvelous book outside of the small group of scholars who have already been associated with Marguerite and her *Mirror* and into my small college.

As I gathered the various pieces of the performances and learned how to splice them together as carefully as possible, I began to realize how this project really brought the *Mirror* to life for me. Even though I had read it several times over the years I had been working on the text, I had only once heard the text read out loud. In Paris, during the conference for the seven hundredth anniversary, several actors had read the parts out of the French Chantilly text. Now here I was hearing several of the texts read aloud by non-actors, and still feeling the power of the words. Zan Kocher as Love, cheerfully chastising Justine Trombley's Reason, while Marleen Cré's Soul kept the discussion moving forward. And Giovanna Czander bringing it all together as the three spectator characters who arrive to cheer on Love and the Soul and presage Reason's death.

Finally, the night arrived to show what we had cobbled together. We were scheduled on Saturday evening just as the parties were getting started at the conference, so we ended up with a very small audience. Half the audience was made up of conference staff and my colleagues, but we did manage to draw a few grad students. I had hoped for a few more. It was not just about having students attend a performance, but actually to get them to be part of a performance that made the difference. My intent had been to get a few volunteers from the audience to read passages from a fifth text in several of the modern translations from all the parts of the world I could find. I had with me modern versions in French, Spanish, Italian, Hungarian, and of course English. So after inundating them with the videos, I asked for volunteers to read from the modern versions.

I was delighted when Ellen Dolgin, who was at first skeptical of the relevance of the *Mirror*, read from the English text. Her own interest lies in nineteenth- and early twentieth-century stage, particularly in the writings of Shaw and the performances of his plays. Her own interest in the stage and in acting brought a whole new beauty to Marguerite's words. Ellen wrote after the experience: "What struck me most about being with the grad students in languages/lit at NeMLA was their own excitement about the power and beauty of Marguerite's concepts in each of the languages and the electricity we all felt when alternating voices and languages to bring the words to life. Watching the video and the exuberance and joy each felt about the courage and vision of Marguerite deepened my own already rich response to Marguerite and my urge to read more on my own."

One of the most amusing stories that came out of this night in Toronto was Zan Kocher's experience at a conference just a few weeks later: "In May 2015, going into a third decade of hearing papers at the International Congress on Medieval Studies at Kalamazoo, I sat down in a lecture hall and received a handout from the person passing them out, a young man I had never seen before. He gave my face a searching look and stated, in the past tense, 'You read Marguerite Porete.' 'Yes,' I agreed, thinking: that neatly sums up a quarter-century of research effort. Then I realized he must have meant that he had been in Toronto and seen the video." A star is born!

The circle then comes back around for me. As a medievalist, my goal is to bring these ancient works back into circulation. By employing the specialties and talents of others — whether it be their knowledge of other languages or their ability to perform — a difficult or obscure author may find new light. What I discovered through this little experiment is that in some sense all scholars are lonely in their specialties and that by working together with other disciplines we can really help clear obscurity no matter what the field. Though we had a very small audience for our first performance, the story of our accomplishment began to circulate and I have had several requests from other members of the Marguerite Porete scholar family, and a few from non-medievalist colleagues who want to perform this book they've heard about from me and from several of the other people in my office. As part of my regular teaching obligations, I have had the opportunity to bring *Beowulf,* Chaucer, and Shakespeare to my students, but I have also uncovered a way to bring a few of the less likely works to them as well.

I suppose I can't really take credit for coming up with the "Let's put on a show" trope, and perhaps we didn't save the orphanage or rescue Granny, but I do believe that our little show could be a way to make the medievalist in a general education college just a little less lonely. With new technologies, medievalists can work together across distances, and with performance, we can reach beyond our own specialty to make these works relevant again to students (and colleagues) in all fields.

Perpetual Invention and Performance-Based Research: The Case of *The Ballad of Robin Hood and the Potter*

Carolyn Coulson, Shenandoah University[1]

When I was in graduate school, I had a secret, albeit not a very well-kept one. Before I moved across the country to study the Middle Ages, I was an actor and director, working consistently in California's regional theaters. I had always been torn between my creative instincts and my intellectual pursuits, and, when I entered my MA program, I thought that intellect had prevailed and I had left theater behind for good. I remember that, when my peers in the English department would lament the state of the academic job market, I would shrug and think, "I was an actor. The job market doesn't get worse than that." I am not sure if I ever said it out loud after the first month because my experience as a theater practitioner was alien to most of my peers and professors. It was not academic. It was not literary. It was not

---

[1] An earlier version of the "written exegesis" of the performance described below was presented at the International Medieval Congress at Leeds in 2013.

historical. Even to me, it seemed to have little relevance to my new field, except for lending me some comfort in front of a class of undergraduates. My past, therefore, was essentially erased, and I reinvented myself as an academic.

Over the next several years, I embraced my new identity and believed that I had left my dramatic interests in the past. I certainly spent my early graduate studies resisting the possibility that the theater of the Middle Ages held any interest for me. Yet, gradually I found myself returning to the connections between the drama and every other aspect of the medieval period, and during my Ph.D. program I specialized in medieval drama. Because of my broad training in medieval English literature, I expected to work in an English department, but job opportunities arose for someone who had skills in theater. In my first academic appointment, my teaching responsibilities were split between the Theater and English curricula. Clearly, my earlier thoughts on the relevance of my practical theater skills to my academic future were proven wrong. However, even when one finds an academic job, medieval drama may be the loneliest of medieval fields. Perhaps because the extant texts represent mere indications of the actual theatrical events and are therefore incomplete artifacts, non-drama medievalists tend to know little about the period's drama, and amongst theater folk, even those who study theater history, medieval drama is generally dismissed as simple and didactic. I had begun a slow process of reassembling my identity — part academic, part artist — but the isolation of being both a medievalist and a hybrid scholar-practitioner provided me no community in which to root that reassembly or find a methodology.

I spent eight years straddling the Theater and English programs in my first position where I found opportunities to mount productions of the Towneley *Herodes Magnus*, the morality play *Mankind*, and the Tudor comedy *Gammer Gurton's Needle*. Both that school and the one where I currently teach are distinctly "teaching institutions," and I have found that pedagogy-based scholarship is not only an outgrowth of what I spend most of my time doing, but also the most meaningful form of scholarship to me as an educator. Although neither school has a community of medievalists, at my previous job I taught medieval literature, so any pedagogical scholarship I produced could potentially be on a medieval topic. Eight years ago, the vicissitudes of life led me to my current institution where I teach in a performing arts conservatory. I direct plays and musicals and teach courses in theater academics and acting Shakespeare. The program's focus is on training young artists to enter the theater profession, and the acting training is rooted in contemporary realism. There is little call for medieval drama in this venue. Fortunately, the scholarship requirements of my institution reflect its emphasis on student learning; indeed, I could live out my days citing my directing projects as my "creative scholarship," and my institutional career path would be safe. I could leave the Middle Ages behind me, and no one would bat an eyelid.

But I don't want to.

My inner medievalist is so alone as to be forgotten for most of the academic year. Occasionally, and largely through medieval academic conferences, I have managed to carve out opportunities to work on the material I not only love, but also have a knack for staging. In particular, I have directed two productions of medieval texts for performances at academic gatherings, the "Octavian and the Nativity" pageant for the 2010 Chester Cycle at the University of Toronto and the *Ballad of Robin Hood and the Potter* for performance at both the Southeastern Medieval Association and the Longwood Medieval Conference. Neither production was curricularly driven or part of our institution's theatrical season. Both were, however, largely funded by support from the university in the form of faculty development grants and competitive student grants. They also represent opportunities for both significant learning for students and performance-based research for me in my chosen field of study.

For those of us who straddle the practitioner/scholar divide and face persistent puzzlement about where we "fit" in the academy, the emergence of "Performance (or Practice) as Research" or performance-based research is something of a Holy Grail.[2] A still-emerging field, its nature and challenges are well-articulated by Shannon Riley and Lynette Hunter:

> While performance practices have always contributed to knowledge, the idea that performance can be more than creative production, that it can constitute intellectual inquiry and contribute new understanding and insight is a concept that challenges many institutional structures and calls into question what gets valued as knowledge. Perhaps the most single contribution of the developing areas of practice as research (PaR) and performance as research (PAR) is the claim that creative production can constitute intellectual inquiry.[3]

While performance-based research may be a discourse which brings together the world of performance creation and the world of academic scholarship, its discourse is fraught with disagreements and questions about what the end result of such research should be (Is it the Art itself? Is it academic discourse about art?). It is characterized by what Baz Kershaw calls the paradox of "boundless specificity."[4] Kershaw argues that this paradox "ensures this type of research will always resist becoming a single discipline as its projects proliferate insights, understandings, knowledges that, over-all, will be part of many disciplines."[5] It

---

2   The terminology for this developing field is not yet fixed. Generally, scholars in the UK and Australia, where it has largely developed, use the terms "practice as research" and "practice as research in performance." US scholars tend to use "performance as research." There are others, including "practice-based research." The terms not totally interchangeable, although I have deliberately used a combination of them in this article.
3   Shannon Rose Riley and Lynette Hunter, eds., *Mapping Landscapes for Performance as Research: Scholarly Acts and Creative Cartographies* (New York: Palgrave Macmillan, 2009), xv.
4   Baz Kershaw, "Performance Practice as Research: Perspectives from a Small Island," in *Mapping Landscapes for Performance as Research: Scholarly Acts and Creative Cartographies*, eds. Shannon Rose Riley and Lynette Hunter, 3–13 (New York: Palgrave Macmillan, 2009), 4.
5   Ibid., 4–5.

is always specific, yet it belongs to no particular discipline. The methodology of performance-based research is far from fixed; it is in fact necessarily re-created for each project in practice. Even within the community of medieval drama scholars, who increasingly value performance as a learning opportunity, a multitude of contradictory research questions are asked of each event. The questions and challenges are specific to each project, and the methods are those of the discipline's practitioners and the researcher's agenda. My Grail has turned out to be a far more complex vessel than I expected, an elusive container that is constantly changing its size and shape, a constantly-reinvented methodology for a reinvented lone medievalist.

It seems to me that the area of most debate within the performance-based research field has to do with the end result, the knowledge delivery system, if you will. What is the form of the scholarship? For some artist-practitioners, those who resist the urge to extract findings from an experience, the performance is the final product. However, the academic educator whose work is embedded in practice and experiential learning can extrapolate from the event, from the discoveries of the rehearsals and the performance. We can preserve the discoveries in what Suzanne Little calls "the written exegesis, which works to facilitate through reflection and record insights and findings in a form that is publishable."[6] Riley and Hunter entitled their collection of essays on performance-based research *Mapping Landscapes for Performance as Research: Scholarly Acts and Creative Cartographies,* and I think the analogy of cartography is a useful one. Maps reflect the agendas and biases of their creators. They are filtered representations of an objective physical space. This article then is my attempt at providing a written exegesis or map of a performance project of the *Ballad of Robin Hood and the Potter.* My cartographic filters might be entitled: Discoveries about the Text; Discoveries about the Creative Process; Discov-

---

6 Suzanne Little, "Practice and performance as research in the arts," in *Dunedin Soundings: Place and Performance,* eds. D. Bendrups and G. Downes (Dunedin, New Zealand: Otago University Press, 2011): 19–28 at 25.

eries about Student Learning; and Discoveries about Myself. In what follows, I have found it impossible to separate them fully as specific moments of discovery are connected to multiple areas of discovery.

When the organizers of the 2011 Southeastern Medieval Association conference (SEMA) at Agnes Scott College announced that they wanted to include live performances, they specified that, rather than typical reader's theater fare, they wanted memorized performances, preferably with costumes and props. I was very keen to bring something as I had shared a great experience taking a group of students to Toronto to perform in the Chester Cycle 2010. When I mentioned to my students the possibility of taking a medieval play in original pronunciation to a conference, five or six of them were nearly overcome with excitement.[7]

By May, at the International Congress on Medieval Studies in Kalamazoo, I was pondering which dramatic text I should propose for performance at SEMA that autumn. During one of those great conference chats that are so important to lone medievalists, a medieval drama colleague suggested that since there was a Robin Hood panel organized for SEMA, perhaps one of the Robin Hood plays would make a good addition to the program.[8] I liked that idea, but was not very familiar with the materials, as they had never fit into any of the parameters of my graduate courses. They so often fall outside the usual "medieval" periodization and, perhaps, fall to the wayside as professors shape syllabi according to "literary value." As Stephen Knight observes, Robin Hood has always retained a "low," popular art form status, but we need not understand that pejoratively. Knight points out that "in artistic terms, the outlaw tradition is a low — and free — form of life, and so is all the more variable, all the more flexible, all the easier for a re-creator to re-create."[9] It is, there-

---

[7] My position in a professional training program, while challenging for the medievalist, certainly provides me with access to dedicated, talented actors.

[8] Special thanks to Gloria Betcher, without whom this project may never have happened.

[9] Stephen Knight, *Robin Hood: A Mythic Biography* (Ithaca: Cornell University Press, 2009), xv.

fore, always prime for experimentation and reinvention, key elements in Performance and/or Practice as Research.

I started making my way through the early materials in search of the right text. From the beginning, my primary interest was in the task of having the students perform in original pronunciation. I wanted to see how that would affect the creative process: rehearsals, character development, and how the actors would rise to the challenge of the language. When it came to choosing the text, my criteria were largely practical: length, size of cast, and at least some roles that could be played by women. I realized that several of the ballads could easily be performed as plays if I included a narrator-figure. So, why did I choose the *Ballad of Robin Hood and the Potter*? It fit my criteria for length and cast-size; the characters suited the students I already had enlisted; and, frankly, moving beyond practicality into aesthetic judgment, I just liked it the best. I liked its clarity, tempo, tidy action, and humor, all elements I look for in any script I may direct. I liked the boyish charm of its Robin Hood.[10] For a ballad, it afforded considerable sections of dialogue. By editors Knight and Ohlgren's calculations, "55% of the lines [are dialogue], as against 45% in *Robin Hood and the Monk* and 50% in *Robin Hood and Guy of Gisborne,* the other two dialogue-heavy texts."[11] As a director, I am drawn to plays that are linguistically and textually rich and interesting, but that speak to my preference for visual processing. From the beginning of any project, I'm thinking about what the play looks like, how the bodies move and the pictures change. How does that movement help tell the story? One of the reasons I chose *Robin Hood and the Potter* was its opportunity for movement; I could imagine it visually and physically. It is curious that a ballad spoke to me in

---

10 As Knight and Ohlgren point out in their introduction to the text, this ballad, while keeping to many of the typical themes of early tales (yeoman, archery, free ethics of forest), incorporates elements of the trickster into this characterization of Robin Hood. Stephen Knight and Thomas Ohlgren, eds., *Robin Hood and Other Outlaw Tales* (Kalamazoo: Medieval Institute Publications, 2000), 58.

11 Ibid., 59.

this visual, physical way, as one would expect the genre to be less active and more descriptive, but perhaps it was the description that painted the pictures in my mind.

For a variety of reasons, practical and aesthetic, the Ballad of *Robin Hood and the Potter* fit my needs and interests. It is not, however, a play, so it required some adapting, although it needed far less than I originally thought it might. The fact that I predicted a need for change that ultimately was not present can be seen as a microcosmic representation of my self-conscious concern over my professional identity when I entered academia. If nothing else, my experiences with a career shift and this performance project (and all others) have taught me to trust my instincts and to stop worrying about categories.

In the end, I didn't change or cut a single word of the *Ballad of Robin Hood and the Potter*. What I did do is assign lines to characters and decide where the lines should be sung. Exploratory rehearsals later revealed the sections that could most effectively (and affectively) be underscored. I chose to use a minstrel character to frame the narrative. I admit this was partly an homage to the Disney animated *Robin Hood* (one of my childhood favorites), and I think it was also a subconscious echo of the minstrel who is part of the musical *Robin Hood* that I performed in when I was thirteen years old. But it is also largely a response to the fact that the text is a ballad, and it just sounds like a minstrel at the beginning, with lines like:

> Herkens, god yemen,
> Comley, corteys, and god,
> On of the best that yever bare bowe,
> Hes name was Roben Hode. (ll. 5–8)[12]

As Knight and Ohlgren point out, this ballad's rapid and dramatic changes in viewpoint have "led to the connection of the ballad to the minstrel style, that is a rather casual technique based on direct communication and emotive effects, assumed to

---

12 Ibid., 62.

indicate a popular context."[13] Evoking the minstrel tradition, we used a ukulele to accompany the singing, to underscore some sections of dialogue, and to achieve a number of sound effects.

We ended up with two minstrel-narrators, again for practical and aesthetic reasons. First, I had two actresses I wanted to use; they would both double as Robin's band and the wives and widows of Nottingham, amongst other characters and objects. Second, the minstrel's lines account for about 45% of the text, approximately thirty-seven stanzas out of seventy-nine. It is far more interesting if that much text is broken up between two people in a dramatic context. Third, two actors make a scene, because they interact with each other, transforming "narrative" into a more dramatically active event. Our minstrel-narrators were also instrumental in the establishment of a relationship between players and audience, one in which both sides have an investment. The ballad's text is divided into three fitts, which correspond to major scene changes: the greenwood, Nottingham, and the greenwood again. I decided to have the beginning and ending of each section sung to help bookend them and clarify the change of scene. We ultimately discovered that a modulation in key was a great auditory cue for the move from Fitt One to Fitt Two and the change of setting.

The theatrical rehearsal process is always one of solving puzzles and overcoming challenges, including those of character psychology, design, staging, and storytelling clarity. This project had some unique challenges to add to the usual ones. First, the performers were non-medievalists, a situation which frequently occurs at institutions where few medieval courses are taught. We lone medievalists must learn how to quickly orient students to the Middle Ages with entry points that engage interest and curiosity rather than relying on depth of study. Fortunately, two of the *Robin Hood* students had been in my troupe that performed the Chester "Nativity" in Toronto, and one of those (who played Robin Hood) had taken my Acting Early Drama class and dabbled in reading Middle English. The rest of them were flying

---

13 Ibid., 59.

on enthusiasm and the willingness to learn and try anything I suggested. Second, due to most of the actors being in another show, we had a very short rehearsal period — two weeks, with probably six group rehearsals during that time. We also had only a brief description of the location in which we would perform.

To tackle the challenge of late fifteenth-century pronunciation, spelling and language, about five weeks before the performance, I sent the actors the text with a facing page modernization for their reference, along with D. Thomas Hanks' one-page handout on Malorian pronunciation and an audio link to the Chaucer Studio's recording of the *Digby St. Paul* play, for which we had used the same guidelines.[14] When we finally met, they had all put in some time on what they called "the dialect." After our first group rehearsal, I met with each of them individually to go through their lines word by word, sound by sound. Here is where I think we venture into a strange new territory for the students' learning experience. None of them had ever had to actually stop and pay attention to every word they had to say in a play, let alone every syllable. As they did so, each word, each sound became foreign and mysterious. Words they thought they understood were revealed to have meanings they had never heard of. The language they thought they knew was suddenly opened up, and they got a glimpse of the mechanics and history of the language. All students working with Middle English experience this to some extent, but for those who are trying to *act* in it — whose job it is to make the words come from them as if for the first time — the responsibilities of chewing, digesting, and literally re-producing that language are immense. I think we all started out thinking that working in original pronunciation would be a technical exercise, and that's what it was to begin with. But, to my actors' credit, they really took on the acting task of making the words spring from their own minds, of reinventing them. In doing so, they took ownership of the text in a way that I have rarely seen young actors do. It was a

---

14 Chaucer Studio's website can be found at http://creativeworks.byu.edu/chaucer/.

milestone in their training as they realized that the same process should happen with every play.

The second major set of creative puzzles were staging challenges, including the following: the action requires the Potter to ride onstage in his cart, pulled by his horse; the Sheriff rides a second horse; Robin steals that horse and sends the Sheriff home with nothing but a white palfrey (a third horse); there is a quarterstaff vs. sword combat sequence; Robin disguises himself as the Potter; the action moves through various locations and includes a dinner party and an archery contest. On top of these narrative specifics, the staging has to help communicate the plot clearly, as the archaic language is obscure for the modern ear, even for medievalists in the audience. And we had no budget and one van to fit all eight of us and our props.

We solved all of these issues as a group, and our collaborative problem-solving yielded one of the most satisfying creative projects any of us has worked on. The process by which we decided how we were going to stage the horses is indicative and worth discussing. After the minstrels' opening where Robin, Little John and the men are introduced, the band spies a Potter come driving over the way in his cart. Robin stops him and lays hands on the Potter's horse, which riles the Potter who twice tells Robin to take his hands off the animal. It is a major confrontation which sets the plot in motion. For the cart, we settled on a stylized solution with two quarterstaffs between two actors, who were the head and rear of the horse. The actors were particularly concerned with "how the audience would know they were a horse," and for a while we talked of re-purposing our donkey mask from the Chester Nativity. As we moved along with our blocking, I realized that if we used a mask for one horse, we would have to use one for the others, and the whole thing became too cumbersome and distracting. So instead, each horse was embodied by an actor in a different way. The Potter's horse was established by sound, physicalization, and the interaction between the horse and Robin or the Potter (call it our cheap and dirty version of Warhorse). The unapologetic, child-like quality of this solution seemed to send a message to the audience about the inventive, imaginative nature of the piece, reinforcing the tone set by the "prelude" we created dramatizing the classic encounter of Robin and Little John on the log — almost completely established in mime.

The second horse is ridden by the Sheriff when he accompanies the disguised Robin-Potter into the greenwood. The text specifies the Sheriff's light-hearted ride:

> Upon the morrow, when het was day,
> He boskyd hem forthe to reyde; (ll. 234–35)

And:

> The screffes hart was never so leythe,
> The feyre foreyst to se.
>
> And when he cam yn to the foreyst,
> Under the leffes grene,
> Berdys there sange on bowhes prest,
> Het was gret goy to se. (ll. 244–49)[15]

The cheery lightness, along with the singing birds and the dramatic irony that the Sheriff is riding into a trap always made us laugh at this passage. We decided that the Sheriff should have a bridle and some reins and just prance along with them, Monty Python-style. The physicality worked directly with the text, and when his mimed trot accompanied the line "the screffes hart was never so leythe / the feyre foreyst to se," I think we struck comedy gold.

The final horse appears after Robin and his men strip the Sheriff of his clothes, money and belongings and send him home to his wife with nothing but a white palfrey (which is a gift to the wife from Robin). Within the narrative of the poem, the horse comes from nowhere. All of a sudden Robin says,

---

15 Knight and Ohlgren, *Robin Hood and Other Outlaw Tales*, 69–70.

"Hether ye cam on hors foll hey,
And hom schall ye go on fote;
And gret well they weyffe at home,
The woman ys foll godde.
Y schall her sende a wheyt palffrey,
Het hambellet as the weynde." (ll. 282–87)[16]

The tricking of the Sheriff is the climax of the plot, and this scene required more bodies than we had. The Potter who had served as the rear of the cart-horse in the first part of the scene merely stood up and grabbed a staff to threaten the Sheriff, and the minstrel who was playing one of Robin's men suddenly became the palfrey when Robin said the word. This was again in keeping with the inventive quality we embraced of necessity, but which gave our piece its signature. It also contributed to the effect that these words were being invented by the actors, that the whole thing had the bit of the feeling of a *commedia lazzi*. In improvisation, when one actor introduces an idea, the other actors' responsibility is to say "yes" and act on it. When Robin said "white palfrey," several of the others repeated the word as if to say "oh, palfrey, whose got that one?" The minstrel whipped off her hat, tossed her mane and pranced up to the Sheriff.

Our experiences clearly support Knight and Ohlgren's statement that "the tone and impact of the ballad may well show more art than has sometimes been assumed; its plot is quick-moving and highly effective, its tone vigorous and direct, with a strong and well-maintained level of irony."[17] Beyond our appreciation for and understanding of the text, however, this project contributed to an empowerment of the students through an exceptionally rich, collaborative learning experience and a truly fulfilling response from the audience. At the beginning of this exegesis, I separated creative process and student learning into two different "filters," but in many ways they are intricately woven together. The learning certainly grew out of the creative process.

---

16 Ibid., 71.
17 Ibid., 59.

My final filter was what I discovered about myself, and this area seems most pertinent to the *Ballad of the Lone Medievalist*. As I said above, in my move from theater to graduate school, I had to reinvent myself as an academic, but later job duties led me to reassemble myself as a hybrid academic/creative practitioner. As I move through my career at institutions with little in the way of a medieval community, I realize the reinvention of self does not end. Those of us who are lone medievalists are constantly inventing ways to be medievalists in the confines of our often non-medievalist duties. Paul Carter's thoughts on invention point toward the larger conceptual picture this project opened for me within the practice-led research field, but they also seem wholly applicable to the plight of the lone medievalist:

> The condition of invention — the state of being that allows a state of becoming to emerge — is a perception, or recognition, of the ambiguity of appearances. Invention begins when what signifies exceeds its signification — when what means one thing, or conventionally functions in one role, discloses other possibilities.[18]

A practice-based approach that belongs to no particular discipline may be the perfect fit for a medieval drama specialist adrift in a sea of modernist theater practitioners, and the willingness to embrace invention and reinvention must surely be a key survival tool for any lone medievalist, no matter what their specialty or discipline.

---

18 Paul Carter, "Interest: The Ethics of Invention," in *Practice as Research: Approaches to Creative Arts Enquiry*, eds. Estelle Barrett and Barbara Bolt, 15–26 (London: I.B. Tauris, 2014), 15.

What's the Message?: Building Community through Tolkien's *Beowulf*

Holly M. Wendt, Lebanon Valley College

When I was asked to participate in a series of summer book talks, I had a number of decisions to make. The first — to participate at all — was easy. As a faculty member finishing up the first year on the tenure track at a new campus, I jumped at the chance to take part in a long-running partnership between my institution and an active, engaged local community. The second decision — the book — was far more difficult. The series' scope ranged wide; the other texts on the schedule leaned heavily toward history, biography, and accessible social and natural science. As someone whose academic interests and teaching responsibilities lay evenly split between creative writing and medieval literature, I was, like Chaucer's Troilus, in *kankedort*.[1] But I found resolution in J.R.R. Tolkien's translation of *Beowulf*. Tolkien's *Beowulf* struck the right balance of intellectually interesting and more broadly appealing; if *Beowulf* itself didn't draw people in, perhaps Tolkien's name might. *The Hobbit* film franchise, after all, had just drawn to a close, and the bulk of the book talk attend-

---
1 Geoffrey Chaucer, *Troilus and Criseyde* (New York: Penguin, 2003), 122.

ees would be seniors. If they had children, those children would have been of an age to discover Tolkien's creative works in their youth. This audience, too, might have better memory of Peter Jackson's screen adaptation of the *Lord of the Rings* trilogy than my current sophomores, who were only four years old when the first movie came out.

Between graduate school, a full-time position at a community college, and the position I now hold as an assistant professor at a small liberal arts college, I've taught the early English literature survey at least once a year for a decade, as well as upper-division Middle English literature and a medieval studies-themed first year writing course. In those courses, especially in the survey, Tolkien has been my populist inroad into *Beowulf,* a more contemporary point from which to enter the text. Sometimes, I feel a bit fraudulent starting there; the niggling scholarly doubt says *aren't I a medievalist?* What do I *need* this fantasy touchstone for? Then sense takes over: I don't *need* it — I *love* it. Tolkien's *Lord of the Rings* trilogy and *The Hobbit,* in parts, are also a love song to medieval studies and languages. And if my purpose in the book talk series was to take *Beowulf* out of the classroom — a space marked by obligation and underwritten by a sense of duty in both the most and the least enthusiastic students — and bring it into a purely voluntary space, on what turned out to be a perfect summer morning, well off-campus, it was the love song I wanted to sing.

***

Convincing people of the value of medieval studies is hard — more than hard. What most will allow is that medieval studies, like other history-based pursuits, has to do with old stuff, and knowledge about old stuff — especially stuff that has actually happened — is a source of cultural capital. There is *Jeopardy!,* after all. But when the focus shifts to literature, especially fragmented, anonymous texts in languages undecipherable without specialized training, it's a harder sell still. As I prepared my talk, I admit to thinking long on that point, second-guessing my choice.

My campus — and the neighboring town where I gave the talk — are in the heart of south-central Pennsylvania, in the shrugging green shoulders of the Appalachians. While we're not so far away from Philadelphia, Washington, D.C., and New York — and from larger universities with medievalists of different stripes across multiple departments — the immediate surrounds are rather isolating despite the reality that, within an hour's drive of my campus home, there are at least half a dozen similar institutions. Geographically, that seems a gift. Practically, the circumstance is far more complex: at those similar colleges, we lone medievalists are also carrying robust teaching loads that often engage other areas of study and wearing multiple hats with regard to service, advising, and developing engaging, productive, and often interdisciplinary ways to bring medieval studies into the wider curriculum. Those myriad duties make it difficult to add building relationships *beyond* the campus borders to the to-do list. The difficulty is increased by the relative isolation even on one's home campus; I'm not only the lone medievalist in the English department, I'm also the only one at the institution whose research connects explicitly to pre-modern Europe. To be fair, of course, multiple colleagues in multiple disciplines face the same challenge; having a limited number of faculty ensures breadth of coverage over depth, and the more specific or arcane one's field — say, Anglo-Saxon poetry, let alone medieval studies at large — the less likely one will find felicitous overlap with colleagues in history or music or art history.

It was, though, within that context of isolation that I found the way to push back against the doubt. The chance to take medieval studies out of the confines of my classroom was a twofold boon: it was an opportunity to share aspects of my own work and my favorite poem with a crowd of people self-selected as interested in learning diverse things, and it was a chance to make a community, no matter how temporary, and to enlarge my own, by however small a measure.

To my happy surprise, sixty people — twice the size of the largest class I teach, which is, incidentally, the English literature survey — attended. Because I'd been told to prepare as though few had read the book in advance — and because I hoped it might inspire some to read the book after — I reviewed the history and content of *Beowulf* and then zeroed in on Tolkien's approach as a translator, closing with the way his translation and linguistic engagement ultimately affected *The Hobbit* and *The Lord of the Rings*. When the Q&A began, I was threefold glad I had chosen this particular text. The audience brought lively questions: further inquiries into the preservation of the *Beowulf* manuscript, some wondering about the linguistic movement between Old and Middle English. Someone asked about the Great Vowel Shift, someone else about the inclusion of the poem in so many high school curricula. It was, in short, the exact kind of curiosity I'd hoped would bubble up: wide-ranging, expansive, and in the context of other learned things.

Someone else, then, asked, "What was Tolkien's message?"

That was a question I hadn't anticipated, one with many possible answers and so weighty that I needed to try. So I started with the translation itself.

Tolkien does not undertake a poetic translation. According to Christopher Tolkien, who had been the one to arrange J.R.R. Tolkien's notes and papers into the book manuscript and also to type up his father's hand-written and annotated translations so many years ago, the primary goal of Tolkien's translation is clarity of meaning as it pertains to understanding the world of the poem.[2] In order to best serve that meaning, Tolkien also opts not to write in a particularly alliterative fashion, focusing instead on choosing the best words in the best order to convey the hero's deeds and the world of the Danes and the Geats, without any extensive formal or poetic constraints.

The predominant theory Tolkien espouses throughout the commentary included in the volume is that Beowulf must have

---

2 J.R.R. Tolkien, *Beowulf: A Translation and Commentary together with Sellic Spell*, ed. Christopher Tolkien (Boston: Houghton Mifflin Harcourt, 2014), 8.

had its roots in a folk tale, a fairy story of some kind.[3] Rather than simply making the claim, Tolkien also wrote an iteration of such a fairy story: *Sellic Spell,* which is included in the volume. In the creation of the tale, Tolkien reinforces his commitment to that textual clarity. Rather than allowing the idea of the fairy story to remain in the abstract, *Sellic Spell* serves as a concrete example of what that story, according to Tolkien's thesis, must have been like. The fairy story is also capped by a rendition of *Sellic Spell* in Old English, an attempt to bring the whole full-circle. Over and over, Tolkien's work shows a devotion to a reader's understanding; even where prudence requires a bit of equivocation — it *might* have been like this — he makes no such equivocation in what the *like this* might be.

But that wasn't the answer to the full question. The asker added another layer, invoking the writing of C.S. Lewis, Tolkien's friend and fellow writer. The man reframed the question as a point of difference: Lewis's writings were allegorical and rife with overt Christian symbolism; Tolkien made all attempts to avoid the same in his own work. To wit, then, the question re-posed had other implications: what was Tolkien's message — with regard to the sense that Lewis's message was explicitly Christian?

I turned to the larger themes of good versus evil: in that regard, surely, Tolkien and Lewis demonstrated agreement. Both writers' and their novels' sympathies align with good. That Tolkien seems less interested in aligning that particular goodness with any immediately recognizable framework does not change his novels' bent toward it.

We had stepped beyond the bounds of *Beowulf,* and yet the same phenomenon occurs in *Beowulf*. Though the Danes and Geats appear to be generally pagan and the poet-narrator moralizes in favor of Christianity from time to time, the poem indefatigably praises certain secularly motivated behaviors via a protagonist who acts to defend others, who keeps his word, who does not abuse the superlative powers given him. That Beowulf is a hero whose greatest concerns are a mortal definition of hon-

---

3   Ibid, 204–13.

or and an earthly fame ultimately does not matter: the poem champions what is admirable, even when it is considered transient in comparison to the poet's own faith.

With that response, the asker seemed satisfied. Someone else signaled for the questions microphone, and on we went. But no matter that the answer didn't feel *un*true, something about what I'd said left me dissatisfied. Something about it wasn't round enough, wasn't full enough. There had to be more to it; on this point, easily articulated reasons couldn't match the physical sensation brought forth in reading these texts, the feeling that *feeling* was too large for the confines of my ribs.

***

A little less than a month later, my English Literature I students read Seamus Heaney's translation of *Beowulf*, and even though Tolkien's text wasn't in front of them, I couldn't resist a little detour. I usually show clips from the 2002 film iteration of *The Two Towers*: King Theoden's grief over his own dead son is an echo of King Hrethel, and the *ubi sunt* passage is a clear hearkening to "The Wanderer" and the elegiac list of Anglo-Saxon poetry.[4] The trappings of the film scenes also offer an opportunity to talk, in more vivid detail, about burial mounds, armor and clothing, and even the Geatish woman's lament that marks the poem's end. But this time, Tolkien's words and scholarship felt nearer still.

The character Unferth, who becomes Unfriend in Tolkien's *Sellic Spell*, is always a point of interest in class discussions. First and foremost, Unferth is the subject of ridicule, recipient of a "shut up, you're drunk" admonition that provides a resonant moment of levity.[5] He's also one of the few characters who appears to undergo change in *Beowulf*; whether it is Unferth's

---

[4] *The Lord of the Rings: The Two Towers*, dir. Peter Jackson (Los Angeles: New Line Cinema, 2002).

[5] R.D. Fulk et al., eds., *Klaeber's Beowulf*, 4th edn. (Toronto: University of Toronto Press, 2008), ll. 530–31.

duty as Hrothgar's *þyle* to challenge and insult Beowulf to test his mettle or whether he is simply a jealous coward, Unferth's treatment of the hero eventually alters such that Unferth sends his own ancestral sword with Beowulf into Grendel's mother's mere. Though the sword ultimately proves useless in that fight, the generosity of the gesture is noteworthy, and Beowulf respects both sword and lender enough to bring the weapon back to the surface with him, despite the burden of the giant-sword hilt and Grendel's severed head that he also carries. The exchange of esteem and the return of Unferth's family sword crystalizes that change: a loudmouth reconsiders his words and behavior, and his adversary forgives him. Perhaps for these reasons, Unferth feels more real to my students than Beowulf, with all of his superlative qualities, and wise, weary Hrothgar. In conversation about Unferth this time, a detail that came up in the summer talk bubbled again to the surface.

In his notes to the translation, Tolkien discusses his choices regarding particular words referring to the Geats' armor as they enter Hrothgar's hall — the apparent manuscript phrase "guþmod grummon" and his proposed emendation to "guþmod grima."[6] Tolkien's point is grammatical — he favors a representative singular instead of a plural — but he draws attention to the word *grima*, a mask or visor that at least partially covers the face. In another later comment, expressly dealing with Unferth, Tolkien calls him "wormtongued."[7] Readers of Tolkien's fiction now recognize a significant character in the land of Rohan: Grima Wormtongue, pawn of the evil wizard Saruman and Theoden's corrupted adviser. In the presentation, this detail served as a pleasing little proof of how Tolkien's linguistic felicity asserted itself in his creative work: the mask-word, plus a reference to a somewhat duplicitous character in *Beowulf,* equals a whole new fictional entity. But the presence of Old English names and referents in *The Lord of the Rings* and *The Hobbit* aren't mere scholarly Easter eggs. Grima Wormtongue appears to be a character

---

6   Tolkien, *Beowulf,* 205.
7   Ibid, 253.

literally born from Tolkien's deep consideration of the poem and its characters, of the translation and notes he made as an educator himself.

The students in my English literature survey are mostly non-English majors. There are some, but the course meets a general education requirement, and so the majority of the students are from disciplines far afield from my own. But the business and biology and actuarial science majors who find their way into the class have chosen this particular course from a pool of several for some reason. It's also the course in which students are most likely to be reading a novel — something that has nothing to do with any of their classes — in the minutes before the course begins. There are always people in the class interested in creative writing. Some of these are the English majors, and many are not. But, like Tolkien, they are people deeply interested in stories.

So if I could go back to that morning in August, I would revise my answer about Tolkien's message thus to add: Tolkien's best message, perhaps, is that there is great power in stories, especially this one. In his 1936 essay, "*Beowulf*: The Monsters and the Critics," Tolkien asserted Beowulf scholarship could only live its fullest life when those studying the poem accepted it as a story, a tale, rather than solely a linguistic artifact or a historical patchwork.[8] It was as a story — a story he taught, translated, reinvented as *Sellic Spell,* and then re-translated in an Old English iteration of *Sellic Spell* — that *Beowulf* rippled through Tolkien's own invented worlds. Even the poem's language — the great hurdle for most students of *Beowulf* and in which Tolkien delighted — was a font of character and motivation in the Middle Earth he built. In reading all of these works, in coming again to the language, to the characters, to the meanings, we make meaning. We build that world anew.

***

---

8   J.R.R. Tolkien, "*Beowulf*: The Monsters and the Criticsm," in *Beowulf: A Verse Translation,* ed. Daniel Donoghue, 103–30 (New York: W.W. Norton, 2002).

Only a few weeks ago — a full two months after the book talk — I received an e-mail from one of the women who'd attended. A "word of the day" subscription brought "kenning" into her inbox. That precipitated her to write to me, as she'd also read that Beowulf's name was derived from the kenning "bee-wolf," or bear; she wanted to know whether that was indeed correct.

Wearing my responsible *Beowulf* scholar hat, I noted first that there were few firm answers where the details of the poem were concerned; the scholarly opinion on "Beowulf" as an overt reference to a bear remains divided. There are the stories of Bodvar Bjarki and Hrolf Kraki, with which the *Beowulf* poem might share some common ground, but excessive strength alone does not a bear-man make. That Tolkien chose to embrace the possibility in *Sellic Spell* by naming his proto-Beowulf Beewulf outright speaks more for the imaginative capacity contained in the word "Beowulf." The entire poem's imaginative capacity was something Tolkien valued. And on I went, certainly for longer than was strictly necessary, but, I hope, not longer than was interesting.

In the moments after I'd sent off the reply, it occurred that she'd sent me the question not only because she'd been to the presentation, but because she had access to a local medievalist, to a person who'd publicly claimed affinity for and fascination with not only one translation but a poem, a period, and all the echoes and flickers of light across the sea of *then* and *now*. She did not send her question to the leading scholars in the field, but rather to someone in her community. In that e-mail, too, I understood that I wasn't really sitting alone in my proverbial boat. She rowed with me, and the man who wanted to know something about Tolkien's message, and the rest; my English Literature I students — nearly thirty new ones each semester, together all of us comprising the strength Beowulf wields in each arm[9] — take up oars together, and so, too, we sing.

---

9   Fulk et al., *Klaeber's Beowulf*, ll. 379b–380.

Why Read *That*?: Selling the Middle Ages

Diane Cady, Mills College

As medievalists, we often do our training in graduate programs with several medievalists on staff, only to find ourselves teaching in places where we are the lone medievalists. As a consequence, we may find ourselves fielding questions from students, colleagues, and administrators about the value—cultural, aesthetic and economic—of studying the Middle Ages. I remember one such question early in my career, during my first semester at Mills College, a small liberal arts college in Oakland, California, with a woman-identified, undergraduate population. How, a student asked, could I love Chaucer? Initially, her question surprised me: I *not* only love Chaucer, but also often wonder how anyone could not love Chaucer. Yet, I also understood the source of her question. We had just finished reading "The Reeve's Tale," a short and troubling story that, like many of the *Canterbury Tales,* presents women's bodies as the terrain on which male rivalry is fought. Does teaching such stories perpetuate the idea that sexual violence is inevitable? Does it reproduce misogyny and gender bias, she pressed? What value, if any, do texts like these hold for us as readers today?

Like many of the questions our students ask, hers were both thoughtful and important. They are questions that not only have pedagogical import but also, in a time of decreased funding for the humanities, are questions we must engage with for professional survival. In this essay, I want to consider why, as medievalists (and especially as lone medievalists in a department or institution), we are more likely to be asked these kinds of questions about value than our colleagues teaching in other fields; what pedagogical opportunities engaging with such questions might provide; and how we can make curricular choices that will make more transparent to students, colleagues, and administrators the larger import of the Middle Ages in contemporary culture and life.

As lone medievalists, we can sometimes feel marginalized in our departments or institutions, perhaps even feel somewhat defensive about questions that seem to challenge the value and viability of the period we have dedicated so many years to studying and, presumably, one we are quite passionate about. These questions can feel particularly annoying if a person feels she is the only professor in a department being asked them. Does an English department's Shakespearean or the History department's specialist in the American Civil War ever get asked such questions? Buried behind these questions, however, is a simple truth: as medievalists we need to make more visible the reason our students might want to study the Middle Ages and that must extend beyond simply covering historical knowledge. When I began teaching medieval literature, I often let the Middle Ages itself serve as the organizing structure behind my classes. I taught survey courses in medieval literature, and courses on single authors, such as Chaucer, or on genres such as medieval drama or medieval women's visionary literature. I taught at an institution in which students were required to take a set number of courses in pre-1600 literature, providing a somewhat captive audience for my classes. This situation changed when I came to Mills as their lone medievalist. I found myself in a department that had no early literature requirements (or any period requirements, for that matter). If I wanted students in my class, I was going to have to figure out how to make a case for why they might want to study medieval literature.

What initially posed a challenge ended up being a tremendous gift to my teaching. Now that I could no longer rely on a set number of students in my classroom, I had to engage more robustly with the question: *why* study the Middle Ages. Historical background or the need for "coverage" seemed like wan answers to such a question. One way that I took up this question was to design courses that take up critical questions and issues that are particularly important to my students, such as the constructions of gender, sexuality and race, biopolitics, literary theory, and the role of literature in colonialist endeavors. All these issues can be explored effectively through the study of medieval texts. One tack I take is to make very clear to my students the critical question or issue operating behind a class: the "so what" of it all. For example, the central question in my "Queer Premodern" course asks, "If, according to Foucault, sexual identity is an eighteenth-century invention, what does sexuality look like in a premodern context?" In that class, we read a wide variety of texts, including *Sir Gawain and the Green Knight, The Complaint of Nature,* "The Pardoner's Tale," and the poems of Juan de la Cruz. In many ways, the class is not that different in content from a traditional medieval literature survey. However, by reorienting the frame to encompass a critical question (versus letting the period be the explanatory narrative), I found students in my class who before had not considered taking a medieval literature class. For these students, what had become clearer to them was the larger cultural and intellectual stakes in studying the medieval past.

These stakes are important to acknowledge upfront since, while often fuzzy about the historical and cultural facts of the Middle Ages, students almost always enter our classrooms with set ideas about what this long, supposedly "middling" period signifies. As Umberto Eco observed thirty years ago, Western culture is still "dreaming of the Middle Ages."[1] In America in particular, that dream takes two seemingly contradictory forms. On the one hand, there is the Middle Ages of fantasy and nostal-

---

1 Umberto Eco, "Dreaming of the Middles Ages," in *Travels in Hyperrealiy,* trans. William Weaver, 61–72 (San Diego: Harvest Books, 1986).

gia, a kind of playground of the imaginary, which serves as the setting for so many popular books, movies, and television series. On the other, there is the Middle Ages of nightmare, a place that conjures specters of authoritarianism, brutality, sexual violence, and gender oppression, an image that only has intensified in the wake of the heightened rhetoric following 9/11, which has frequently deployed "the medieval" as part of its arsenal.[2]

While popular culture and media are largely responsible for these images of the Middle Ages, scholars have also contributed to their construction and circulation. (And indeed, depending on our institutional culture, our own colleagues may contribute to that construction as well). In scholarly discourse the Middle Ages occupy an odd and contradictory role. They are often presented as a time radically different from the periods that follow, with their close heralding the beginning of modernity. And yet,

---

2 Indeed, the week I sat down to write the initial draft of this essay, then Republican presidential candidate Carly Fiorina was touting her degree in medieval history and philosophy as a qualification for fighting ISIS, an organization that she claimed makes use of medieval "techniques" ("the crucifixion, the beheadings, the burning alive") and one that "wants to take its territory back to the Middle Ages." See Jordyn Phelps, "Carly Fiorina Says Knowledge of Medieval History Will Help Her Defeat ISIS," *ABCnews* (last modified 5 October 2015), http://abcnews.go.com/Politics/carly-fiorina-medieval-history-degree-helps-defeat-isis/story?id=34256597. Although never stated outright, the implicit logic seemed to be that a commander-in-chief familiar with a medieval past would be especially well equipped to confront its modern manifestations. As a number of commentators have noted, ISIS's origins, methods, and technologies are decidedly modern, even ultra-modern. However, associating ISIS with the Middle Ages has less to do with a misunderstanding of history and more to do with a nostalgic investment in a fictional past which can conveniently serve as a screen onto which can be projected anything that a society wishes to distance itself from. For a discussion of the link of ISIS to the Middle Ages, see John Terry, "Why ISIS Isn't Medieval," *Slate* (last modified 19 February 2015), http://www.slate.com/articles/news_and_politics/history/2015/02/isis_isn_t_medieval_its_revisionist_history_only_claims_to_be_rooted_in.html. For a response to Fiorina's association of ISIS with the Middle Ages, see David M. Perry, "No, Carly Fiorina, a degree in medieval history doesn't qualify you to fight ISIS," *The Guardian* (last modified 6 October 2015), http://www.theguardian.com/commentisfree/2015/oct/06/carly-fiorina-medieval-history-degree-fight-isis.

the Middle Ages are also viewed as foundational for modern ways of thinking. It is why, for example, Edward Said can locate in a medieval text like Dante's *Inferno* the origins of colonialist thinking, while Benedict Anderson can suggest that colonialism is a decidedly modern phenomena, one rooted in nationalism and unknown to the feudal Middle Ages.[3] Or why Michel Foucault can claim that the medieval confessional is essential to the invention of the modern sexual subject, while simultaneously arguing that medieval and modern thinking about sexuality are radically different.[4] As Kathleen Davis has argued, there is a "split temporality" that often exists in deployments of the Middle Ages, which allows it to be both "the immature stage from which modernity developed, and an inert, temporal space incapable of change."[5] The supposed alterity of the Middle Ages allows for it to function as a blank space onto which various historical periods and places can project their fears and fantasies. It is a blank space that is configured, at once, as both empty of meaning and, because of that emptiness, full of cultural significance.

---

[3] For a discussion of Edward Said's use of the medieval in Orientalism and how medievalists have traditionally replicated Anderson's idea that colonialism is not a medieval phenomenon, see Kathleen Biddick, "Coming Out of Exile: Dante on the Orient Express," in *The Postcolonial Middle Ages,* ed. Jeffrey Jerome Cohen, 35–52 (New York: Palgrave, 2000). For a sense of the diverse ways in which the Middle Ages is both a period of colonization and central to theoretical understandings of colonialism, see the essays in Jeffrey Jerome Cohen, ed., *The Postcolonial Middle Ages* (New York: Palgrave, 2000) and in Lisa Lampert-Weissig, *Medieval Literature and Postcolonial Studies* (Edinburgh: Edinburgh University Press, 2010).

[4] On Michel Foucault's seemingly contradictory use of the medieval in *The History of Sexuality, Volume I,* see Karma Lochrie, "Desiring Foucault," *Journal of Medieval and Early Modern Studies* 27, no. 1 (1997): 3–16. Carolyn Dinshaw has argued that Foucault's misreading of the Middle Ages is strategic and an effort to imagine a time and place unencumbered by the constraints of modern sexuality. See Carolyn Dinshaw, "Getting Medieval: Pulp Fiction, Foucault, and the Use of the Past," in *Getting Medieval: Sexualities and Communities, Pre- and Postmodern* (Durham & London: Duke University Press, 1999), 183–206.

[5] Kathleen Davis, "Time Behind the Veil: The Media, the Middle Ages, and Orientalism Now," in *The Postcolonial Middle Ages,* ed. Jeffrey Jerome Cohen, 105–22 (New York: Palgrave, 2000), 107.

It is the simultaneous alterity and centrality of the Middle Ages in contemporary culture that makes it a particularly productive place for students to not only contemplate the legacy of the past, but also its uses in the present. One strategy that I use in my classroom to highlight this ideological work is to read medieval and modern texts alongside one another. In doing so, students discover that ideas they identify as modern often have their roots in earlier periods. They also discover that ideology often lurks in modern texts behind the mask of liberation and, conversely, that medieval texts are not as hegemonic in their ideology as they might seem at first.

For example, I teach a course called What's Love Got to Do With It?, which attends to the decidedly unromantic concerns of medieval romance. For many of my students, this class is their first encounter with actual medieval romance, and they are often surprised to discover that these texts contradict the idealization of chivalry and romance they so often find in movies and books. While the language of respect and adoration exists on the surface of classical and medieval "instructional manuals" on love, such as Ovid's *The Art of Love,* Andreas Capellanus's *Art of Courtly Love,* or Lorris de Guillaume and Jean de Meun's *Romance of the Rose,* these texts also reveal that respect and adoration are primarily performances a man must enact in order to "win" a woman. When we turn to specific romances, students see that heterosexual love serves not as an inspiration for chivalric deeds, but rather as an impediment to their fulfillment and as a constant threat to homosocial bonds. Students are particularly surprised by how often sexual violence or the threat of sexual violence appears in these romances. Generally, by the midpoint of the class, students begin expressing relief that they now live in a more equitable age, when women are more empowered in their romantic relations.

It is at this point that I like to introduce a modern text that invites students to challenge their narratives of progress when it comes to gender ideology. One example that I find particularly useful for my students is the HBO series *Sex in the City.* Although now off the air for a number of years, the show continues to circulate in the form of reruns and movies. In 2013, the CW launched a spinoff series, *The Carrie Diaries,* which supposedly chronicled the teenage years of the main protagonist, Carrie Bradshaw. Although only on air for a year, this series introduced the franchise to a whole new generation of viewers. Some scholars have seen potential empowerment and cultural critique (albeit circumscribed) in its portrayal of women who have high-powered, glamorous jobs, spend money on themselves (rather than on partners or families) in the form of expensive dinners and drinks and fashionable clothes, and speak frankly about sex and the pursuit of pleasure.[6] While all this seems very modern, what often struck me about the show as I watched was how medieval it was in its presentation of women, particularly in its treatment of women's pursuit of both sexual pleasure and luxury goods.

While these themes traverse all six seasons of the show, it is made most explicit in an episode from the first season called "The Power of Female Sex." In this episode Carrie, the columnist played by Sarah Jessica Parker, inadvertently becomes a prostitute. Carrie has a serious addiction to high-end footwear, and, while making her most recent purchase, her credit card is denied. A casual acquaintance, described as an Italian party girl with a revolving door in her bedroom, swoops to her rescue, insisting she pay for the shoes with her new boyfriend's credit card. Carrie somewhat reluctantly accepts the offer. Later, she finds herself hanging out at a posh restaurant with the woman and her friends, including a beautiful Frenchman. She spends the next day showing him around Manhattan and that night sleeps with him at his hotel. It is only when she wakes up the

---

6 See, for example, Jane Arthurs, "*Sex and the City* and Consumer Culture: Remediating Postfeminist Drama," *Feminist Media Studies* 3, no. 1 (2003): 83–98; Diane Negra, "'Quality Postfeminism?': Sex and the Single Girl on HBO," *Genders* 39 (2004), http://www.iiav.nl/ezines/IAV_606661/IAV_606661_2010_52/g39_negra.html; Emily Nussbaum, "Difficult Women: How 'Sex and the City' Lost Its Good Name," *The New Yorker* (29 July 2013), http://www.newyorker.com/magazine/2013/07/29/difficult-women.

next morning to find a thousand dollars on the bedside table that she realizes he thought she was a prostitute.

There is much worth examining in this episode: its association of sex work with foreigners; its depiction of this labor as high-paying and glamorous; even the shoes that are the object of Carrie's desire — baby blue mules with a large poof on top that look, perhaps not surprisingly, like bedroom slippers. However, the aspect of the episode that caught my attention as a medievalist was the idea that a woman's love of luxury goods will inevitably lead her to engage in sex. As medievalists we know this claim is perhaps one of the most hackneyed accusations lobbed at women during the Middle Ages.[7] While the episode presents

---

7 A few examples illustrate the point. In Jean de Meun's portion of *The Romance of the Rose,* the allegorical figure "Friend" tries to comfort the rejected poet-lover by assuring him that he will eventually obtain the object of his desire if he simply plies her with enough small gifts: "if you have the means to do so without ruining yourself, give them such gifts as you can now hear me describe: chaplets of flowers on wicker frames, purses or hair-ornaments, or other pretty, charming, elegant little trinkets […]. For just as the noble hawk is trained by the lure to come to the hand night and day, in the same way the gatekeepers are influenced by gifts to show mercy and favor to true lovers; all are conquered by them" (Guillaume de Lorris and Jean de Meun, *The Romance of the Rose,* trans. Frances Horgan [Oxford & New York: Oxford University Press, 1994], 114–15). Chaucer's *Wife of Bath* affirms Friend's advice, announcing not only that "al is for to selle" (III.D.414), but also that "with empty hand men may none hawkes lure" (III.D.414–15). See, "The Wife of Bath's Prologue," in *The Canterbury Tales Complete,* ed. Larry D. Benson (Boston & New York: Houghton Mifflin Company, 2000), 105–16: And Andreas Capellanus directly links women's avaricious desires to their anatomy by playing on the crude double entendre of *bourse* ("purse") in Old French: "Because of their avarice all women are thieves, and we may say they carry purses. You cannot find a woman of such lofty station or blessed with such honor or wealth that an offer of money will not break down her virtue, and there is no man, no matter how disgraceful and lowborn he is, who cannot seduce her if he has great wealth. This is so because no woman ever has enough money — just as no drunkard ever thinks he has had enough to drink. Even if the whole earth and sea were turned to gold they could hardly satisfy the avarice of a woman" (Andreas Capellanus, *The Art of Courtly Love,* trans. John Jay Perry [New York: Columbia University Press, 1960], 201).

Carrie's fall into prostitution as inadvertent, when read through the lens of medieval gender ideology, it is also inevitable.

Although appalled the next morning, Carrie is intrigued by the financial possibilities that sex work might afford her. Nonetheless, by the end of the episode, she clearly rejects this job, preferring to support herself through her writing. Her decision to sell her words, rather than her body, might seem like an affirmation of her intellectual assets, rather than her physical. However, while the episode's conclusion makes it clear that Carrie is not going to engage in sex work, the series as a whole continually underscores that a woman should attach herself sexually to a man who can take care of her financially. As if to underscore this point, Carrie's man is called "Mr. Big" by her and her friends throughout the series. Significantly, Mr. Big is the potential suitor who is, like the favorite husband of Chaucer's Wife of Bath, the most "daungerous" with his love, and much like Chaucer's Alisoun, Carrie loves him the best.[8] My students are somewhat surprised to discover that Carrie Bradshaw and the Wife of Bath share a number of other similarities as well: both are purveyors of words and use their sexual exploits (five marriages, in the case of the Wife of Bath) as the fodder for their narratives and both women have a penchant for "luxuria."

Perhaps the most glaring similarity between these two characters is the most important: both women seem to affirm, rather than challenge, patriarchal ideas about women. While Chaucer's Wife of Bath appears to question the "auctoritas" of the Church fathers, she also embodies the stereotypes of the consumptive woman. More troubling, she is someone who loves a man who is not just "dangerous" in the Old French sense of the word, but also in the modern sense as well: a man who beats her to such an extent that she is rendered deaf in one ear. In a similar way, *Sex in the City*, like the "Wife of Bath's Tale," undercuts many of the supposedly progressive messages that it seems to deliver. The series ends with Carrie fleeing the arms of one powerful man and flying into the arms of Mr. Big, with whom she is recon-

---

8   Chaucer, "The Wife of Bath's Prologue," III.D.514.

ciled. Like Carrie, her three friends all end up in monogamous, heterosexual relationships, two married, one not. Thus, for all of the series' celebration of pleasure, experimentation, and casual sex, the final message seems to be that women want — or should want — to be with one man. Like the heroine in an early modern comedy, in Sex in the City the unruly woman dwindles into the domesticated wife.

While ideology works in similar ways in the construction of both of these fictional women, I find that my students are often more willing to interrogate the ideological work of a medieval text than they are a piece of modern popular culture. One reason is that due to the historical distance of the Middle Ages (and my students' perception of that distant past) they are often more quickly able to see the ideology in medieval texts. This willingness, of course, does not mean that medieval texts are more ideological (as one former colleague tried to convince me). Rather, that ideology is rendered more visible to my students' critical eyes. By juxtaposing medieval texts alongside modern narratives that include similar messages, students are invited to question narratives of progress and to grapple with the ideology that they consume in contemporary culture, often packaged in clandestine ways.

Just as the mask of emancipation and liberalism often disguises modern misogyny, the presence of misogyny in medieval texts may be more complex than it at first appears. As Jane Burns notes, while medieval romance often privileges masculine desire, imparts misogynistic stereotypes and reaffirms heteronormativity, it also presents resistant voices that trouble the values and beliefs displayed on the surface of the texts.[9] While Burns' focus is on French and Occitan romances, her observation applies to a wide variety of medieval texts and gives students a tool for complicating their readings of medieval literature. One of

---

9   Jane E. Burns, "Courtly Love: Who Needs It? Recent Feminist Work in the Medieval French Tradition," *Signs* 27, no. 1 (2001): 23–49.

the texts I find particularly productive for this task is *Sir Gawain and the Green Knight*.[10]

In the past, this romance has been read as an exploration of the tensions between courtly love and chivalric responsibility: Gawain tries to balance the obligations of friendship with the expectations of romance. More recently, scholars have focused on the romance's queer play.[11] Indeed, it is hard to imagine another text — medieval or modern — that narrates so explicitly the homoerotics of homosociality. For if Gawain sleeps with Bercilak's wife, isn't he obligated, based on the terms of their agreement, to sleep with Bercilak as well? The fact that Bercilak not only proposes the game, but also instructs his wife to seduce Gawain, makes her, quite literally, the kind of conduit and substitution Eve Sedgwick describes in *Between Men*.[12]

How the romance grapples with this homosociality is both complex and contradictory. After nicking Gawain on the neck for taking his wife's girdle, Bercilak tries to laugh off the incident

---

10 *Sir Gawain and the Green Knight* is a text I teach frequently, both to beginning students in a lower division survey, and to advanced undergraduates and graduate students in a course on the queer premodern. The Pearl-Poet's NW Midlands dialect can be difficult for my students to decipher, even those skilled in reading Chaucer's Middle English. I like to use William Vantuono's dual-language edition of the poem: *Sir Gawain and the Green Knight*, trans. William Vantuono (New York & London: Garland, 1991), which provides a translation of the text while giving students an opportunity to consult the Middle English. All subsequent references are to this edition and will be cited in text.

11 See, for example, Carolyn Dinshaw, "A Kiss is Just a Kiss: Heterosexuality and Its Consolations in *Sir Gawain and the Green Knight*," *Diacritics* 24, nos. 2–3 (1994): 205–26; Tison Pugh, "Gawain and the Godgames," *Christianity and Literature* 51, no. 4 (2002): 526–51. Scholars have also taken up the colonialist impulses of the poem. See, for example, Patricia Ingham, *Sovereign Fantasies: Arthurian Romance and the Making of Britain* (Pennsylvania: University of Pennsylvania Press, 2001); Geraldine Heng, *Empire of Magic: Medieval Romance and the Politics of Cultural Fantasy* (New York: Columbia University Press, 2003); and Lynn Arner, "The Ends of Enchantment: Colonialism and *Sir Gawain and the Green Knight*," *Texas Studies in Literature and Language* 48, no. 2 (2006): 79–101.

12 Eve Kosofsky Sedgwick, *Between Men: English Literature and Male Homosocial Desire* (New York: Columbia University Press, 1985).

and invites Gawain to return to his castle to enjoy the rest of the holiday season. Gawain refuses and proceeds to blame Bercilak's wife for his downfall. In doing so, Gawain writes himself into a long genealogy of biblical men who also have been "bigyled" by women (3.2409–2948). Here, misogyny serves both as an excuse for his behavior and as a signifier of his worthiness.

Often, when my students first encounter this passage, they throw their hands up in disgust at what seems its blatant misogyny. However, this moment is more complicated than it might at first appear. These lines are not Gawain's initial response when he realizes that the Green Knight is Bercilak. Rather, his first reaction is to blame Bercilak for the betrayal and chastise himself for accepting the girdle:

> "Corsed worth cowarddyse and couetyse boþe;
> In yow is vylany and vyse þat virtue disstryeȝ."
> Þenne he kaȝt to þe knot, and þe kest lawseȝ,
> Brayde broþely þe belt to þe burne seluen.
> "Lo, þer þe falssyng; foule mot hit falle!
> For care of þy knokke, cowardyse me taȝt
> To acorde me wyth couetyse, my kynde to forsake,
> Þat is largeȝ and lewté þat longeȝ to knyȝteȝ.
> Now am I fawty and falce, and ferride haf ben euer
> Of trecherye and vntrawþe; boþe bityde sorȝe
>   and care.
>   I biknowe yow, knyȝt, here style,
>   Al fawty is my fare;
>   Leteȝ me ouertake your wylle,
>   And efte I schal be ware. (3.2374–2388)

["Accursed be cowardice and covetousness also;
In you are villainy and vice that virtue destroy."
Then he took the neat knot, and unties the contrivance,
Hurled the belt angrily toward the green man himself.
"There is the false favor; may misfortune befall it!
Because of concern for your clout, cowardice taught me

> To reconcile myself with covetousness, to go against my nature,
> Which is liberality and loyalty that belong to knights.
> Now I am faulty and false, and have foolishly followed
> Treachery and untruth; both betide sorrow
> and care.
> As my host, I honor you still;
> I know I have not been fair.
> Now let me work your will;
> To be false I will never dare."]

Gawain's first response, then, is to criticize Bercilak and then take personal responsibility for his misdeeds, rather than to blame women for them. Interestingly, Bercilak, too, provides two explanations for his behavior. His first reaction also is to take responsibility for his actions. He tells Gawain, "ffor, hit is my wede þat þou wereȝ, þat ilke wouen girdle; / Myn owen wyf hit þe weued, I wot wel, forsoþe. / Now know I wel þy cosses, and þy costs als, / And þe wowing of my wuf I wroȝt hit myseluen" (3.2358–2361). ["It is my gear you are gripped with, that girdle of green, / My wife wished it on you, I know well, indeed. / I am cognizant of your kisses, the circumstances attached, / And the wooing of my wife I wrought myself"]. It is only after Gawain's misogynistic outburst that Bercilak provides a second explanation for his behavior, one that also indicts women. According to this second explanation, the whole episode was an elaborate scheme concocted by Morgan le Fey who hoped that the shock of seeing the headless Green Knight speaking in Arthur's court would kill Guinevere (3.2446–2460). Thus, both a woman and a rivalry between women, rather than a man and a rivalry between men, are made responsible for what has transpired. In a relatively tight poem, these are curious circumlocutions, circumlocutions that suggest the residue of ideology and call for a closer look. As I note to my students, if the Pearl-poet wished to lay the blame unequivocally at the feet of women, why have both Gawain and Bercilak initially take responsibility for their actions? What alternative motivations might lie behind these misogynistic outbursts?

One possibility is an anxiety about reputation. Throughout our reading of the poem, we have discussed as a class Gawain's obsession with his reputation. It is his fear of a loss of reputation that causes him to accept the Green Knight's challenge when no other knights of the Round Table step forward. It is Gawain's fear that he'll lose his reputation as a knight courteous to women that enables Bercilak's wife to cajole kisses from him, as the poem's narrator repeatedly observes. And it is perhaps Gawain's confidence that no man will see the girdle (thereby protecting his reputation as a courageous knight), which motivates him to accept it. For Gawain, his reputation and his sense of self are one and the same. Gawain's initial reaction is so forceful not simply because he has been caught in a lie, but because the lie that he has been caught in has produced a crisis in his sense of masculinity and in his sense of self.

Gawain has an opportunity at the end of the poem to reevaluate his investment in reputation and chivalric masculinity. Perhaps in his initial speech, in which he takes responsibility, he is grappling with that possibility. In the end, however, he retreats from this potential epiphany by blaming women for his mistakes. In structuring the men's exchange in this way, the poem invites the reader to consider how personal shortcomings, as well as contradictions and conflicts in the social and cultural fabric, are projected onto women. Bercilak's behavior mirrors Gawain's and may be motivated by the same desire to distance himself from the personal and social fallout from what he has set in motion. Just as Gawain distances himself from this crisis in selfhood by blaming women, Bercilak perhaps tries to rehabilitate the homosocial bonds he has established (and damaged) with Gawain (and therefore by extension with Arthur) by blaming Morgan le Fey for what has happened. While Arthur's half-sister might be the puppeteer behind the scenes, the supposed purpose of this elaborate plot — to scare Guinevere to death — strikes the reader as patently absurd. Surely there would be easier ways to end Guinevere's life. In pulling Morgan le Fey into the narrative at this moment and in such an implausible way, the poem intentionally or unwittingly makes transparent how misogyny serves as a cultural *deus ex machina,* which helps restore social order and male relationships. Much like the girdle that Gawain picks up and ties back on, misogyny is the social bond that allows him to restore the homosocial bonds he almost discarded.

Just as Gawain and Bercilak offer two alternative explanations for their behavior, the girdle, too, is a sign with shifting meanings. Returning to King Arthur's court, Gawain explains that the girdle he wears is a badge of shame and a mark of his "untruth." However, the assembled knights and ladies laugh off his explanation and promise to wear a similar girdle themselves, converting it into a sign of honor and an insignia of membership in the Round Table (3.2507–2510). Thus, an act of rereading once again brings Gawain into the homosocial fold. Arthur and the court's rereading of the girdle, like Gawain and Bercilak's rereading of their behavior, accommodates a socially acceptable narrative — one that insulates the participants from scrutinizing their society and its beliefs. However, for the reader, there still lingers the original meaning of the girdle and a sense of unease, an unease that the poet has built into the very structure of the poem. Like all of the Pearl-poet's texts, the end of Sir Gawain and the Green Knight echoes the very first line of the poem: "Þus in Arthurus day þis aunter bitidde; / Þe Brutus bokeȝ þerof beres wyttenesse. / Syþen Brutus, þe bolde burne, boȝed hider first, / After þe segge and þe asaute wat sesed at Troye, / iwysse" (3.2522–2526). [Thus in Arthur's era this adventure occurred; / The books of Brutus bear witness thereof. / Since Brutus, that brave soul, first settled here, / After the siege and the assault had ceased at Troy, / indeed]. The repetition of the initial lines of the poem could be read as a sign of stagnation. Nothing has changed in Arthur's court as a result of this adventure; what could have served as a transformative lesson is diluted into a "Christmas game" (1.463–490) and, as the reinterpretation of the girdle suggests, as a sign of honor. Significantly, the poem ends not with a heroic image of Aeneas' descendants, but rather with a reminder of Troy's destruction. As both the first and the last lines in the poem, the image of Troy going "amiss" lingers in the reader's mind. The repetition may serve as a warning that a society that blames women for its shortcomings is not only prone to social stagnation but also to eventual destruction.

Certainly this reading of *Sir Gawain and the Green Knight* is just one of many possible readings. We could never confirm that the Pearl-poet set out to make these points intentionally, any more than the writers of *Sex in the City* intended to draw on medieval models of femininity. Nor would that confirmation really tell us anything. Perhaps what we have in the case of both texts is an example of how misogynistic discourse, like all ideology, is replete with logical gaps. Ideology's effectiveness relies, among other things, on not looking ideological, and two of its most effective tools are projecting onto the past and narratives of progress. Students are generally more than willing to see medieval texts as ideological, making such works an ideal place to teach students the close reading and critical analysis skills necessary for uncovering ideology, particularly in its more covert forms. At the same time, medievalists can demonstrate how certain ideological assumptions about medieval culture tend to lead us to read medieval texts in ways that deny to the Middle Ages the rich complexity readily recognized in other periods. These ideas can serve as a starting point for conversations about where ideas about the past come from and what they can tell us about the fears and fantasies of a particular moment, including our own.

It may seem unsatisfactory, perhaps even a bit unsavory, to suggest, as I have in this essay, that as teachers we need to sell the Middle Ages to our students and colleagues and that the best way to sell it is to show its centrality to contemporary culture. Shouldn't the rich diversity of this complex and fascinating period be enough of an inducement for study? Certainly, for some of our students, it will be. Even more students will undoubtedly come to our classrooms through exposure to Tolkien, *Game of Thrones,* or some other form of popular, "medieval" culture. A larger group still, will come to college having read very few (if any) medieval texts, with only the briefest exposure to the "dark ages" in history classes. This group is perhaps the largest group of students that I encounter at a school where the vast majority of students are first-generation college students, many of whom did not do the kind of college prep courses found at high schools where one can earn more than a 4.0 GPA. I don't lament this situation; I see it as an extraordinary opportunity. History is always a fabrication: a product of human hands that says more about the present moment than it does about the past. Working in a field where that process is so transparent, offers us a terrific pedagogical opportunity. Empowering our students to recognize how the present uses the past and the gaps in ideology, particularly in its most disguised forms, is some of the most important work we do as teachers. It is work that, as medievalists, we are particularly well positioned to do.

A Trip to England: Discovering the Ties between Medievalism and Pop Culture

Danielle Girard, Sarah Huff, Justine Marsella, Alicia Protze, Abbie Rosen, Jacki Teague, Fitchburg State University Alum

In early March of 2014, a group of eager undergraduate students sat huddled in a classroom at Fitchburg State University discussing with ill-disguised excitement the trivial fact that *The Hobbit: The Desolation of Smaug* might be a screening option on the plane to England. Our Lone Medievalist — our study abroad course instructor — listened with an amused expression. The following night we boarded said plane to embark on our adventure to walk in the footsteps of medieval England. As we moved through the country it became clear that there was an indisputable link between the medieval sites we visited and the fan culture that we so thoroughly immersed ourselves in daily. Not a single day passed during which we failed to find a link between the medieval past and contemporary "nerd-dom." In a trip that lasted the duration of nine days, we learned that, while the world of academia may marginalize medieval scholars in favor of contemporary scholars, the world of popular culture embraces and profits from the fascinating and diverse stores of medieval culture.

In the contemporary world that is beginning to favor "nerd culture," it is no secret that J.R.R. Tolkien's Middle Earth is one of the most popular fantasy realms. Peter Jackson's two trilogies of films based off Tolkien's *The Lord of the Rings* and *The Hobbit* both grossed $2.9 billion, earning the entirety of the Middle Earth saga a stunning $5.8 billion,[1] a hoard fit for a dragon. Beyond the monetary figures, though, Tolkien's world stretches deep into the recesses of fan culture. In 1960s America, the counterculture developed by the baby boomers would spray paint "Frodo Lives!" and "Gandalf for President" throughout the subway systems.[2] To them Tolkien's love of the natural world was the standing feature of his work. From the 60s to the internet-prolific age, Tolkien's popularity has yet to fade. It takes only a simple Google search to discover the plethora of ways contemporary fans have created to learn and teach others how to speak Elvish[3], including YouTube videos, numerous websites, and even an app that can be downloaded to a mobile phone. It is obvious that Tolkien has succeeded in bringing the reader into his world, using characters and settings and even languages of his own invention. As a linguist he once stated, "The invention of languages is the foundation. The 'stories' were made rather to provide a world for the languages than the reverse."[4]

Because of his extensive background in medieval literature, Tolkien was able to create a complex world that brought medieval themes into mainstream culture. In fact, there is so much medieval influence in today's culture that it makes the idea of being a lone medievalist somewhat ironic. As we traveled to Tolkien's grave in Oxford, England in that same March of 2014, what

---

[1] "Lord of the Rings Showdown," *Box Office Mojo* (2015), http://www.boxofficemojo.com/showdowns/chart/?id=vs-lotr.htm.

[2] Jane Ciabattari, "Hobbits and Hippies: Tolkien and the Counterculture," BBC (20 November 2014), http://www.bbc.com/culture/story/20141120-the-hobbits-and-the-hippies.

[3] One of several languages Tolkien created for his works.

[4] "National Geographic Lord of the Rings — Languages & Culture," Beyond the Movie, *National Geographic* (2001), http://www.nationalgeographic.com/ngbeyond/rings/language.html.

we discovered was a tombstone heavily decorated by fans that had made the pilgrimage before us. As we made our way from Tolkien's grave to the pub he used to frequent with his writing group, The Eagle and Child, our conversation began to shift from the medieval-influenced Middle Earth to other fandoms that we cherish. While Tolkien's status as an Anglo-Saxon professor is relatively well known, what we then discovered was that it is not only Tolkien's world that is shrouded in medieval influence.

The obvious progression from Tolkien himself would inevitably lead to the man who has been dubbed "an American Tolkien."[5] George R.R. Martin is the author of the series "A Song of Ice and Fire," which in recent years has been turned into an award-winning[6] HBO television show that is also a dominate force in contemporary pop culture. George R.R. Martin has credited Tolkien as being a major source of inspiration for his book series. Here we have another case of an extremely popular fantasy series that is rooted in medieval influence. While Martin veers away from the "good versus evil" trope that tends to persist in Tolkien's work, he also compares Tolkien's work with other fantasy writers, stating, "From the 1970s, Tolkien imitators had retreaded what he'd done, with no originality and none of Tolkien's deep abiding love of myth and history."[7] Due to the enduring popularity of his works, Tolkien is not a "lone medievalist" any longer. His works have inspired many readers over the years, and continue to do so today. Tolkien paved the road for Martin and his contemporary popularity as his works of heavy fantasy introduced a new audience to an insatiable craving for stories with a medieval twist. However, Martin cites another

---

5   Lily Rothman, "Why TIME Declared George R.R. Martin 'An American Tolkien,'" *Time* (12 April 2015), http://time.com/3774280/george-r-r-martin-tolkien/.
6   The show has been nominated for 83 Emmy Awards, 26 of which it won. "Game Of Thrones: Awards & Nominations," *Television Academy* (2015), http://www.emmys.com/shows/game-thrones.
7   Mikal Gilmore, "George R.R. Martin: The Rolling Stone Interview," *Rolling Stone* (23 April 2014), http://www.rollingstone.com/tv/news/george-r-r-martin-the-rolling-stone-interview-20140423.

creator as having been "the greatest literary influence on me."[8] The man Martin bestows this honor upon is none other than Stan Lee, the renowned creator of the Marvel Comics Universe.

Martin comments on this icon, "Stan Lee introduced a whole concept of characterisation to comic books and conflict; maybe even a touch of grey in some of the characters."[9] One of the most famous medieval characters with "a touch of grey" would be the outlaw Robin Hood. Contemporary pop culture is no stranger to the arrow-slinging rebel archetype. Despite the seemingly intimidating nature of medieval studies, it is comforting to know that medieval literature is actually responsible for a plethora of works that we are surrounded by on a daily basis, and Robin Hood is just about everywhere. The influence of the honorable thief with the bow and arrow can be seen in the aforementioned *The Lord of the Rings*, *The Hunger Games Trilogy*, the *Green Arrow* comic books and their television adaptation Arrow, as well as another of the most popular contemporary franchises, the Marvel Cinematic Universe.[10] The archers in these stories all have the same goal: to protect the innocent and punish the greedy and evil. Beyond this Robin Hood has always stood as an adventurer; it would be a difficult thing to find so much as a child in contemporary society without knowledge of the basic concept of the bandit hero. Throughout the centuries, the popularity of the trope of challenging social norms that are immoral has remained at its peak high. There is an endless list of films that have capitalized on this idea, including but not limited to the *Ocean's Eleven* films and *The Legend of Zorro*. There's something inherently intriguing about an outlaw doing the right thing guided only by their moral code. Recognizing archetypes like Robin Hood in contemporary literature creates a link to the medieval and makes it more relatable and less overwhelming. It

---

8   Fiona Macdonald, "Who Inspired the Game of Thrones Creator?" *Culture* (21 October 2014), http://www.bbc.com/culture/story/20140826-who-inspired-george-rr-martin.

9   Ibid.

10 Based on Stan Lee's Marvel Comics Universe, the MCU has released several films to date, three of which featured the arrow-wielding Hawkeye.

lends these newer stories more depth through their connection to these old tales. What is strange is that the stories themselves have not even remotely disappeared from popular knowledge.

Arguably more prominent than Robin Hood, though the issue of popularity remains unresolved, is the once and future king. The story of King Arthur, along with his knights, wife, and wizard, has evolved into a vital portion of our storytelling traditions, no matter what the medium. Our televisions are filled with modernized courtly love triangles that mimic Arthur, Lancelot, and Guinevere. Novels whose audiences range in age feature Merlin-esque wizards such as Dumbledore from the *Harry Potter* series[11] and Gandalf from *The Hobbit* and *The Lord of the Rings*. Both of these pop culture wizards share a resemblance to the aged Merlin with their long white hair and waist-length white beards. While Tolkien's works continue to pop up because much of his novels' stories were taken directly from medieval counterparts, such as Smaug, the dragon who was lifted from the epic of *Beowulf,* Tolkien is just a small fraction of the contemporary canon of work that was inspired by medieval times.

After we watched Smaug rain his desolation on Bilbo thanks to the inflight cinema service, we arrived in England where we were lucky enough to visit the medieval Warwick Castle, built circa 1068. This castle, rich in medieval history, is now a well-known tourist attraction. Upon entering the grounds we were faced with the opportunity to explore just about every area the castle had to offer, including the dungeon and the ramparts. During our visit we got to see in person the ways in which this antiquated castle has evolved with the roaring trade of pop culture as they were at the time hosting an exhibit on the popular BBC One television show *Merlin*. *Merlin,* of course, is a television show about the legendary King Arthur and Camelot. The exhibition, which featured wax figures of the cast, was erected due to the fact that Warwick Castle's contemporary claim to fame is that is was used as a filming location for the show. This type of pop culture phenomenon, in essence visiting locations that re-

---

11 The popular and most profitable children's book series of all time.

late to fandom, creates an interesting juxtaposition between pop culture and the lone medievalist. While the pop culture chalice overflows and then sinks under the weight of medieval influence, fandom moves in and seeks almost to replace centuries of history with a contemporary enthusiasm for the human consciousness that allows us to love deeply, and often obsess, over our respective fandoms. In essence the pop culture group races straight to see where their favorite actors stood to film scenes, and overlook the history and the stories that are exponentially older than they are, and the medievalist stands alone again. This form of pop culture, a TV show based off of a medieval legend, made the visit to Warwick castle lose some of its original essence. It did not feel like a medieval castle, but instead felt like the tourist attraction it has become.

Despite that pitfall of pop culture, the fact remains that the general constraints of what constitutes an entertaining story have remained the same. Today's stories drip with the centuries-old influence of medievalism, whether they're told through the medium of television, film, books, or even video games. As students of a lone medievalist, the term doesn't quite make sense to us as we have learned that much of our contemporary world is sheathed by influence from the Middle Ages. A class discussing the origins of the most popular fan cultures would essentially be a class on medieval literature. While it may be true that many students are daunted by the prospect of tackling medieval literature, we would hope that pop culture's obsession with the subject would calm their worries.

The Lone Medievalist as Scholar

Opus Clamantis in Deserto

From the Monk's Cell to the Professor's Office

Kisha G. Tracy, Fitchburg State University

Despite the title of this essay, I am not going to spend much time in the monk's cell—this regardless of the common habit of equating academics with monks, generally with negative connotations. This image was evoked by Nicholas Kristof in his much-discussed (by academics at least) *New York Times* article, "Professors, We Need You!," advocating for public engagement by academics in less arcane language. He ends with the cry, "So, professors, don't cloister yourselves like medieval monks—we need you!"[1] Earlier, he defines what this "cloistering" means: "A basic challenge is that Ph.D. programs have fostered a culture that glorifies arcane unintelligibility while disdaining impact and audience. This culture of exclusivity is then transmitted to the next generation through the publish-or-perish tenure process. Rebels are too often crushed or driven away." Essentially, he is denigrating, if not the lone medievalist by name, then certainly the lone academic. With due respect to Mr. Kristof, he clearly has not been a student of medieval studies. Peter Bu-

---

1 Nicholas Kristof, "Professors, We Need You!" *New York Times* (15 February 2014), http://www.nytimes.com/2014/02/16/opinion/sunday/kristof-professors-we-need-you.html.

chanan offers a reply to Kristof's article on his blog Phenomenal Anglo-Saxons that cannot fail to make a medievalist smile — if not smirk. He writes, "And since my PhD is in medieval studies, it's not clear that he would want me […] although I could at the very least let him know that medieval monks were often active figures in their world, preserving and transmitting knowledge, producing art and literature, and serving as public intellectuals shaping the course of local and international political affairs."[2] Of course, such a discussion would necessarily get into eremitic vs. cenobitic monastic traditions, the various rules of orders, and the determination of the effects monks had on public life. Nonetheless, Buchanan's response is well-aimed.

Not all comparisons between monks and academics are negative, at least in the sense of condemning the latter. A few years ago, I was reading an article in *The Chronicle of Higher Education* — "The Professor and the Would-Be Monk" by David Evans.[3] While necessarily brief in its ruminations, I found much to consider in the article. Evans' main point concerns his reading of Pierre de Calan's *Cosmas, or the Love of God* and how the title monk — a modern, not a medieval, one — struggles to reconcile his ideal expectations of his calling with its reality. Evans equates this with encountering reality upon embarking into the academic profession. His definition of reality is probably familiar to most lone medievalists: committee responsibilities, the demands of teaching, departmental and university politics, and the general claims on an academic's time beyond the quest for knowledge. Some of these issues I will address further in a moment. The comparison between the calling of monkhood and the calling of academia (most poetically, medieval studies) — the passion, commitment, fit of personality, seclusion, to name a few

---

2   Peter Buchanan, "Nick Kristof Needs Me," *Phenomenal Anglo-Saxons* (16 February 2014), http://phenomenalanglosaxons.wordpress.com/2014/02/16/nick-kristof-needs-me/.

3   David Evans, "The Professor and the Would-Be Monk," *The Chronicle of Higher Education* (16 August 2012), http://chronicle.com/blogs/onhiring/the-professor-and-the-would-be-monk/33007.

characteristics — has possibilities. Indeed, John Van Engen likens members of a university to "members of religious orders."[4]

As I thought about Evans' comments, it made me curious. How much has academia changed? As an academic, and a lone medievalist in my department at a university, it is both interesting to note the origins of my profession as well as illuminating to think about the requirements, realities, challenges, and rewards of university life. What can we learn about ourselves and what we do by exploring the history of intellectuals and teachers? How do we define ourselves today, particularly as medievalists and teachers of medieval studies? Especially at a time when, as Richard Demillo states, educators are "on a path to marginal roles in a much different world than they are designed for"?[5] Perhaps being lone medievalists gives us much-needed perspective, not to mention practice.

Rather than turning to the monastery, I'm going to turn to the medieval university. "Every society," Van Engen states, "has devised means to educate its young and to prepare a next generation of leaders. Not every society has had universities. These guilds of scholars and students, the invention of twelfth-century Europe, receive the highest acclaim from modern scholars."[6] Perhaps much of this acclaim is related to our genealogical link to these institutions. Perhaps it is also a sense of kindred spirit. Anthropologists at Boise State University are studying what they call *Homo academicus*, and an article summarizing their current findings appeared in an online journal dedicated to "bridg[ing] the worlds of academia, journalism and the public interest." While their sample size is at present small, their findings are nonetheless intriguing in considering the shape of the modern academic:

---

4   John Van Engen, "Introduction," in *Learning Institutionalized: Teaching in the Medieval University,* ed. John Van Engen, 1–4 (Notre Dame: University of Notre Dame Press, 2000), 1.
5   Richard A. DeMillo, *Abelard to Apple: The Fate of American Colleges and Universities* (Cambridge: MIT Press, 2011), 3.
6   Van Engen, "Introduction," 1.

[F]aculty spent approximately 17 percent of their workweek days in meetings. These meetings included everything from advising meetings with students (which could be considered part of teaching or service depending on the department) to committee meetings that have a clear service function. Thirteen percent of the day was spent on email (with functions ranging from teaching to research and service). Thus, 30 percent of faculty time was spent on activities that are not traditionally thought of as part of the life of an academic. Twelve percent of the day was spent on instruction (actual lectures, labs, clinicals etc.), and an equal amount of time was spent on class preparation. Eleven percent of the day was spent on course administration (grading, updating course web pages, etc.). Thus, 35 percent of workweek days was spent on activities traditionally thought of as teaching. Only three percent of our workweek day was spent on primary research and two percent on manuscript writing.[7]

This in a nutshell is who we are. The study also determined that we are solitary creatures: "The surprising finding was the amount of time spent alone (57 percent). Only 17 percent of participant time was spent doing activities with colleagues and 15 percent of our time was spent doing activities with students. Being a faculty member appears to be a lonely occupation."[8] This statistic might explain, more accurately than Kristof's assumptions, why we are

---

7 John Ziker, "The Long, Lonely Job of Homo academicus," *The Blue Review* (31 March 2014), https://thebluereview.org/faculty-time-allocation/. For a more specific breakdown from one academic, see Mary Collins, "What's a College Professor Do? I'll Tell You," *Hartford Courant* (1 November 2015), http://www.courant.com/opinion/op-ed/hc-op-collins-heres-how-professors-spend-their-time-1101-20151030-story.html. These studies and anecdotes contradict a seemingly widespread belief that academics should "do more work." See, for instance, Lucy Mccalmont, "Walker Urges Professors to Work Harder," *Politico* (29 January 2015), http://www.politico.com/story/2015/01/scott-walker-higher-education-university-professors-114716.

8 Ibid. See also Maggie Berg and Barbara Seeber, *The Slow Professor: Challenging the Culture of Speed in the Academy* (Toronto: University of Toronto Press, 2016).

often likened to the popular conception of secluded monks. It certainly quantifies the world of the lone medievalist.

And, yet, is this solitary lifestyle as surprising as Ziker intimates? Let us consider it in light of the first of the holy triumvirate: research. The question often arises about what a scholar needs in order to be a scholar. Stephen Ferrulo in his article on the medieval university recounts the story of University of Paris chancellor Peter Comestor who was overlooked for the position of prelate because he "wasn't suited for the active life" and eventually resigned the chancellorship to enter the abbey of St. Victor [as he] seems to have preferred the life of a "reclusive scholar."[9] In this case, the active life and the scholar's (reclusive) life are at odds with each other. Consider *Piers Plowman* and Haukyn the Active Man, although his plight is not that of the distracted scholar, or *The Cloud of Unknowing*. Ferrulo's article title — "Quid dant artes nisi luctum?" [What do the arts give other than trouble?] — is taken from a 12th-century poem by Walter of Chatillon, who laments, as he cannot find a job, the years of "self-denial" in being a "poor scholar."[10] Turning again briefly to the monastic, the Rule of St. Benedict states, "there shall certainly be appointed one or two elders, who shall go round the monastery at the hours in which the brothers are engaged in reading, and see to it that no troublesome brother chance to be found who is open to idleness and trifling, and is not intent on his reading; being not only of no use to himself, but also stirring up others."[11] The implication is clear. Study requires concentration, focus. Other people are a distraction. Here I am reminded of Francis Bacon, although a bit beyond the medieval period, who implies much the same in his essay "On Marriage and Single Life," asserting pithily that the best works have come from

---

9   Stephen C. Ferrulo, "'Quid dant artes nisi luctum?': Learning, Ambition, and Careers in the Medieval University," *History of Education Quarterly* 28, no. 1 (1988): 1–22, at 16.
10 Ibid., 1.
11 "Rule of St. Benedict, c.530," *Internet Medieval Sourcebook*, Fordham University (1996), http://www.fordham.edu/halsall/source/rul-benedict.asp.

those who are not married and have no children — or perhaps those who do not teach 4/4 loads.

To return to the findings of the Boise State study, the time we spend alone, at least during the school year, is less about research and more about the second area of academia: teaching. Class preparation, email with students, grading — solitary activities (we can argue out whether or not e-communication is actually time alone). The nature of teaching and the amount of solitary activity, including the types of activity, have changed since the work of our medieval counterparts. Although, as John Scott points out, "In today's universities, the basic teaching mission and many features of the medieval model from Europe remain intact. This pattern exists worldwide in the Americas, Asia, Africa, and Australia. Major organizational features are the power to confer degrees, curriculum, examinations, commencements, as well as colleges."[12] This rather sweeping statement is reductive, particularly, as "[i]n most universities […] these matters [teaching or the curriculum, the textbooks used, the schedule of lectures and disputations, or the stages of advancing to the master's degree] seem to have been regulated by unwritten customs, by practices imprinted upon the collective memory of the institution by the regularity of their occurrence."[13] There is much that we cannot know.

Perhaps what we can say with certainty then is simply that teaching was key to the roles of university faculty from the beginning. James Weisheipl finds that "the bachelor was a practice-teacher, an apprentice to a master whose obligation was to teach and hold disputations … Actual teaching, therefore, was an essential part of a cleric's education. He had to teach in order to merit the grand title of Master."[14] He claims that "[a]t the time of inception the young candidate had to take an oath that

---

12 John C. Scott, "The Mission of the University: Medieval to Postmodern Transformations," *The Journal of Higher Education* 77, no. 1 (2006): 1–39, at 9–10.
13 Ferrulo, "'Quid dant artes nisi luctum?'" 5.
14 James A. Weisheipl, "The Structure of the Arts Faculty in the Medieval University," *British Journal of Educational Studies* 19, no. 3 (1971): 263–71, at 271.

he would lecture in that faculty for at least two years ... One who failed to fulfill his oath to teach was a perjurer and could not rightfully claim the title of master."[15] The exact nature of this apprenticeship is an intriguing topic. The amount of emphasis that faculty today put on being teachers depends on many factors, not the least of which is their institution's teaching load and departmental and institutional attitudes towards teaching. To be faculty, according to the medieval model, is to teach, and yet college teachers today often receive little to no training in teaching. Further, teaching is often marginalized. Ken Bain, in *What the Best College Teachers Do,* argues that successful college teachers perceive teaching as "an important and serious intellectual (or artistic) act, perhaps even as a kind of scholarship,' one that requires 'the attention of the best minds in academia.'"[16] Also, he remarks that "a teacher should think about teaching (in a single session or an entire course) as a serious intellectual act, a kind of scholarship, a creation."[17] Thinking of teaching as scholarship is a field that has been developing for decades, and yet we often do not consider it in the same category as our discipline-specific research. Teaching is, as Bain states, an "intellectual act," deserving of the same attention and application of process as our other work.

The developing field of teaching and learning scholarship has much to offer us as we think about the medieval connection. On one hand, we can argue that the new research and pedagogical techniques are a significant sign of progress from the medieval university. Scott remarks that certain scholars are "call[ing] for revitalizing the 'collegiate ideal' [set by the medieval model] of traditional residential institutions: student development, active learning pedagogies, and integration of academic and experiential learning."[18] Another angle is to apply understanding of the changes faced in medieval education to our own current situ-

---

15 Ibid., 267.
16 Ken Bain, *What the Best College Teachers Do* (Cambridge: Harvard University, 2004), 49.
17 Ibid., 169.
18 Scott, "The Mission of the University," 10.

ations. For instance, William Courtenay writes that, in medieval universities, the "emphasis on the written record may have resulted from the difficulty of proving heresy on the basis only of reports of oral teaching. Yet one has the sense that accusers found the written form of heresy to be particularly offensive, perhaps because it gave the elevated status of the written word to those views and had the power to spread them through manuscript copies."[19] I will revisit the concept of heresy in a moment. With respect to the development of the written record as opposed to oral teaching and the complexities as related to teaching, I cannot help but think of the innovative practice now of recording oral lectures, particularly in flipped classrooms. Can we not see another shift occurring and can we not look to our medieval counterparts and their adaptation to the written word to shed light on what are surely going to be complexities — positive or negative — we need to address?

A third avenue of thought is considering how the study of the Middle Ages can influence current scholarship of teaching and learning. In a volume entitled *Burn After Reading*, which is a collection of miniature manifestos concerning Post/medieval studies, Joshua Eyler discusses another way we might approach the (seemingly endless) fight to argue for the value of the humanities:

> Brain-based learning theories, which lie at the intersection of cognitive neuroscience and the scholarship of teaching and learning, have made tremendous gains in articulating what physically happens in students' brains when they learn. Using this methodology, I have begun a project to try to show that the humanities profoundly and permanently affect the structures of students' brains in a way that is different from

---

19 William J. Courtenay, "Inquiry and Inquisition: Academic Freedom in Medieval Universities," *Church History* 58, no. 2 (1989): 168–81, at 172.

other fields and, thus, these modes of inquiry cannot be replaced.[20]

Eyler demonstrates that learning involves the brain translating material into "stories and metaphors," which he argues makes medieval studies "well positioned to contribute to our knowledge here, if we take advantage of the multiple kinds of narratives embedded in our field to study how our students are learning."[21] Personally, I find the idea that medievalists — especially lone medievalists who teach a considerable amount of liberal arts courses — could hold a significant key to the humanities debate delightful. Additionally, we could also use the structure of the medieval university to make a supplementary argument that the humanities, at least in its incarnation as the medieval "Arts," was and is the foundation of all other study: "When the universities were finally organized in the thirteenth century the arts faculty was a prerequisite to the three higher faculties of theology, medicine and law. Without preparation in arts at some recognized *studium,* no one could matriculate in one of the higher faculties; at least this was the general rule."[22] Of course, this line of thought does fall back into what Eyler addresses, that our arguments tend to revolve around proving that the humanities are "important," rather than proving that they are "necessary" — thus, his persuasive and alternative approach outlined previously.

From teaching, let us turn to the third traditional area of academia: service. Generally, service (at least in contracts and by tenure committees) is broken down by service to the campus community and service outside the university. I will focus here on the latter, particularly its incarnation as public engagement, which brings us back to Nicholas Kristof's concern for academ-

---

20 Joshua R. Eyler, "This Is Your Brain on Medieval Studies," in *Burn After Reading,* eds. Jeffrey Jerome Cohen, Eileen A. Joy, and Myra Seaman, 25–27 (Brooklyn: punctum books, 2014), 26.
21 Ibid., 26.
22 Weisheipl, "The Structure of the Arts Faculty in the Medieval University," 263.

ics' involvement in (or, in his opinion, lack of involvement in) public concerns. Consider this concept from the medieval angle. Were medieval university faculty interested in and engaged in public discourse? The short answer is yes. Ferrulo comments, "chancellors and other masters 'were not academic recluses living in isolation from the wider world of affairs' ... The tensions and conflicts that did arise were about the responsibility and the accountability of the university to society."[23] What about, some might ask, the influence of the institution of the Church, especially as it was heavily involved in and heavily invested in the university's production of students versed in theology? There is no doubt that the Church asserted its influence over the universities. We can look at this from different perspectives. We can consider this restrictive, and, to return to the concept of heresy, there were certain teachers who were accused and condemned for their teachings, which supports considering the Church's influence in this light. We can also consider other possibilities, such as the effect of this influence on the university responsibility to society. Jacques Verger states, "[T]he church imposed on universities the idea that the mere love of science, the pure research of truth, could not be the only aim of learning. Learning had to carry out two other requirements: it had to be socially useful [...] and it had to respect and even support religious orthodox as defined by the papacy."[24] Here we have these two ideas in one context. Learning had to go beyond study for the sake of study and it had to support orthodox beliefs — service to the community and restriction at one and the same time. Weisheipl emphasizes this: "Masters could lecture on any book they chose and they could hold any opinion not directly opposed to the Christian faith. Students could choose any master they wished

---

23 Ferrulo, "'Quid dant artes nisi luctum?'" 17.
24 Jacques Verger, "The First French Universities and the Institutionalization of Learning," in *Learning Institutionalized: Teaching in the Medieval University*, ed. John Van Engen, 5–19 (Notre Dame: University of Notre Dame Press, 2000), 13.

to work under."²⁵ The sense of academic freedom exists in the ability of teachers to shape their own curriculum and of students to choose their own instructors, not to mention the prominent practice of university personnel maintaining autonomy and authority over their own members, but with the caveat that the opinions expressed must not oppose "Christian faith." The "tensions and conflicts" that Ferrulo mentioned arising out of the university's responsibility to society are reflected in the circumstances surrounding certain punishments of masters and students. Courtenay argues:

> [T]he most serious penalties were imposed or were attempted in those cases in which a bachelor or master allowed or encouraged his controversial views to influence a wider public […]. The issue was whether a scholar knowingly and willingly maintained views contrary to the faith (which most did not), whether his views were disseminated outside the university, and, if so, whether or not he could rely on political protection.²⁶

It is important to note the emphasis on dissemination of ideas outside of the university to a "wider public." This seems to be the crux. Faculty were responsible for engaging with the public and yet that act could rebound on them, placing them in a precarious position. Has all that much changed?

Many of the discussions concerning university faculty and public engagement center on the idea that what actually needs to change is the acceptance of public engagement within the university itself. By gaining support and approbation (particularly from those reading our tenure files), the argument is that more academics would be so engaged. Here is where we can see the clearest adjustment from the medieval. Faculty sought less the

---

25 Weisheipl, "The Structure of the Arts Faculty in the Medieval University," 271.
26 Courtenay, "Inquiry and Inquisition: Academic Freedom in Medieval Universities," 180–81.

approbation from within and more the approval from without. This is a result of changes in purpose. As Ferrulo comments:

> In view of their impressive record of worldly success, the masters must not have been any less ambitious for social advancement or any more reluctant than their students to make practical use of their learning when the right opportunity presented itself. [...] A mastership in the medieval university was not regarded as a permanent, lifelong profession. The masters did not seek nor did they want tenure. The value of the title *magister* rested above all in the prestige and promotion that it likely would bring someday outside the schools.[27]

This appears contrary to modern academia. The anxiety to complete portfolios, including the requisite and "correct" research, often comes first for practical reasons if nothing else. This anxiety can have consequences to the mission to be "socially useful." David Perry, himself a medievalist and frequent writer for *The Chronicle,* asks in a post on his blog responding to Kristof, "How would you count public engagement in your field and institution?"[28] His question arises from the concern as to how public engagement factors in tenure and promotion decisions. The formula is not an easy one, particularly if an institution does not consider public work in the same light as scholarship. Perry speculates on examples such as, "Does a 'well-read' [...] blog equal a conference presentation? Do 6 op-eds for national media equal a lower tier journal article?"[29] These are not easy questions. Add in the argument by Valéria Souza, a PhD in Bra-

---

27 Ferrulo, "'Quid dant artes nisi luctum?'" 18.
28 David M. Perry, "Academics in Public (belated response to Nicholas Kristof)," *How Did We Get Into This Mess: On Language, Power, and Privilege* (18 February 2014), http://www.thismess.net/2014/02/academics-in-public-belated-response-to.html.
29 Ibid. For futher discussion of this subject, see also Margaret A. Post, Elaine Ward, Nicholas V. Longo, and John Saltmarsh, eds., *Publicly Engaged Scholars: Next-Generation Engagement and the Future of Higher Education,* (Sterling: Stylus, 2016).

zilian studies, on her blog *It's complicated* that public engagement is only thus when it serves no ulterior motive and seeks no exterior reward, such as "counting" towards tenure,[30] and the complexities build even further. Do we even have the time to be truly publicly engaged?

The question of public engagement also must consider opportunity and access. Ferrulo states that "the masters whose subsequent careers did bring them worldly success were far more likely to be remembered, and to have their scholarly writings preserved, than those who spent their entire lives teaching."[31] This sentiment is echoed in a *Chronicle* article by Perry:

> [T]he general public perceives faculty members as isolated from reality, holding cushy jobs, and uninterested in open communication. The public has little access to the broad diversity of knowledge, experience, and background inside higher education, because those academics who do achieve broader platforms generally come from only the most elite universities.[32]

Perceived worldly success continues to drive the supposed public face of academia, as does the belief in a hierarchy of publication venues. In yet another response to Kristof's article, Corey Robin, a professor of political science, posted, "[Kristof] only reads *The New Yorker*, and then complains that everyone doesn't write for *The New Yorker*. He doesn't see the many men and women who are in fact writing for public audiences. Nor does he see the gatekeepers — even in our new age of blogs and little

---

30 Valéria M. Souza, "'Public Engagement': You're Doing It Wrong," *It's Complicated* (22 February 2014), http://valeriamsouza.wordpress.com/2014/02/22/public-engagement-youre-doing-it-wrong/.
31 Ferrulo, "'Quid dant artes nisi luctum?'" 9.
32 David M. Perry, "My Initial Public Offering: Why More Academics Should Write for a General Audience," *The Chronicle of Higher Education* (22 July 2013), http://chronicle.com/article/My-Initial-Public-Offering/140407/.

magazines — that prevent supply from meeting demand."[33] The truth is, despite concerns about how it will "count" in tenure and promotion, not to mention the fear of public scrutiny — which our medieval counterparts faced as well — there are many faculty members of institutions of all kinds who do engage in public discourse. Lone medievalists have often commented that they find public engagement, at local, regional, and national levels, an effective method of bridging the gap between their scholarship and non-medievalists, those within academia and without. Arguably the most significant to medieval studies is the rise of the digital humanities as medievalists are some of the foremost leaders in this field, not to mention that they are platforms that medievalists spread out all over the world use to stay connected and involved. Why is this so important? As Perry comments, "Although many of those public intellectuals [who come from elite universities] are brilliant writers and speakers, they represent only a tiny percentage of the expertise available in the academic world. That expertise lies not just in our subject fields but also in the habits of mind we bring to bear on countless other kinds of issues."[34] Bruce Holsinger, on his blog *Burnable Books*, comments on Perry's article: "[E]xpertise is not just discipline-based, limited to the immediate subjects of our research, but the product of more general 'habits of mind' cultivated within and by the institutions of higher education in which we teach and work."[35] We, as lone medievalists, have a great deal to offer in multiple arenas and that without sacrificing quality and rigor.

So what can we learn from studying our medieval academic ancestors? For me, it is that we defy definition. We are individuals and institutions. Teachers and researchers. Experts and students. Centralized and marginalized. Restrained and limitless. Bloggers and peer-reviewed article writers. Medievalists and

---

33 Corey Robin, "Look Who Nick Kristof's Saving Now," *Corey Robin* (16 February 2014), http://coreyrobin.com/2014/02/16/look-who-nick-kristofs-saving-now/.

34 Perry, "My Initial Public Offering."

35 Bruce Holsinger, "Expertise and Habits of Mind: A Medievalist's IPO," *Burnable Books* (24 July 2013), http://burnablebooks.com/perr/.

generalists. Praised and condemned. Rebels and stereotypes. Academic and popular. Public intellectuals and cloistered scholars. Alone and in communities. We occupy all of these spaces, even the contradictory ones, simultaneously. We may have defined responsibilities, but how we shape those responsibilities is our choice. An understanding of our professional genealogy and its roots in the medieval university, beyond providing a sense of belonging and kinship, can help us determine these choices, shaping us both as lone medievalists and academics in general.

Embracing the Medievalist Margin

Alicia Spencer-Hall, Queen Mary, University of London

What a loaded phrase it is, "the Middle Ages." What does it denote, exactly? Medievalists have long critiqued the terminology as an empty — and intellectually partisan — marker of otherness.[1] Certainly, the term is useful for historicists, classicists, and modernists as a delimiter of the end of the age of Antiquity and the beginning of the Renaissance. Yet, the phrase is tainted for researchers in the medieval trenches, actively working to dem-

---

1   See, for example: Catherine Brown, "In the Middle," *Journal of Medieval and Early Modern Studies* 30, no. 3 (2000): 547–74; John Dagenais, "Decolonizing the Middle Ages: Introduction," *Journal of Medieval and Early Modern Studies* 30, no. 3 (2000): 431–48; Margreta de Grazia, "The Modern Divide: From Either Side," *Journal of Medieval and Early Modern Studies* 37, no. 3 (2007): 454–67; Paul Freedman, "The Medieval Other: The Middle Ages as Other," in *Marvels, Monsters, and Miracles: Studies in the Medieval and Early Modern Imaginations*, eds. Timothy S. Jones and David A. Sprunger, 1–24 (Kalamazoo: Western Michigan University, 2002); Jennifer Summit and David Wallace, "Rethinking Periodization," *Journal of Medieval and Early Modern Studies* 37, no. 3 (2007): 447–51. Scholars practising neomedievalism (or research into the "New Middle Ages") actively push back against the impulse to quarantine the medieval period from the modern era. See, for example: Stephen G. Nichols, "Writing the New Middle Ages," PMLA 120 (2005): 422–41; Karl Fugelso, ed., *Defining Neomedievalism(s)* (Cambridge: Brewer, 2010); *Defining Neomedievalism(s) II* (Cambridge: Brewer, 2011).

onstrate the fecundity and importance of the period to intellectual and cultural history. The formulation itself, "the Middle Ages," deflect us from the temporal period supposedly under study: what are those ages in the "middle" of? The Middle Ages, paradoxically, take center-stage in their function as the margins of other more exciting periods of study. Without the essential instrument of "the Middle Ages," modernists and Classicists would struggle to frame their own work. Even the adjectival form, "medieval," offers us few benefits. As Margreta de Grazia notes, the term "medieval" "works less as a historical marker than a massive value judgement, determining what matters and what does not".[2] To research the Middle Ages, to be a medievalist, is to be irrevocably tied to "a millennium of middleness," and to exist "in the [marginalized] middle" in our professional academic lives.[3]

The middle is a tricky thing. The *Oxford English Dictionary* can't really offer us a shoulder to cry on here. That which is "middle" is "situated at the center, central," but also "intermediary," of middling quality, of arguable value, or worse — that ultimate academic slur — average. Being "in the middle" is no less problematic. We are, apparently, "in the midst of," surrounded by crowds of (receptive?) people — the life and soul of an intellectual party, at last. Let's not get ahead of ourselves yet: working "in the middle," we are also "in a difficult, dangerous, or untenable position; in trouble." Medievalists, alone in the whirling academic crowd: so often isolated in our institutions, unable to profit fully from inter-disciplinary collaborations, with our outputs ultimately warehoused adjacent to "properly relevant" research. After all, the fruits of medieval research are "difficult," "inaccessible," "arcane." And won't anybody think of the children? Apologies, I misspoke: won't anybody think of the students? How will medieval studies ever draw in big enough crowds of undergraduates to help sustain the university coffers? And so, as medievalists,

---

2   De Grazia, "Divide," 453.
3   Leo Patterson, "On the Margin: Postmodernism, Ironic History, and Medieval Studies," *Speculum* 62, no. 1 (1990): 87–108, at 92.

we find ourselves "in the middle," in that strange (dis)location of betwixt and between, of being both in some sense central and at almost all times marginal.

Medievalists have long struggled with such professional and institutional problems; our current situation is — sadly — nothing new.[4] Nothing short of tectonic shifts in institutional and intellectual *praxes* will remedy such circumstances. I'm not naïve enough to believe that all will be peachy keen in academe if medievalists just "bootstrap" ourselves out of this quagmire. Be more commercial! Teach all the things! Don't sleep! But, I do think that we can ameliorate our current situation in the status quo, and speed the advent of desperately needed changes in our industry, if we strategically embrace — dare I say weaponize? — our marginality. Not just any marginality: a specifically medieval kind of marginality, drawn from the hermeneutic power of manuscript margins. Operating in this critical space, for a time at least, will ultimately allow us to de-marginalize ourselves, and medieval studies as a discipline.

In 1992, Michael Camille brought medieval margins front and center.[5] Developing earlier (scant) research into images found in the margins of medieval manuscripts from scholars such as Lilian M.C. Randall and Lucy Freeman Stadler, Camille was the first to theorize on a grand scale the power dynamics at play between "central" texts and the images which surround them.[6] For Camille, the margin of a medieval manuscript is a "powerful" place: marginal annotations, glosses, and images often "interact[] with and reinterpret[] a text which has come to

---

4   See, for example, ibid., 107–8. Patterson summarises medievalist angst relating to relevance and accessibility to other disciplines dating to the 1920s and 1940s.

5   Michael Camille, *Image on the Edge: The Margins of Medieval Art* (London: Reaktion, 1992). See also his later work on the topic: "Glossing the Flesh: Scophophilia and the Margins of the Medieval Book," in *The Margins of the Text*, ed. D.C. Greetham, 245–67 (Ann Arbor: University of Michigan, 1997), in particular 254.

6   For an overview of the discipline, see Domenic Leo, *Images, Texts, and Marginalia in a "Vows of the Peacock" Manuscript (New York, Pierpont Morgan Library MS G24)* (Leiden: Brill, 2013), 76–86.

be seen as fixed and finalized."⁷ The margins are a site of potential resistance to proffered textual significations, spaces for dissent and discussion of that with which the reader is presented, the textual status quo. In this way, then, marginal inscription(s) are "radical" as they challenge the concept of any singular totalitarian signification.⁸ As Rosemarie McGerr remarks, medieval margins are discursive and dialogic:

> The margins of medieval manuscripts can thus be read as spaces of ambiguity and dialogue that allow for interrogation of constructions of otherness, hybrid areas resistant to traditional systems of classification.⁹

What if we acknowledge our "marginal" position as medievalists in such terms? The medievalist borderlands become a fertile, provocative zone for breaking free from traditional research paradigms and methodologies, for pushing ourselves — and our colleagues — beyond comfortable disciplinary lines. Our job in the medievalist margins, then, is to trouble the dominant narrative(s), to push for alternate analytical perspectives and advocate for neglected objects of study. What if we embrace our medievalist marginality on our own terms, and glory in challenging the central texts and *praxes* which govern our intellectual work? A marginal image, found in an English Book of Hours from ca. 1300, illustrates the capacity of the margins to manipulate the central text.¹⁰ Owing to a forgetful or overworked scribe, perhaps, Psalm 127 in this manuscript is missing its fourth verse. Help is at hand from the margins, however. A man extends him-

---

7   Camille, *Image on the Edge*, 16, 20.
8   Camille, "Glossing the Flesh," 261–63.
9   Rosemarie McGerr, *A Lancastrian Mirror for Princes: The Yale Law School New Statutes of England* (Bloomington: Indiana University Press, 2011), 2–3.
10 *Book of Hours,* Baltimore, Walters Art Gallery, MS 102, fol. 33v; Camille, *Image on the Edge*, 24; Lilian M.C. Randall, *Images in the Margins of Gothic Manuscripts* (Berkeley: University of California, 1966), fig. 491. The image can be viewed online at: "Book of Hours, Baltimore, Walters Art Gallery, MS 102, fol. 33v," *The Digital Walters,* http://www.thedigitalwalters.org/Data/WaltersManuscripts/W102/data/W.102/sap/W102_000070_sap.jpg.

self on tip-toe just to the left of the text column. The forgotten verse has been inserted at the bottom of the page, and the man hoists it forcefully into its correct place in the main text. We, like this "textual construction worker[]," are in a position to supplement, correct and extend the "central text" of academia itself. [11]

The margins, it turns out, are crowded and noisy places. Catherine Brown chronicles her experience reading a twelfth-century manuscript of Augustine's *Confessions,* seemingly "reading with" — and reading *as* — a medieval commentator who littered the text with marginal notes.[12] By reading with/as her medieval colleague, Brown and the commentator become two subjects with connected consciousness united in a moment of unsettling simultaneity. The marginal space enables potent moments of connection and community, even across wide temporal divides.[13] What if we consider ourselves as annotating the "central text" of academia, as laying down our tracks in the margins for others to find? Acting as "lone medievalists," we each leave marginal marks of our experiences as medievalists — vastly different in terms of, say, career development, institution, research priorities and so forth — on the central text of academe which unites us. The margins are a space for heterogeneity — for nonsense doodles, corrections, scholarly glosses, *obscenae,* the works — but all that exists in the margins are bound together by the "off-centre" relationship to the main text. If we work to read each other's marginal notations, to read with — and in some instances *as* — each other despite our myriad differences, then we may unite "in the middle," finally, of a welcoming crowd. I'm advocating, then, for a conscious push to establish supportive inclusive networks for and of medievalists, interlocutors in the

---

11 Camille, *Image on the Edge,* 24.

12 Brown, "Middle," 551–68, in particular 551–53. She refers to Augustine, *Confessions,* Chicago, Newberry Library, MS 12.7, fol. 22r.

13 I draw upon Brown's experience to theorize the ways in which contact with manuscripts facilitates cross-temporal communities of readers and collocutors, a process I term "coresthesia," in more depth in Spencer-Hall, *Medieval Saints and Modern Screens: Divine Visions as Cinematic Experience* (Amsterdam: Amsterdam University Press, 2018), 136–45.

margins with whom we find much-needed fellowship.¹⁴ I see the present volume as a vital step in establishing the kind of energetic community frameworks that will enable us, ultimately, to move to the center of the academic page.

Margins are not just a space for reflections on and of the "real" world. Images of bizarre monsters and fanciful hybrids, for example, are commonplace. The marginal space is "a site of reworking of the imaginary," a territory to imagine not just social changes, but alternate psychological possibilities too.¹⁵ Marginal monsters enable an individual to visualize different versions of the self, of the known world, and of humanity itself. Alongside finding academic interlocutors in the medievalist margins, we may also find the strange specimens that populate our own intellectual imaginations, fanciful flanges of our analytical priorities which tend to overspill into all areas of an academic's life. Instead of rejecting such specters as unimportant — marginal — to our bread-and-butter medieval research, I affirm that we should actively welcome these random stragglers into our intellectual life. In my office, I have two such marginal imaginary friends who have come to symbolize for me the power of medieval marginality: a giant poster of Jessica Fletcher, the heroine detective from *Murder, She Wrote*,¹⁶ and a soft toy unicorn head (called Hildegard) that hangs above my desk. Somewhat bizarrely, I admit, Jessica and Hildegard operate as two members of an intellectual community which encourages

---

14 In a keynote paper I delivered at the 21st Gender and Medieval Studies Conference (Corpus Christi College, University of Oxford, UK; 8–10 January 2018), I urged for the development of a medievalist-feminist politics of professional and personal visibility, predicated on practices of genuine inclusivity of all kinds of academic bodies and lives, and supportive action for colleagues of all career stages. Much of that paper's content is relevant to my comments here. For the full text of the paper, see "Hagiography, Media, and the Politics of Visibility," *Medieval, She Wrote* (blog) (5 February 2018), http://www.medievalshewrote.com/blog/gms2018-fulltext.
15 Camille, "Glossing the Flesh," 249.
16 *Murder, She Wrote*, created by Peter S. Fischer, Richard Levinson, and William Link (prod. by Universal Television, Corymore Productions [1992–1996], 1984–1996).

me to confidently and provocatively engage within and beyond medievalist circles. Camille urges us "to stand on the margins with the monsters and see what vantage point that reveals."[17] What does it mean for me "to stand" with Jessica and Hildegard? Frankly, I'm not sure that I can answer such a question precisely.[18] At the very least, these marginal "monsters" remind me of my wider identity in the world, offering me a way out of medievalist solitary confinement. Perhaps more importantly, they remind me to reach ever outward in my research — to push beyond facile concrete categorizations, and to work to raze boundaries separating medievalists from other academics, and academics from the general public.

A note of warning is necessary. Whilst marginalia can and often do challenge and reshape their central texts, they are nevertheless ineluctably "tethered to texts which they can 'play' upon but never replace."[19] Indeed, Camille notes that the vivacious blossoming of Gothic marginalia in the late twelfth to the late fourteenth century is directly related to the "absolute hegemony of the system it sought to subvert."[20] Once that "system" was actively being dismantled, such marginalia went into rapid decline. As the center depends on the margins, the reverse is also true. Though the strenuous efforts of the marginal man in the Book of Hours that I described above meaningfully interacts with the central text, he hauls into place a textual fragment that should already have been in the Psalm, rather than introducing genuinely challenging material. In other words, marginal activity can work to reinstate coherent dominant narratives just as much as it can succeed in offering necessarily audacious correctives to traditional paradigms. Inhabiting the "medieval marginal" should not be an excuse for us to isolate ourselves from

---

17 Ibid., 255.
18 I flesh out my thoughts on this more fully on my personal blog: "'That Gives Me an Idea': An Explanation, of Sorts," *Medieval, She Wrote* (blog) (25 June 2015), http://www.medievalshewrote.com/blog/2015/6/25/that-gives-me-an-idea-an-explanation-of-sorts.
19 Camille, *Image on the Edge,* 47.
20 Ibid., 160.

collaborating across disciplines, sharing our knowledge with the public, taking on the unglamorous administrative work which underpins access to institutional power, or actively working to reshape that which forces us to reclaim "the marginal" as a position of power.[21] "Medieval marginality" is — or at least should be — a transitional state: a means of advocating for ourselves and our work on the long road to definitive change in institutions and intellectual frameworks. If we must be marginal, then let's be medievally marginal.

---

21 On the importance and difficulties of taking up the role of "public medievalist", see Spencer-Hall, "Some Thoughts on #s406 at #IMC2015 — Medievalists, Public Engagement & Budgy Smugglers," *Medieval, She Wrote* (blog) (7 July 2015), http://www.medievalshewrote.com/blog/2015/7/7/some-thoughts-on-s406-at-imc2015.

The Medievalist's Soliloquy: Struggles and Advice for Lone Medievalists

Tiffany A. Ziegler, Midwestern State University

Many scholars of medieval studies enter their first job after leaving supportive graduate programs where other graduate students understood their woes. Once teaching at an institution where scholarly studies may not be a priority, many quickly discover that they do not have much time, especially for research and writing. Moreover, they lack the supportive community that they once had.[1] As a lone medievalist, the struggle to produce scholarship and writing is difficult and complicated. Creating classes, curriculum planning, committee work, etc., all eventually become routine. Sadly, the same cannot be said of research. From lack of library resources, to the reliance on oneself as an audience, the research process proves to be difficult. Despite these obstacles there are a number of ways to better facilitate researching and writing while still performing one's teaching du-

---

1   The lack of community is compounded for those individuals who do not teach graduate classes and do not have the pleasure to engage with more advanced students.

ties as the lone medievalist. The solutions and advice[2] — focusing on the categories of research and collegiality — draw from *The Rule of Saint Augustine*. The solitary medieval monk serves as a surprising parallel to modern lone medievalist.[3]

Rule four of the Augustinian Rule instructs the brothers to "call nothing your own, but let everything be yours in common."[4] Embrace teaching survey courses. Many professors at teaching-oriented institutions dread the teaching of generalist courses when they should not. Survey courses provide the opportunity to develop teaching techniques that can be refined in the upper level courses. Survey courses also provide commonality and create collegiality. Be it activities, teaching techniques, or even stories of being in the trenches, the survey classes belong to the entire department are shared "in common." Moreover, teaching broadly about one's subject area and teaching other subjects outside one's research focus provide professors with knowledge and context both inside and outside of their field of interest, which helps one to become a better specialist.[5] While some classes will

---

2 Many thanks to Rebecca Stephenson, Jennifer N. Brown, Mary Valante, Maire Johnson, William H. Campbell, Janet Snyder, and Janine Larmon Peterson who provided suggestions for those who struggle to complete research at teaching-oriented institutions. As part of this project I created a dialogue on the *Facebook* page "Teaching in the Middle Ages" to gather suggestions from faculty who not only value teaching but who have also managed to complete research. Each offered sound advice and each comment provides proof that there are support groups and people out there willing to help. See "Teaching in the Middle Ages," *Facebook* page (24 September 2015), https://www.facebook.com/groups/219963604761327/.

3 As an exercise of my own advice, I am using the *Rule* of Saint Augustine as a basis for the categories of discussion. The brothers and sisters of the thirteenth century Hospital of Saint John in Brussels followed this Rule. My research centers on the Hospital of Saint John, and I am currently writing the early history of the institution. See Tiffany A. Ziegler, "Medieval Healthcare and the Rise of Charitable Institutions: The History of the Municipal Hospital" (unpublished manuscript, Palgrave Macmillan, August 2017).

4 *The Rule of Saint Augustine*, trans. Robert P. Russell based on the critical text from Luc Verheijen, *La Règle De Saint Augustin* (Paris: Études Augustiniennes, 1967), 1.

5 Jennifer N. Brown put forth this idea, and I can fully agree with her. Teaching Western Civilization I and II provides a necessary context that better

be unavoidably limited in scope, such as your Western, World, and American surveys, others will be open to more development. For upper level and special topics courses, create classes that overlap with your research and will allow you to engage with your research material while teaching simultaneously. In addition, the classroom provides a venue for the discussion of your findings. Even the simplest discussions of your research topic can be fruitful: although lectures, readings, and discussions will have to be adjusted to the students' level, focused explanation of complex topics proves to be an excellent way to give voice to your work before you send it on to more advanced colleagues.

Time is precious for those at teaching-driven institutions. Survey courses, upper division classes, student advising, and committee work all take precedence over research. Thus, it is important that you schedule research as part of your weekly plan, but then it is imperative to keep to your plan: Rule eleven warns that "no one should do anything other than that for which was intended and from which it also takes its name."[6] This means not scheduling committees, student meetings, and other items of business during the time that you have set aside to research and write.[7] When are you most productive and creative? Be honest with yourself and "figure out the two hours out of the day that you are most productive. Ensure that you write during those two hours,"[8] otherwise you are wasting your time and ef-

---

    helps me to situate my research. Teaching World Civilizations, though, profoundly developed the ways in which I thought about my own period of study. Jennifer N. Brown, "Teaching the Middle Ages," *Facebook* page (25 September 2015), https://www.facebook.com/groups/219963604761327/.

6 *The Rule of Saint Augustine*, 2.

7 Rebecca Stephenson and Maire Johnson both argue for setting aside a specific time and for not allowing anything to come between you and that time. "Teaching the Middle Ages," *Facebook* page (25 September 2015), https://www.facebook.com/groups/219963604761327/.

8 Rashawn Ray, "Prepare for the Unexpected: Surviving Your First Year on the Tenure Track" *Conditionally Accepted* (12 September 2013), http://conditionallyaccepted.com/2013/09/12/prepare-for-the-unexpected/. Many of the sources provided here relate to first year experiences. The advice for the first year applies to later years as well.

forts. Then, treat those times as work hours, just as you would treat hours in the classroom or office hours.

Moreover, in a profession with such limited blocks of time, you must capitalize on the little that you have. For example, "if I teach a 3 credit hour class, it may appear that I'm only working 3 hours/week. [...] You also have student office hours [...], time grading assignments [...] and exams, and professional development [...]. So, a 3 credit hour class can easily take 15–20 hours/week. Depending on the school, a full-load might be two or four classes. So, it's pretty easy to get to 30–40 hours/week with just *two* [emphasis added] classes."[9] You must be firm and you must not be "hindered by those who think something else must be done."[10] If the regular schedule during the week is not enough, consider spending breaks, such as Spring and Summer Break, writing. Make a research plan and stick to it.[11] The research plan provides direction and a semblance of a planned timeline. Without a deadline, it becomes easy to give up your research time for other needs as they arise. You can also consider working on multiple projects at once to vary your focus and to "help to keep your research line flourishing in case there are setbacks on any one project."[12]

---

9 David Kroll, "Top 10 Reasons Being a Professor Is a Stressful Job," *Forbes* (5 January 2013), http://www.forbes.com/sites/davidkroll/2013/01/05/top-10-reasons-being-a-university-professor-is-a-stressful-job/.

10 Rule 11, *The Rule of Saint Augustine*, 2.

11 Although specified to the field of science, the suggestions here for writing a plan apply to history as well. Jim Austin, "Writing a Research Plan," SCIENCE (26 July 2002), http://sciencecareers.sciencemag.org/career_magazine/previous_issues/articles/2002_07_26/nodoi.4611149009600202486.

12 Stephen Reysen and Lacy E. Krueger, "How to Survive and Thrive During Your First Years in a Tenure-Track Job" *Observer* 26, no. 1 (January 2013), http://www.psychologicalscience.org/index.php/publications/observer/2013/january-13/how-to-survive-and-thrive-during-your-first-years-in-a-tenure-track-job.html. Although this work is directed at psychologists, it provides fundamental advice that can be used across disciplines. The article also has a fairly extensive bibliography from which other ideas can be drawn. A similar article can be found at *Inside Higher Ed*: Shari Dinkins, "Surviving the First Year," *Inside Higher Ed* (16 August 2007), https://www.insidehighered.com/views/2007/08/16/dinkins. If this advice is not enough,

Rule fifteen wisely suggests that "when you come to table, listen until you leave to what is the custom to read, without disturbance or strife. Let not your mouths alone take nourishment […]."[13] Attendance at conferences and professional meetings[14] is a great way to create a network of people who can aid you in your research and writing, not to mention a good way to vent about your work to a more specialized group. My policy is to do at least one conference a year, but I often do as many as two or three. Go. Present. Listen. Bring ideas back. Most importantly, though, make professional acquaintances, especially with those people who do research that is similar to yours.[15]

While some professors may be the only Europeanist in their department, others will have the good fortune of a community of early modern or even ancient scholars to whom you can reach out. These early and later European periods tend to overlap, and more likely than not your peripheral colleagues will have done

---

there are manuals out there that might help, such as Paul J. Silvia's *How to Write a Lot: A Practical Guide to Productive Academic Writing* (Washington, DC: APA, 2007) and Patricia Goodson's *Becoming an Academic Writer: 50 Exercises for Paced, Productive, and Powerful Writing* (Washington, DC: Sage Publishing, 2013), that is, of course, if you can find the time for the extra reading.

13 *The Rule of Saint Augustine*, 2.
14 International Congress on Medieval Studies at Kalamazoo (https://wmich.edu/medievalcongress), International Medieval Congress at Leeds (http://www.leeds.ac.uk/arts/info/125137/international_medieval_congress), Medieval Academy of America (http://www.medievalacademy.org/), Haskins Society (http://www.haskinssociety.org/), Society for Medieval Feminist Scholarship (http://list.uiowa.edu/scripts/wa.exe?SUBED1=MEDFEM-L&A=1), etc. Many of these groups offer additional benefits, such as receiving a subscription to *Speculum* as part of the MAA membership. Janet Snyder also suggested MAHS, AVISTA, and SECAC. "Teaching the Middle Ages," *Facebook* page (26 September 2015), https://www.facebook.com/groups/219963604761327/.
15 Often scholars working on similar topics are willing to share sources. Maire Johnson suggested that "if you know someone who is working on things that you are working on, or even something ancillary to your own project, it's worth seeing if you can get pdfs and other [sources] from them." Maire Johnson, "Teaching the Middle Ages," *Facebook* page (6 October 2015), https://www.facebook.com/groups/219963604761327/.

some work in medieval Europe. They may not be able to speak directly to your particular scholarship, but they are there to help. The prudent advice from Rule twenty of walking "together, and when you reach your destination, stay[ing] together"[16] suggests the importance and benefits of cooperation. In addition, reach out beyond your university to other medievalists in nearby communities. Online support groups,[17] writing workshops, and blogs[18] create a semblance of togetherness even when you find yourself all alone in your department.

The most important factor in successful research is your ability to acquire the sources you need.[19] Some institutions and faculty are restricted by the size of the library, the size of the collection, the scope of the collection, and especially limited funding. All too often, the lone medievalist experiences a struggle similar to that of a medieval monk: "books are to be requested at a fixed hour each day, and anyone coming outside that hour is not to receive them."[20] At your institution, take some time to meet your librarians. Introduce yourself and your research. Be nice to them, especially when it comes to Interlibrary Loans and book funds. If your library cannot facilitate your needs, you can look for a nearby institution that may have a bigger collection or even better databases. Take a weekend or evening to visit outside libraries and use them to your benefit. If these options fail,

---

16 *The Rule of Saint Augustine*, 3.
17 Janine Larmon Peterson furthers this point when she argues that creating a community will reaffirm your scholarship, but it will also "energize" you to work. See Janine Larmon Peterson, "Teaching the Middle Ages," *Facebook* page (25 September 2015), https://www.facebook.com/groups/219963604761327/.
18 See, for example, Lois Huneycutt, "Conference Report, 'Beyond Exceptionalism,'" *Royal Studies Journal* (blog) (5 October 2015), https://royalstudiesjournal.wordpress.com/2015/10/05/conference-report-beyond-exceptionalism/. This post in particular was an overview of the recent conference, "Beyond Exceptionalism." Other blogs include discussions of an Overview of Kalamazoo 2015 and interviews of various medieval scholars.
19 Nicole Jantzen, Jenifer N. Brown, Mary Valante, and William H. Campbell all echoed this sentiment. See "Teaching the Middle Ages," *Facebook* page (25 September 2015), https://www.facebook.com/groups/219963604761327.
20 Rule thirty-nine, *The Rule of Saint Augustine*, 6.

consider research, reading, writing groups, and source-sharing groups.[21] A wonderful network of scholars is out there; many are willing to share ideas and sources because they too know the struggle.[22]

Researching and writing as the lone medievalist can be a challenge, one that can even be compared to that of the life of a medieval Augustinian monk. It is not, however, impossible. Manage your time, make your research a priority, and reach out to others. If there is anything that the Augustinian monks can teach us, it is to work together as a community. If a medievalist decides to keep something "secretly […] given to him,"[23] that is his or her prerogative. She/he will not be "judged guilty of theft" as a monk might.[24] If, however, we choose to function as more of a community and help each other out, we naturally advance the progress in the greater field of study.

---

[21] See, for example, "Medieval History Reading List Crowdsourcing," *Facebook* page (24 September 2015), https://www.facebook.com/groups/292481914241580/. Teaching the Middle Ages is another group where the focus is on teaching. Get ideas from similar groups to better facilitate teaching so that you have more time to write. See, "Teaching the Middle Ages," *Facebook* page (25 September 2015), https://www.facebook.com/groups/219963604761327/.

[22] A word of advice for graduate students entering the job market regarding sources: try to have your records readily available, be it in digital or printed form when you leave your degree-granting institution.

[23] Rule thirty-two, *The Rule of Saint Augustine*, 5.

[24] Ibid.

Reflections of an Embarrassed Medievalist

Michael Elam, Regent University

While many medievalists find themselves alone in their departments, ranging from History to English, etc., many medievalists often find themselves just as alone, lonelier in some cases, among other medievalists, especially in professional contexts in which shared specialization ought to help them feel they belong. Lone medievalists in their academic departments, though they may feel a sense of isolation, may find that acclimation to teaching, service, and other responsibilities has its own separating effect, an effect that makes the lone medievalist feel doubly alone among other medievalists, especially at conferences, at which the expectation to make significant, independent, meaningful contributions to further medieval studies can be stifling. Such an expectation, frankly, may not be entirely reasonable. This may seem shocking, but many, if not most, medievalists do not have the personal resources to offer the kind of discipline-changing studies tacitly expected from them (from any scholar, really). At least it is shocking to say it out loud. The custom among academics is to refrain from saying what most are thinking and experiencing in the hopes that somehow one will stumble into something that peers will claim is brilliant; it has been my custom, anyway, and I know from candid conversations with others that I am not alone.

What is more reasonable to expect, given the limited resources and energy of a scholar trying to get by in the world, is the desire to share ideas and feel a sense of belonging than stumble into something seemingly brilliant. More often than not, I have an idea that seems to me like an odd piece belonging to some larger puzzle, and I am anxious that what looks odd may seem insignificant to others. What if they have seen the puzzle put together already, and I make a fool of myself trying to make sense of my piece? Should I be shamed for not having done my research, for not having found time in the midst of grading papers from multiple first-year composition courses, serving on institutional committees, taking care of my family, maintaining a home, among other things? I find myself alone among medievalists, those with whom I should feel most free. I am no longer like them; I am an outsider. But perhaps a change in perspective can actually reveal belonging during those times but in different ways. That has been my own growing experience, even if the experience itself has not always been easy.

Years ago, I never imagined while I was going through the process of completing and defending my dissertation that my zeal for medieval literary study would ever diminish.[1] At that point I thought I was at the top of my game, and I wanted to invest more and more of myself into my interests. I imagined that my search for a tenure-track job would be the next step in establishing my own enclave where I could cloister myself and focus on this or that work of medieval literature and produce astonishingly brilliant works of scholarship about it. Sure, I would have to emerge occasionally and teach a class, likely, I thought, in my area of specialization, but I would be professing my discipline and specialization all along. My search had been built on my assumption that my medieval scholarship was my best asset, and the teaching experience I had only relevant insofar as

---

1 My PhD is in English with an emphasis in medieval literature, and I have an interdisciplinary certificate in Medieval Studies as well.

it was related to medieval topics. The search for an academic job, however, quickly opened my eyes for the need to be flexible with my expectations. (I laugh when I think about how I understood flexibility at that time — expecting more acquiescence of others than of myself.) I realized that in order to get a tenure-track position, I would have to teach outside of my area. No matter, I thought: I would still be able to cultivate my expertise as a medievalist at conferences among my peers. My expectations were perhaps still not as flexible as they needed to be.

Long months of fruitless job searching and rejection after rejection left me wondering if I had anything to offer, if there were any place I belonged as a medievalist. During the times of fruitlessness, the main support my medievalist colleagues offered was more often personal than professional, which was frankly what I needed most. I noticed, moreover, that I had begun to pour most of my time into looking for jobs rather than keeping up with scholarship or maintaining my specialist interests. Already, I was on the path towards feeling out of touch with my discipline. Were my doctoral studies, my dissertation, a fluke? Did I belong in academia as a medievalist, or was I only valuable as a commodity, someone who could dispense course content to a mass of educational consumers who care little or nothing for medieval studies? When I found a job, then, the very one I still have now, I felt I belonged in the academy, even in a place where being the only medievalist meant mainly teaching courses in composition and literature up through the eighteenth century — and sometimes beyond. Perhaps it was okay to cultivate the generalist in me, one who could teach a variety of literatures to students. Being a teacher could be as fulfilling as being a researcher; both are scholars, I thought.

I felt a sense of belonging, as I said, of a different sort. I settled into my new place and finally started teaching, but I secretly wanted the same fellowship I found with my medievalist colleagues. I had only experienced a sense of belonging with my fellow medievalist colleagues based on what I thought was our discipline. What I found in my new job was an entire cadre of people who needed me for other reasons. My departmental teaching load included and still includes teaching courses ranging from significantly before to significantly after my own area of specialization, and for medievalists such loads are often no different. For example, I may find myself teaching literature courses covering material of the classical period or material through the eighteenth century, and this spring I actually taught the later American Literature survey — post-Civil War through the present. Still, I have found such duties rewarding. I am proud of the contribution I make to my department. Developing close relationships with other members of a department has been a positive outcome of such a workload. Often because such workloads are the result of small departments needing to cover a lot of material with few teachers; a kind of professional closeness can develop among such a small group.

I experience such professional closeness at my own institution, and I even see my training as a medievalist not only as something I bring to our department, but also something that endears me to its members. Indeed each of our specializations seems to endear each of us to the others. My colleagues needed me because none of them were medievalists and were uncomfortable teaching literature from the eighteenth century back. And there was a personal facet to such need. They needed someone to rescue them from the dread of teaching literature they did not know so well, and they were happy to say as much. Their delight at my arrival was very congenial to me. I thrived and soon found myself part of an integrated department, a band of sisters and brothers fighting the good fight of literary study and championing its cause as a necessary component of students' intellectual and personal, indeed holistic development. There was no sense of being an outsider. We all belonged together. My identity as a medievalist was fading into the background.

Many will be familiar with such experience. Teaching requirements that force one to cover expansive time periods and materials, especially at institutions that emphasize teaching over research, can dissipate a medievalist's working knowledge of the things that set her apart in the first place. Unless one finds oneself in a position to teach a 2/2 or maybe a 3/3 load, most of one's professional time is spent in duties such as course preparation, grading assignments, serving on committees, and other non-specialist tasks. The medievalist in such a position may find it hard to keep up with scholarship current in her own field, creating a kind of embarrassing scholarship lag, even lapse. Some may trade satisfaction in specialization for satisfaction in fulfilling departmental or institutional obligations, sometimes grudgingly and sometimes happily. Some may do so without knowing it. Such a trade of satisfaction often brings about a new feeling of belonging. In a sense, one becomes a specialist of the institution, which is not necessarily bad. Nevertheless, the net effect of such redirection is that many once-alone medievalists, now integral parts of their departments, find themselves in a conundrum where they feel alone amidst the very colleagues who share their original scholarly interests. The medievalist integral to a department may feel like the lone incompetent among other medievalists.

Indeed, I found myself losing much of the specialized knowledge that had given me a sense of purpose. As I kept up with the demands of a 4/4 teaching load being my department's only Early British Literature "specialist," much of the minutiae I had proudly learned in preparing and defending my dissertation seemed to fade into the general landscape of my mind. Preparing to teach courses such as Milton and the Seventeenth Century, Western Literary Tradition, and first-year Composition courses preoccupied me. No longer did I need my knowledge of Middle English exercised and standing by in case a point of language should come up in class. No longer did I need to remember who was ruling England during the time the *Pearl* Manuscript was compiled. I did not even need to remember, scandalous as it may seem, that the Normans had conquered the English in 1066. Instead, the most useful information to have at hand was why a sentence did or did not convey enough information in a student's personal narrative, how heroism is defined and portrayed differently in modern popular culture from ancient Mediterranean cultures, or how to disentangle the syntax of the opening sentence of *Paradise Lost* (or any sentence of *Paradise Lost* for that matter). Readiness for the classes I taught had to be in the forefront of my mind if I was to show myself a valuable member of the department's faculty, and so the readiness I needed to discuss why Boethius was relevant to understanding poems in the Exeter Book (or how even to read the poems in the Exeter Book) seemed no longer a readiness but a diversion, a misplacement of personal academic and scholarly resources. Even in teaching the Early British Literature survey, class discussions focus on general liberal-arts concerns, how a work might evince qualities valued in the study of humanities at large. Although I might read something like *Sir Gawain and the Green Knight* in an original language edition, how people experience the kinds of anxieties that Gawain experiences (even if the details of the experience are not our own) were the kind of discussion most fruitful to my students, not whether or not they could detect characteristics of a West Midlands dialect.

I found myself discharging a responsibility to teach large numbers of students how to succeed in their university studies in general. Discussions with colleagues centered on things like the best ways to maximize peer review experiences in College Composition and in Research and Academic Writing. My colleagues began seeing me as more than someone mercifully teaching early literature, but as one indispensable for carrying out our department's contribution to the general development of the university's students. Rather than focusing on deepening knowledge in a smaller pool of study, I developed students' breadth of knowledge. I pushed students, and myself, to see, for instance, how knowing a poem by Robert Herrick might help them understand a general human admiration for asymmetry, perhaps even a psychological need for it.

In fact, what occupies my academic thoughts most of the time is not medieval at all. While discussions about Ricardian courtly customs may be on the lips of a colleague at a large conference, on my mind may be recent preparation for teaching the Cavalier Poets, or Dryden, or, horror of horrors, American Lit. And though conversation about Ricardian courtly custom may have seemed like an anticipated balm, the reality is that a medievalist such as myself may have more to say about Penshurst, Thomas Shadwell, or Brooke Farm than about fourteenth-century aristocrats. Among other medievalists, I may feel more like the lone generalist, the lone jack-of-all-trades — early trades at least — in a moment poised on the edge of panic: does one admit to having nothing new or interesting to say about one's medieval specialization? Surely there have been classes to cover, committees to serve on, and papers to grade; but as surely too is the understanding that such things are the very things one has come to think of as excuses for not keeping up with one's discipline. Having legitimate excuses or not, the medievalist in me may believe that he is no longer as qualified to participate in his specialization as he once was.

Such a feeling, often associated with "imposter syndrome,"[2] however, need not be an alienating force. While the idea of the imposter syndrome should not be denied to have some power (real or imagined), the feeling that one has real gaps in one's knowledge can open opportunities for building networks and advancing scholarship based on interpersonal interestedness. The sense of being an imposter in one's own field is more widespread than one might imagine and should encourage medievalists to find ways to connect with each other in order to share openly their anxieties and also to cross-pollinate, as it were, to build ideas that might lead to fruitful scholarship and other work in the specialization. Doing so is still risky, and often implies a kind of weakness, that one is not ready to be counted among the perceived elite in the discipline. Indeed, one must acknowledge the reality of elitism among academics, a way to confirm biases about what passes as aptitude or legitimacy. Elitism can have devastating effects on specialists trying their best to get along, to fulfill institutional, professional, and personal obligations. I have felt on the fringe of medieval studies, out-

---

2 The editors of this volume pointed me to an interesting online article by on the topic: Carl Richards, "Learning to Deal with the Imposter Syndrome," *New York Times* (26 October 2015), https://www.nytimes.com/2015/10/26/your-money/learning-to-deal-with-the-impostor-syndrome.html.

side the fold, so to speak, not knowing which medievalist/academic custom to cultivate in a given situation. I have made my awkward attempt at aloofness and feigned confidence only to find myself reverting back to the earnestness that drove me into medieval studies in the first place. That earnestness has elicited many an awkward glance, meant to be recognized by me as a warning shot over the bow of my enthusiasm: "Watch out," it implies, "Your zeal reveals your ineptitude." Such elitist attitudes can be found in any profession and will always be a barrier to advancing one's own professional development, but the barrier need not be insurmountable. I believe, in fact, one of the best ways to deal with elitism is not only with a healthy sense of self-purpose but also an equally healthy sense of apathy toward trying too hard to be perceived as being elite. Frankly, I have given up trying to fit among others as a professional medievalist and tried to engage others as my colleagues (and they are my colleagues whether they think so or not), as people I might like to get to know personally. This practice has been cultivated by my experience as the lone medievalist in an English department where the common bond is not so much time-period specialization in literature as it is the need to band together and work as a team, supporting each other both professionally and personally.

Indeed, such a disposition helped me establish the connection with my colleagues I discussed above. I refused to be alone. The perception of being alone was a powerful catalyst for breaking its influences. Such an experience should not be surprising in theory, or even in practice.[3] Indeed, medievalists within their departments may find that there is much help available to

---

3 Craig M. Rawlings et al., "Streams of Thought: Knowledge Flows and Intellectual Cohesion in a Multidisciplinary Era," *Social Forces* 93 (2015): 1715–18, found that cohesion can be found among faculty in diverse disciplines when they engage in collaboration, and, although the collaboration under discussion is inter-/multi-disciplinary, such collaboration furthermore seems to strengthen a sense of unity among members of an institution. It should be noted that the study focused mainly on the intellectual cohesion formed among faculty at Stanford University, which may or may not reflect possibilities for cohesiveness and unity at other institutions (1718).

them from other departmental colleagues, and such help — be it pedagogical, institutional, personal, etc. — can go a long way to building in one a sense of belonging that might ameliorate the trauma of being separated from a previous cohort of specialists.[4] In my own experience, a thriving reading group of medievalists at Saint Louis University, Woode Walkers, helped me quite a bit in navigating through the academic rigors of my doctoral studies, but their support was based on their personal connections to me, connections that replaced initial shared interest in medieval matters. When going on to the job market, I found myself nervous that I would not be able to find the same sense of supportive community that I did among them, the ones who saw me more as a person than merely a medievalist. But I did find such community. I found a strong sense of departmental unity went a long way to match much of the support structure I had among the Woode Walkers. I felt a sense of belonging in my new department, initially by my knowledge of medieval material and willingness to teach beyond it, but eventually by my getting to know them as people.

Still, I could not deny that I was able to get a good position teaching in a university in part because of my medieval specialization, and the evolution from medievalist to institutionalist was not easy. Learning to belong in a different context was a hard lesson. After being steeped in the responsibilities that attend teaching a lot outside my specialization, my knowledge of medieval things seemed to gather dust without me realizing it. Going to conferences reminded me again that although my academic pedigree is primarily as a medievalist, what occupies my thoughts is rarely exclusively medieval. I did not realize, therefore, that the first academic conference I would attend as a me-

---

4   David A. Wicks et al., "An Investigation into the Community of Inquiry of Blended Classrooms by a Faculty Learning Community," *The Internet and Higher Education* 25 (2015): 59–60, at 62, reveal that the sense of being in the same boat with others, so to speak, can move from mere collaborative unity, toward a sense of holistic unity. Their study suggests that when faculty are more engaged in learning communities within their own institutions, they are more likely to experience professional satisfaction, even "fun" (59).

dievalist since starting my work as a university professor might expose knowledge lapses to other medievalists. Thank goodness for alone time in my room to fret without witnesses before giving my paper. Such alone time, though, did not alleviate my stress at realizing just how dissipated my specialist knowledge was. Wasn't there a point of language I had been so hung up on before that might be relevant to my discussion at this conference, and how do I find it again? Who was reigning during the great heathen army's incursions into the English landscape, and did the invasion coincide with *Beowulf*'s composition, or was it with the preparation of the manuscript, Cotton Roman-Emperor-or-Other A (it's often A) Roman-Numeral-Something? Yikes! Relief, alas, must come at the merciful end of my session, when, hopefully, no one would ask a question that might expose my self-consciousness about widening gaps in my knowledge. Perhaps the end of the conference will offer the additional relief of returning to and covering courses in one's department.

Though I have experienced such relief before and since, it was not to be the case in my first conference as an assistant professor, however. I had delivered my paper without embarrassing incident, so I looked forward with some relief to the remainder of the conference. In an unusual turn of events, however, I found myself in the audience of a very popular session at this very popular international conference of medievalists. The session was meant to be humorous, a way to unwind from the stress of academic performance anxiety, and I suspect I was not alone in needing such relief. One of the presentations included a number of slides with session titles on them, actual session titles from the very conference we were all attending. While the presentation was being given, however, I could not tell if the titles were made up or not. I laughed along with the audience, and at one point I must have checked my phone for something, because after the session was over, a friend of mine asked me about how I felt that my paper title was included among those most laughed at. I was floored. I had not seen my paper title on the slide, but everyone else had. The humorous session had certainly not been meant to lampoon me specifically, but I had no idea that the unimaginative title of my own paper would be made an exemplar of the kind of thing one might ridicule as academically pedestrian. To this day I do not believe that the presenter meant any tremendous harm, and, of course, I survived both the night and the conference. What I realized, however, was just how alone one could feel among one's peers. And, paradoxically, I was not alone. I was one of only a few people among hundreds of presenters, an inverted elite, whose paper titles were meant to represent, among other things, what may seem ridiculous about those trying their best to build or maintain their specialist knowledge. We were all alone together, none of us knowing the others, and I did not even know if I was the only one who had taken the joke badly.

Despite being quite embarrassed, however, that experience helped me realize that I did belong among my peers, but that my peers were not necessarily medievalists, and I do not mean that in a backhanded way. Perhaps I was an outsider at that conference, but I was still making meaningful contributions. I just did not realize where those most important contributions were being made: at home, at my institution, among my friends, and in other places where people actually know me. In a way, it was, and is, probably a mistake to think, as I did, of any abstract group as one's peers. Abstract groups often give me the impression that their members matter less than the abstraction for which they stand. There are no peers in abstractions. Instead, I now realize that my peers are those interested in my personal and professional development and welfare. They include the faculty members in the department where I teach, who have lunch with me and wonder how my classes are going. They include my medievalist colleagues in the Woode Walkers, who still want to know how my family and I are getting along. They included close friends, who help me when life gets unavoidably crowded with responsibilities.

The irony is that I had been an imposter when I most feared I might become one, and it took a semi-public embarrassment during a time when I was in an important life transition to realize it. I had staked my identity on a professional abstraction, a group identified by a specialized academic interest. I never really belonged to that group, and I am not sure that any actual people can ever be part of it anyway, which is for the best really. Specialized academic interest is necessary, but it in no way validates the personhood of those pursuing it. None should feel like an imposter because their pursuit reveals limitations to their knowledge; that is a positive side effect of scholarship and should be seen as such. Those I see at conferences should not feel alienated from each other. They belong to those around them who care for them and their well-being. Perhaps we can be more mindful of appropriately caring for those trying to see how their small puzzle piece might fit into something larger, not because of any contribution it may make to our specialization, but for the contribution it will make to them and to us.

The Unicorn Learns Accountability

Misty Urban, Muscatine Community College

In the spring of my first year at Lewis-Clark State College in Lewiston, Idaho, I stood before a standing-room-only crowd in the on-campus coffee shop, prepared to give an informal talk as part of the Humanities Division's ongoing colloquium series. Other professors had run small but intellectually substantial discussions about, for example, tigers in Romantic poetry. I was here to talk about monstrous women, Middle English romance, and the fairy Melusine. I had a set of PowerPoint slides. I had a packed audience, composed not just of my colleagues and seminar students but, I suspected, other students earning extra credit. Giving this talk on my research felt like a good way to introduce myself as the new assistant professor of English. It felt like a good way to give students a small taste of medieval literature that might lure them into further study. It felt like one of the many ways I was still attempting to prove, to the division and to myself, that, though the hiring process was long complete, I was indeed the right person for this job.

I have a history of being the only X in the room. The only woman in the department manager meeting at the bookstore. The only female in the board room when my consulting team met with the client. The only non-traditional student in the creative writing class, then the only creative writer in the Old English literature class, then the only combination MFA/PhD candidate in my cohort at Cornell. I had learned to assimilate, to switch codes, to volunteer for everything, and to put forth extra effort while adopting a pose of humility.

When I interviewed for the pre-1800 English literature and creative writing line at LCSC, however, all my differences were prized. I began to recall "The Unicorn in Captivity" tapestry hanging in The Cloisters in New York. My predecessor had been a combination medievalist and fiction writer, and the search committee worried they'd never find another one, or at least not a person trained in, published, and equally committed to both fields. (There are more of us than anyone suspects.) As a young(er) female, I was welcomed by my older, mostly male colleagues for adding to the diversity profile. They were all feminists already, but happy to defer to my claims of representation. I wasn't just the lone medievalist in the Humanities Division; I was the only medievalist on campus, as the historians over in Social Sciences were all Americanists. In fact, apart from the professor whose position I was filling and our linguist, who taught Nez Perce as well as HEL, I was the only medievalist for miles.

But, unlike many others in my position, I was fortunate enough to start my assistant professorship knowing my place was secure. The English program took pride in its rigorous curriculum, which included the early Brit Lit survey as a lower-level requirement and one pre-1900 lit seminar at the upper level. I wouldn't have to fight to defend my territory, since the praxis exam for secondary education majors still included a segment on early English lit. I would get to teach Beowulf, Chaucer, Malory, and Marie de France in the fall, and in the spring, the Medieval or Renaissance Lit seminar along with the Shakespeare course. That unicorn in the enclosure started to feel rather full of herself: petted, well-fed, and safe.

I had vaguely anticipated, as the lone medievalist, that I would need to find ways to make my work and my field intelligible to my department and accessible to students who had never read anything earlier than *The Scarlet Letter*. That proved not to be the case, at least where my literature colleagues were concerned. They were all generalists by necessity, versed in teaching everything from ancient Greek tragedy to the contemporary novel; any of them could have taught Chaucer, and likely better than I could. My first year as an assistant professor was not so much about learning how to be the Early Lit Guy and a creative writing teacher than it was about learning how to become a professional: in short, how to go from a senior graduate student fortunate enough to have a job and a dissertation prize to a professor, an advisor, a faculty member, division member, college employee, and tenure-track medievalist with a book. I learned to worry about things that graduate students never have to think about: how to recruit bodies into upper-level seminars, how to properly mentor a senior research project. Advising can expand to fill all available time. So can committee work, especially if, as the new hire, you volunteer for all the committees. Learning how a division, a college, an administration, and a State Board of Education operates takes time, observation, and a measure of delicacy. Three — or four — different class preps can fill your whole day, particularly when you have been ambitious enough to add an entirely new class to the curriculum, for instance a seminar on literary theory.

For the first time, I was designing syllabi without direct supervision or approval, though I did have to submit copies for my file. I felt the heady glee at creating my first Renaissance Lit course infused with self-doubt and panic — what did I know about Milton, anyway? My dissertation committee was no longer there subtly urging me to reframe my focus, deepen my analysis, or test my argument when my colleagues asked wonderful questions about my research. When I rambled at length about monstrous women and medieval romance, no one seemed to challenge my methodology, question my argument, or urge me to check my facts. At my talk for the colloquium, my anticipated 40 minutes stretched to an hour-and-a-half-long question-and-answer session, for which even the extra-credit seekers stayed to listen. It struck me then that my colleagues had given me a dangerous gift. I had to become the expert, even when I had so much yet to learn. I no longer had a dissertation committee or fellow students to cover my errors or fill the gaps in my knowledge. The unicorn had to perform. And she was in charge of her own professional development, now.

This is not to say I lacked support or oversight. My division chair was a wonderful mentor and gave excellent advice. Syllabi and student evaluations went on file for annual reviews; statements and letters of recommendation were necessary for the tenure committee. But it was my colleagues to whom I felt accountable, and my students who were evaluating me. As LCSC was a teaching college and I had accepted a 4/4 load, my job description anticipated that I would spend about 70% of my time teaching and advising. About 10% I could expect to devote to committee and service work, with 20% of my effort dedicated to creative writing and scholarship. As the unicorn, I still wanted to scatter some sparkle about the field of medieval literature, but I had to be a workhorse, too. I threw myself into becoming a better teacher, to live up to the high standards my colleagues had set.

This effort was greatly supported by a collegial division climate that welcomed collaboration and exchange. I audited classes like History of the Novel or the Modernist seminar so I could learn new subject matter and new pedagogical approaches. I invited other teachers to guest lecture in my seminars. I accepted every invitation to give talks in other classes, whether it was stage production in Shakespeare's time or applying feminist theory to *Wuthering Heights,* and when colleagues audited my classes, I followed up by asking for a letter for my personnel file. These were always glowing commendations, because those are the type of people I worked with, but I read with care to determine what about my teaching style might be working, and what I might continue to improve. After every class, I jotted down notes about what was going well and what problems I needed to address.

As a one-woman field, I realized that I needed to provide my own content *and* my own oversight. I started the habit of creating a typed self-review of each class at the end of the semester.

It was a simple document: a brief description of my philosophy and approach, a narrative of the semester, a list of aspects I'd reinforce the next time I taught the class, a list of things I'd change, and sometimes quotes from the narrative evaluations I asked my students to write. It began as a tool for personal development and then, to have a hard copy backup, I started putting it in my file. This simple document was hugely welcomed by my chair, my annual reviewers, and, in time, my promotion review committee. My chair once asked if she could share examples with the division, to encourage them to keep similar documents on file.

I created extra course evaluation tools, short essays and the like, so I could get detailed feedback from students on what they were learning. I frequently asked students permission to keep copies of their papers — with my comments — that I could use in future classes, and I put copies in my annual review file. When the time came, my promotion portfolio filled a 2 ½" binder — the recommended size was 1" — but it sailed through the review process. I still keep it on display in my office, not just as a record of what I accomplished, but of all I learned.

Going from a deeply-integrated, on-site graduate medieval community to a department of one responsible for English literature from its beginnings to 1800 meant, as most lone medievalists find, I had to find ways to keep up with developments in my fields. I signed up for a lot of listservs. I went to conferences and attended as many panels as possible in fields I taught, to learn what new work was being done and make contacts who could share syllabi, pedagogical tips, and favorite teaching resources. I felt very pushy at first, approaching strangers at talks and conferences, but once I could put faces to the other medievalists in my region, my sense of community grew, and so did my joy in my work.

The largest sense of accountability I felt was toward my students. While I could rely on their learning sound techniques of literary analysis from my literature colleagues, and good creative writing practices from the other writers, there was little chance someone else would fill the gaps on the subject matter. The survey gave me one chance to show students the heroic beauties of *Beowulf*, the ironies and provocations in Chaucer, the gender ideology at work in Malory and Marie. In the upper-level seminar, whether it was Shakespeare or Spenser, Marlowe or Milton, I had to make sure our English lit majors could hold their own in graduate school, in conferences, and in publication. Any failures of our education majors with the pre-1800 questions on their praxis exams would be laid at my door. My colleagues were well-versed in many periods and far more well-read than I, but if our seniors were writing their thesis on anything before 1800, their logical mentor was me. I felt an intense responsibility to make sure my secondary criticism was broadly informed, my arguments were up to date, the analyses I introduced in class were sound, and my comments on papers pointed students to research extending their interests. For everything from Cynewulf to Virginia Woolf, I had to know my stuff.

Added to that challenge was my growing sense that some anticipatory defense-building was called for. If the administrative axe were ever directed to my areas — and there was talk among the Idaho Board of Education about changing our core curriculum — I would need proof of rigor and evidence of worth to defend the outposts of my medieval kingdom. It wasn't enough just to be the unicorn; I had to be able to prove why the unicorn was needed, even indispensable. Outside of the classroom, I jumped at every chance to make my work more visible to the college and beyond. I donated my book to our library (which felt so self-aggrandizing, but I did it), gave talks at colloquia, and participated in conference panels organized by my colleagues. Each year for the Women's History Month programming, I volunteered to give a talk on medieval women. Some of these activities felt like trying to create a cult of personality — love me, love medieval lit. But engaging broad-based support for the study of literature was necessary to justify the importance of work in the humanities to local and state-wide governance bodies that seemed frequently suspicious, if not overtly hostile to the work of higher education, at least when it was not business, nursing, or STEM.

The price for all this extra activity and accountability was steep. The 80% of my job allotted to teaching, advising, and service spread to 85, then 95, then 99% of my time, including nights and weekends. As I prepared my promotion portfolio, I noticed that while my CV had expanded in other places, my recent publications were all things I'd developed in graduate school and revised since then. Some of my conference talks came from my teaching — for instance, a paper on domestic utopias in early modern women's writing, which evolved from the Renaissance Lit class — but for the most part, I was still mining research from my monograph. The one short story I'd published was an old one I produced upon request for LCSC's student-run journal. Despite starting and abandoning a new novel over every vacation break, I'd written one new short story in four years, and it was still unpublished. As it happens, my trickle of publications didn't impede my promotion to associate professor, and the effort I invested in teaching paid off in other ways: in the spring of 2012, I was awarded the President's Award for Excellence in Teaching. It was a deeply humbling honor, and I proudly display that plaque in my office, too.

I missed my writing, though, and my own research. When my husband received a job offer that would substantially increase his professional happiness as well as move us closer to our families still living in the Midwest, we decided to take it. I left LCSC to become a truly lone medievalist in the sense of being an independent scholar, which requires that one work even harder to find community, and that one make good friends at the nearest research library. For an independent scholar, there is truly no one to hold you accountable for your work, either in rate of production or in quality.

Looking back, I believe that the kindness, collegiality, professionalism, and support from my colleagues was the single most important factor in my survival as the lone medievalist at LCSC. This, of course, does not translate into useful advice for a job seeker, who can only hope she lands in a department full of fantastic people. But the tactic of finding or creating a supporting network of medieval scholars, using technology where we must, is, I think, key for any lone medievalist to survive in the wild.

My own experience has convinced me that the other most useful strategy to our survival, and happiness, is to make our fields accountable in both senses of the term: answerable to the broader objectives of the curriculum and the college's goals for students, and able to be explained to administrators and students not just in terms of numbers but of value. The best way I found to foster visibility and produce interest in medieval scholarship was through frequent exchange within classes and at events both on and off campus. I integrated medieval lit into my literary theory class and referenced it in my surveys, my early modern seminars, and my creative writing courses. I kept as samples, and included in my review file, student papers that incorporated "The Wife of Bath's Tale" or *Gawain and the Green Knight* into their analysis. In many ways I felt I was simply butting my unicorn horn in everywhere I could find an opening. But I made these efforts to show students — as well as annual reviewers, colleagues outside the division, and hopefully also the college administration and Board of Ed — that the study of medieval literature was just as rigorous and yielded as much to scholarly analysis as any other literary field, as well as offering all the traditional, oft-rehearsed benefits that learning in the humanities provides to the minds and well-being of a citizenry.

While the devotion to teaching meant a sacrifice of time and energy for my own research, true, I also felt that I reached more students through my teaching than I did through my articles or books. Many of us in teaching-focused institutions find that our work in the classroom constitutes our major contribution to medieval scholarship, even when we bring students to medieval lit through the gateway of medievalism, and even when their knowledge of the history and literature of the period only marginally informs the work that eventually earns their keep. Most of our major medieval associations think in some ways about teaching, and many sponsor awards for excellent scholarship, but I wonder if there ought to be more recognition in the field of the contributions of teaching, to recognize that the students, not the profession, are really the ones we serve.

And I often wonder if we do need to kill the unicorn after all. By this I do not suggest that we eliminate or absorb medieval studies but that we resist the entrenchment that periodization creates. If the unicorn escapes the silken bridle and the golden corral to trample at will over other less-contested fields — those considered less dusty — she just might leave her hoofprint on them. We should not feel alone, isolated, or embattled in our medieval outposts; we are ambassadors from a vibrant and important part of history that bears deeply on the other conversations about literature, meaning, relevance, and humanity taking place within our departments.

The most satisfying thing about designing my classes at LCSC was that I truly felt that medieval lit was not treated as a special case, an adumbration of our curriculum that showed our commitment to a fading nineteenth-century ideal of a university. Early lit was considered an integral piece of our curriculum, a body of work essential to students' larger understanding of the scope and meaning of English literature. My territory tended to seem more distant and superficially strange, but students quickly realized that Chaucer, Petrarch, and Christine de Pisan were having lively discussions about problems still relevant in our own time. Rather than the exotic pet, a proof of departmental wealth in that they can afford to house and feed us, medievalists need to be considered an essential voice, if not a core foundation, of a healthy conversation about what literature is and means, what history means and does. It is this sense of accountability to our students, our schools, and the work of the humanities that will, I believe, best ensure the longevity of our field and the survival of the unicorns.

How to Stop Being a Lonely Medievalist

M. Wendy Hennequin, Tennessee State University

If you are reading this essay, chances are you are a Lone Medievalist. So am I. I am the only medievalist in my department (Language, Literature, and Philosophy, comprising the disciplines of English, foreign languages, literature, linguistics, and philosophy). I teach at a historically black college, where medieval studies doesn't even register on the academic radar. My historically-minded students are generally more interested in American or African history. Many students, and indeed many of my colleagues, see the Middle Ages as irrelevant to our studies and disciplines.

Yet my purpose here isn't to enumerate the challenges of being a Lone Medievalist. We all know what they are, and other essays in this volume examine our situation and its inherent issues and frustrations in detail. Instead, I intend to discuss the problem of a Lone Medievalist's loneliness and suggest some concrete ways to deal with it.

Lone Medievalists tend to get lonely; it's only logical. We're surrounded by colleagues, both outside our departments and sometimes within it, who don't understand what we do. I once had a conversation, for instance, with a colleague with a health science administration background about how difficult it is to get funding for medieval research. She suggested I co-write a grant with a psychologist to study students' reactions to *Beowulf*. My well-meaning colleague wanted to help, but clearly she doesn't understand the sort of research we do. I'm a literature specialist, not a pedagogical specialist. I study medieval languages and texts, not modern readers; other medievalist colleagues study historical documents, artwork, religious and folk practices, government, archaeology, and artifacts. We don't need scientific grants or large studies to practice our craft. We need books, time and mental space, and colleagues to share our ideas.

Thanks to the amazing powers of Interlibrary Loan and the Internet, we can easily get books, and digitization has even made many manuscripts available long-distance. Time and mental space are harder to come by — a challenge we share with all academics. Our most pressing, and most grievous, problem as medievalists emerges from our lone status: we lack colleagues in our own discipline to discuss our ideas with. We work in isolation, trying to develop our ideas on our own, without encouragement, feedback, and suggestions. Certainly, this is part of our process: we need time alone to think and write. Because we aren't talking about our ideas, however, we aren't developing those ideas as fully or as efficiently as we could. We lose our trains of thought, and our sparks of our inspiration die for lack of fuel. For this reason, many of us find that we develop our best ideas when talking to our colleagues at conferences or other scholarly gatherings, like National Endowment for the Humanities (NEH) seminars. A colleague's suggestion or connection can open up new ideas, help us remove scholarly roadblocks, or point out a new avenue of research. Like our academic ancestors, we still write copious correspondence to colleagues, digitally, to try to combat this lack, but there is no substitute for face-to-face feedback and exchange of ideas. A Lone Medievalist needs colleagues and collaboration just as much as books and time; otherwise, our professional loneliness hamstrings our work.

But we don't have to be lonely. Yes, we should reach out to each other through digital means, such as the Lone Medievalist site, discussion boards, Twitter, Facebook, and the ever-reliable e-mail. And, yes, we should attend large conferences like Leeds and Kalamazoo where we can find old friends and colleagues and discuss [insert your obscure medieval interest here] to our hearts' content. But those opportunities don't necessarily relieve the professional loneliness nor give us means to talk about our work in our immediate, day-to-day lives. Yet, I argue, we can employ several simple strategies to prevent ourselves from becoming Lonely Medievalists — and they all come down to one thing: *Make friends.*

I'm not being sarcastic here, nor even facetious. In order to stop being lonely, we need to find relatively local, medievally-minded people so we can talk shop. Yes, I know what you're thinking — we're *Lone* Medievalists. Of course we can make friends — anyone who's been to the International Congress on Medieval Studies knows that we're generally a sociable bunch — but if we had relatively local, medievally-minded people around, we wouldn't be reading this essay.

But you can find our tribe around you. You have to know where to look. With a little research, you may discover that you may be a Lone Medievalist, but you may not be as alone as you thought.

1. Find your local colleagues

- *Find the other medievalists at your university.* We have often trained only with other medievalists in our own departments and don't think of looking outside our disciplines for other medievalists. But you may find you have other Lone Medievalists scattered around the campus, separated by discipline, department, and buildings. Check in English, history, art and art history, foreign languages, economics, philosophy, even theater. I myself have a medieval colleague in History (not unexpected) and another in the Writing Center (who knew?). Your colleagues are probably just as lonely as you are and would love to hear from you. An added bonus: you might collaborate on courses and projects or exchange guest lectures. Your colleagues also may have other local contacts.

Look for the ancient, classical, and early modern scholars as well; they're lonely too, and they often understand our research problems and perspectives.
- *Find the medievalists at other "local" universities.* If you work in a city, or in a densely settled area, this can be very local; you probably have many universities and colleges within easy driving distance. If you're in a more isolated area, check what's reasonably nearby. If you're part of a university system or consortium, check for medievalists at your sister universities. Either way, use your Google-Fu, and discover who the medievalists are, and *contact them*. Go to your local medieval conferences, not just the big ones like Leeds and Kalamazoo. Find and join your local medieval association. I have met several local medievalists — and made several friends — in these ways.
- *Start a research group.* Once you find your colleagues, start getting together to talk about research. Yes, I know, scheduling is always a problem, but it's well worth it to keep in touch and have an outlet to talk about our research. I'm lucky enough to have a Liberal Arts research symposium at my university and a research group of medieval, classical, and early modern colleagues hosted at Vanderbilt University, about fifteen minutes away.

2. Find your local nerds.

No, they're not academics, and they won't have the expertise a colleague might have. But the Middle Ages and medievalism are popular with non-academic audiences, and reaching out to them gives us a rare chance to talk about our field to an interested audience. These non-academic, medievally-minded people often have questions that help us refine our ideas or open new avenues of thought and research.

- *Find the campus geeks.* Does your university have a science fiction, fantasy, or video game club? Contact them. Tell them you can teach them about Tolkien's languages or make his-

torical and cultural connections between *Skyrim* and medieval Scandinavia. They'll love you forever.
- *Reach out to your local high school and middle school teachers.* All the teachers I know love to pick our brains and hear what we're working on. If they are working on something medieval in the curriculum — and sometimes even if they aren't, but can make a connection — they may want you to come in and speak.
- *Consult your local library.* Local libraries often sponsor workshops, book groups, and activities for adults and children, and the popularity of such books and television series such as *Game of Thrones* and *The Vikings* has sparked a great deal of popular interest in the Middle Ages. Librarians (who, despite stereotypes, are often some of the friendliest people on earth) are always looking for new speakers and very happy to allow us to show off and make use of our expertise. I participated in a "Hobbit Day" at a local library where I taught children — and their parents — about Old English and Old Norse runes. Yes, I know — it's not exactly academic. But it allowed me to teach and think about something in my specialty which I hadn't been able to consider in a long time.
- *Discover your local nerd culture.* You may find yourself spoiled for choice. Look not only for the hard-core medieval hobbyists, such as the Society for Creative Anachronism (SCA) and Renaissance Faire enthusiasts, but also gaming clubs, book clubs at the local bookstore, and non-profit acting companies. These people often make some of the best students we could wish for — they love the Middle Ages, and they *want* our knowledge. Since they rarely have access to scholars, they are often very grateful to hear us speak. Some of the best classes I have ever taught — on Old English poetics, on medieval "fan fiction," even on academic citation — have been for SCA groups. I gave a "scholar's talk" for the Nashville Shakespeare Company's production of *Henry V,* and most of my very enthusiastic audience asked thoughtful and interesting questions not only about the play, but about its medieval setting and history.

Granted, these strategies take time and effort — the very resources we desperately need and which we already desperately lack. On the other hand, many can be done piecemeal, and some, such as reaching out to the librarians and the campus and off-campus nerds, can be implemented while coping with our daily email barrage. I suggest saving the more difficult strategies, such as starting a research group, for the quieter times of the academic year, such as winter break. I promise that the time will be well spent. Administrators, budgets, and the evolving values of the academy may limit our ability to change our status as Lone Medievalists. But our tribe surrounds us, hidden in other buildings and other campuses, lurking among the stacks of the libraries and in the medieval corners of the Internet; your quest is to seek them out. We are not — and do not have to be — alone.

Blended Medievalist Careers: Staying Optimistic While Balancing Passion and Job Market Realities

Timothy R.W. Jordan, Ohio University Zanesville / Zane State College & Aubri Anne McVey, Wabash College[1]

University teaching is by nature an optimistic profession. To invest in the time and energy for graduate-level training and then go on to work with our own students is to invest in the belief that despite the ills of war, political corruption, social conflict, and natural disasters, there is hope that human beings can overcome the obstacles that we face. This hope springs not just from a vague sense that "everything will be okay" but also

---

1 This paper developed in tandem with a roundtable discussion entitled "Blended Medievalist Careers" delivered at the Fall 2015 meeting of the Medieval Association of the Midwest at the Hill Museum & Manuscript Library of Saint John's University, Collegeville, MN. We extend deep appreciation to the other discussants: William F. Hodapp (Professor of Technical Writing and Program Coordinator of Medieval and Renaissance Studies at the College of St. Scholastica), Matthew Z. Heintzelman (Curator of Austria/Germany Study Center and Cataloger of Rare Books at the Hill Museum & Manuscript Library), and Chad Judkins (PhD, English, 2013, Purdue University and First Lt. in the United States Army).

from seeing our own liberal arts educations help us solve "real world" problems.

Along with this optimism, the pursuit of graduate studies brings a passion for research within a given discipline or specialization. In the cases of this essay's authors and many of its readers, that passion is for medieval studies. We share a conviction that our subject matter is valuable and worth sharing. That conviction may stem from our understanding that lessons from history and philosophy can shape our reactions to current events. It may also arise from the awareness that human self-expression in art, music, and literature can stretch across centuries and still resonate with us, suggesting that people of any time or place are not as radically different as they sometimes first appear. Indeed, there is a poetry to learning and teaching these lessons of medieval history, philosophy, art, music, and literature because they revive the very roots of the university as an institution developed in the Middle Ages.

Unfortunately, the decline of tenure positions presents a harsh counterpoint to the ideal of university teaching as a way to share these passions. We medievalists may bare the brunt of this reality; we certainly have enough colleagues and mentors whose retirements are tarnished by the news that their medievalist tenure-lines will not be filled. As this essay collection illustrates, many medievalists are already the sole individuals in their departments if not their institutions who engage in this area of specialization. Thus, the news that a colleague or mentor's tenure-line will be ended impacts with extra poignancy contingent medievalists trying to carve out time for research and opportunities for specialist teaching.

We speculate to a degree in the preceding statements, but regardless of whether medievalists disproportionately are perceived as "impractical," a September 2015 article in the *Chronicle of Higher Education* presents a drop in graduate students in the arts and humanities. It states, "first-time doctoral enrollment in history, English, and other arts-and-humanities disciplines fell 0.5 percent from 2013 to 2014, according to a report published last week by the Council of Graduate Schools."[2] It is worth pondering whether those who might have enrolled in graduate studies in the humanities will experience the same passion for their chosen career or develop the skills that those who complete advanced degrees do. There may be many reasons for this reduced enrollment, but one almost certainly is the lack of full-time positions and stability of such a career path.

Those of us who do remain optimistic about the possibility of eventually finding a tenure-track position should not succumb, however, to a false idealism about when such a job will present itself. In the current market, opportunities for blended career paths need to become serious considerations. Graduate students and graduate programs alike have been called for some time to give greater consideration and discussion of how advanced degrees can benefit non-academic professions.[3] A statement from the MLA in 2014 is the most significant to our backgrounds, stating the need to "validate the wide range of career possibilities that [humanities] doctoral students can pursue."[4] However, these statements often have been broad calls for action, so we hope our discussion will provide two working models that seek to strike a balance between a passion for medieval studies while transferring graduate training to complementary professions outside of academia.

---

[2] Vimal Patel, "Enrollment in Humanities Ph.D. Programs Decline as More Graduate Schools Slim Down," *The Chronicle of Higher Education* (17 September 2015), http://chronicle.com/article/Enrollment-in-Humanities-PhD/233175.

[3] "The Alternative Career," *Chemistry in Australia* (July 2014): 40; Natalie Henderson, "Questioning the Promise," *Chronicle Of Higher Education* 51, no. 24 (18 February 2005): C1–C4. Alexandra M. Lord, "Whose Job Is It, Anyway?," *Chronicle Of Higher Education* 56, no. 26 (12 March 2010): A39–A40; Thomas Magaldi, "The Backup Plan," *Inside Higher Ed* (29 June 2015), https://www.insidehighered.com/advice/2015/06/29/essay-need-new-phds-do-job-searches-more-dream-jobs; Patel, "Enrollment."

[4] Quoted in Leonard Cassuto, "The MLA Tells It Like It Is," *Chronicle Of Higher Education* 60, no. 39 (20 June 2014): A32.

Job Market Background

A broad marker of the changes to academic teaching appears through the drop in number of tenured positions across all disciplines. In 1975, 57% of all faculty positions were tenure-track, but this figure had dropped below 30% by 2009. Projections place 15–20% of all positions as the new normal for tenure.[5] Additionally, a 2013 report found that since 2005 "the proportion [of full-time professors] that are untenured but on the tenure-track declined […] from 11.3 percent to 9.9 percent."[6]

From the narrower perspectives of our own disciplines in English and French, the Modern Language Association's 2013–14 report on the *Job Information List* reveals that advertised English positions are down by 8.4% and foreign language positions are down by 6.8%. These declines are for the second year in a row, with the 2012–13 report showing drops of 7.5% in English and 2.3% in foreign languages.[7] Put differently, last year's numbers come to 1,046 in English and 1,027 in foreign languages compared to the 10-year high in 2007–8 of 1,826 in English and 1,680 in foreign languages.[8]

Furthermore, when we consider recent postings in the job market, we notice a dichotomy: institutions request applications from academics with either a highly specialized, narrow, "trendy," "sexy" field or an incredibly difficult combination of skills (e.g., the ability to teach both French and Arabic from beginning to advanced levels with a native command of

---

5 Stephanie Findlay, "Whatever Happened to Tenure?" *Maclean's* 124, no. 2 (24 January 2011): 46–47; Robin Wilson, "Tenure, RIP: What the Vanishing Status Means for the Future of Education," *Chronicle of Higher Education* (4 July 2010), http://chronicle.com/article/Tenure-RIP/66114/ .

6 Peter Schmidt, "'Temporary' and 'Part Time' Part Ways in Faculty Hiring," *Chronicle Of Higher Education* 61, no. 22 (13 February 2015): A8.

7 Lindsay Ellis, "MLA Reports Modest Decline in Job Ads Posted in 2012–13," *Chronicle of Higher Education* (30 October 2013), http://chronicle.com/article/MLA-Reports-Modest-Decline-in/142687/.

8 Posted by Anna Chang, "Report on the MLA Job Information List, 2013–14," *MLA Commons* (19 November 2014), https://news.commons.mla.org/2014/11/19/report-on-the-2013-14-mla-job-information-list/.

French, Arabic, and English). Because the academy is moving to a model of doing more with less, is it any wonder that those with advanced degrees fill contract, visiting appointments, or adjunct positions?

The realities of this job market also have an impact on full-time faculty. Fewer tenure-track positions increase the amount of pressure upon the professors in them to meet research quotas and to perform administrative service.[9] One Canadian study even suggests that these pressures link to strains on mental and physical health. In a sample of 267 assistant professors, only 30.7% met recommended levels of exercise, compared to 50% of non-academic professionals.[10] A Harvard-conducted study found that "only 70% of [those on the tenure-track] at research institutions said they would choose to work at their universities if they had it to do over again."[11] Hard work that promises reward is one thing, but inescapable stress is something else.

Although these numbers suggest bleak job prospects, they do not paint a full picture of the motivations for pursuing graduate studies. Graduate degrees represent far more than simply job credentials and are much more integral parts of our identities. The process of completing graduate school has taught us practical skills for performing research, highly developed writing, presentations, and teamwork. We also gain such mental skills as the focus for analyzing problems, the discipline for pursuing long-term projects, the organizational skills for dealing with complexity, and an understanding of how different disciplines complement and relate to one another. In short, graduate study develops passion in us for our subject area, medieval or otherwise, and from that passion, we derive a precise framework for how we understand the world.

---

9   Findlay, "Whatever Happened to Tenure?"
10 Quoted in Claire Potter, "The Only Good Professor Is A Dead Professor: Or, Is The Decline of Academic Labor A Health Risk?" *Chronicle of Higher Education* (29 April 2011), http://chronicle.com/blognetwork/tenuredradical/2011/04/only-good-professor-is-dead-professor/.
11 Wilson, "Tenure, RIP."

Equally important to these practical and mental skills are the relationships that we build with others through these passions. The best interactions with students in the classroom create a two-way exchange that stimulates both parties, forging connections that can be important both for the short-term and for lifetimes. Through conference attendance, we also create networks with other scholars who have completed similar courses of study and share our beliefs.

Although all of these benefits are less tangible than the financial benefits of having a tenure-track job, they are just as important to our satisfaction in life. Indeed, we should view the academic job crisis as having as much to do with the choice of walking away from these passions and relationships as with the shortage of faculty positions for PhDs on the market. It is because of these stakes that we are attempting to forge middle paths for ourselves.

Personal Histories

Tim became involved with two closely related Native American historical sites in Licking County, Ohio — Flint Ridge and the Newark Earthworks — in 2013. He was hired to work as an interpretive guide for these sites, which provided supplemental income to the adjunct teaching he was doing while pursuing his academic job search. To earn a livable income, adjuncting was requiring him to take on five courses per semester, plus summer classes, cutting significantly into his time and energy for research and the job search itself. The interpretive work was seasonal and intermittent, but it significantly required less time than teaching additional classes because there was no prep or grading at the end of a tour.

In October 2014, the current site managers of Flint Ridge approached Tim with the proposition of taking over as the part-time curator of the park and its museum. If not the beginning, their proposal marked a defining moment for the model of his blended career path due to the close geographic and cultural relationships of the sites in the area. The Newark Earthworks consists of a pair of two-thousand-year-old geometric enclosures called the Great Circle and the Octagon. They respectively enclose thirty and seventy acres. The Great Circle and Octagon are also part of a World Heritage package projected for advancement as soon as 2018 and making Licking County an international tourists' destination.

Although not explicitly part of the World Heritage package, Flint Ridge's proximity of just 11 miles from the Great Circle and Octagon will also make it of interest to visitors. Its significance is its one thousand flint quarries from which ancient Native Americans made their stone-chipped tools beginning thirteen or fourteen thousand years ago. The quarries and earthen mounds build a complementary picture of the area's early people wherein Flint Ridge is the technological base for the civilization and the earthworks are the culture's self-expression.

By taking on site management of Flint Ridge, Tim has been able to take a step back from teaching, paradoxically leaving open more time for course prep and for professional development. In the six months since beginning to take on responsibilities as site manager, he began organizing a cast of readers for a recording with the Chaucer Studio, contributed to this article, and co-organized three conference sessions. Just as significant as opening up time, if not more so, has been allowing more energy for these professional activities. As many of us probably find true, outlining lesson plans, writing assignment sheets, and grading student papers require the same energy reserves as research. Tim's experience has often been that, even if time at the end of a day allowed for his own reading and writing, he simply could not maintain focus.

Like Tim and many other graduate students in the humanities, Aubri has chosen to adjunct to continue in her profession and to teach medieval French literature. She finds teaching French and medieval French highly fulfilling and rewarding. However, because of the current climate in the Academy and the paucity of available full-time and adjunct positions, she applied for a language-related job for a major medical company in August of 2015. Ironically, she applied for the same position she was unable to take a few years before because she was presented with a full-time temporary teaching opportunity. She had begun an academic job search and then received a job announcement for French speakers in the international medical company. However, when the academic job search proved fruitful, she decided to continue teaching in academe.

Aubri decided to apply for the position in the medical industry again because it would mean speaking French and aiding French-Canadian customers who purchased medical devices. It would also allow her to use the communication and presentation skills gained during her graduate study, and she would work in a team of others completing the same tasks. Aubri felt she was qualified for the position because of past jobs she had in the pharmaceutical industry and in healthcare facilities during her undergraduate studies and because of her fluency in French. Her previous experience as an assistant in the Office of Medical Affairs communicating with healthcare professionals, interacting with healthcare staff, verifying medical privileges, and acting as a liaison between her supervisor and physicians prepared her to understand the inner workings of a company based on service. She also had prior experience in Quality Control for a pharmaceutical company which included testing, storing, and disposing of medications in specified environments as directed by the corporation. As a result of that position, she was familiar with corporate management structure, protocols, and manufacturing. She decided to include these positions in healthcare and pharmaceuticals on her application along with her teaching and academic experiences.

During Aubri's second application process for the medical position, her application was accepted, and she had a conversation with the human resources recruiter about the position within days of submitting it. During the application and screening processes, she went through several phone conversations and interviews. In addition to the necessity of practical use of the French language, she found the benefits and retirement package that were offered very attractive because these are rare in part-time and in some full-time academic appointments.

Aubri assumed she might have time to teach a class or two around her work schedule, but then learned that the hours were based on Canadian time and that she would never be presented with a regular nine to five corporate shift should she take the position. The odd hours and the necessity of a commute would not allow her to teach even one French course in the role of adjunct faculty. That fact and some prior commitments that conflicted with the company's training schedule prevented her from taking the job. However, she currently receives job announcements from the medical corporation tailored to her profile on an almost weekly basis. Tim once remarked that this corporate "courtship" was indeed medieval, to which Aubri agreed, citing the theme of the persistent knight and the reluctant lady. She has continued her search for a full-time position with more reasonable hours or at least a part-time position that would allow her to continue in her current role as adjunct faculty.

Teaching within a Blended Career

Our statements about cutting back our amounts of teaching are not to dismiss its satisfaction as a second major component of involvement in academia. They are instead describing a recalibration of expectations in order to strike a more sustainable balance. Admittedly, many of the courses taught by adjunct faculty are the introductory and general education courses whose students bring wide ranges of ability and enthusiasm for the subject matter. Although these courses can demand great deals of patience, depending upon the student make up, the arrangement of working a second, nonacademic job provides a case of less being more. Fewer students in fewer sections in a term allows for more focus on the classes for which we are responsible.

Moreover, general education courses do not entirely preclude the possibility of bringing in specialized content upon occasion. Our specializations help us to see the world in unique ways, and taking opportunities to draw on that knowledge provides students with learning experiences that we can uniquely offer them, even if the course does not strictly demand that content.

One of Tim's most successful examples has been to incorporate a mini-lesson on the history of the English language into the composition classroom. Within a single class session, he briefly demonstrates how English evolves through Old and Middle English before reaching Modern English by reading aloud for students texts in all three forms and by demonstrating different etymological influences that have shaped English through invasion. He also discusses modern dialects and neologisms with his students to demonstrate how language still is not stable. Tim's hope is to provide a context for students to think about why standardized language is important, especially when they might exclusively associate language study with the tedium of grammar and mechanics.

Literature surveys present even greater opportunities for incorporating medieval content. These courses cannot be exclusively medieval, but their thematic nature obviously allows anyone to incorporate specialized material into the study. The theme of "the mythic and the heroic" allowed Tim to incorporate the Genesis creation story, Ælfric's *Life of Saint Edmund*, and J.R.R. Tolkien's neo-medieval *The Hobbit* alongside the Iroquois creation story, John Steinbeck's *Of Mice and Men*, and Malala Yousafsai's *I Am Malala*. These discussions drew on older definitions of "myth" as "origin stories" and allowed the students to consider how we still to look to ideals such as the American Dream or empowerment through education as guiding narratives in our lives. Heroes then are the people who fulfill these narratives. Tim makes these kinds of thematic connections from medieval and Renaissance works to other periods, and being an adjunct does not prevent him from taking these opportunities, which are just as, if not more, satisfying for exploring specialized material with students as they would be for full-time colleagues. Additionally, having his doctorate has caused Tim to be invited with more frequency to teach these more desirable literature surveys that allow him to incorporate his specialization. In time, he may also be asked to teach period surveys.

Aubri has also had extensive experience in teaching general education courses such as French 101. Like Tim, she has incorporated her medieval specialty by introducing language students to Old French and Middle French, thus showcasing the evolution of modern French. Students often do not realize that language is not static. They are also unaware that there was a complex process of written communication before the invention of the printing press. Aubri has had opportunities to incorporate discussions and experiences related to textual studies and manuscript culture into her basic language classes. She has taken her French 101 students on excursions to rare manuscript libraries where they have heard presentations by experts in the field. Students were also introduced to French cuisine during course excursions. They were delighted to discover that they were eating lunch at a locally owned French buffet on a trip to the Lilly Library. Students were presented with several authentic French dishes they had never eaten, and they adventurously tasted each one. On a later excursion to the Art Institute of Chicago, students had lunch at the oldest crêperie in the US after they completed their assignments on different periods of French and Francophone art. They curiously studied the menu, competing to see who would order the best meal! Students' enthusiastic responses indicate that they enjoy experiential learning, and they often comment that these are their favorite activities at the end of the semester. Because of the success in student engagement and experiential learning, Aubri infuses her specialty into her teaching rather than focusing on presentations of verb conjugations. Students in her basic language courses are fulfilling their language requirements and are often from different backgrounds and specialties. She finds their reactions and observations intriguing.

Aubri also enjoys teaching medieval and Renaissance surveys in addition to basic language courses. These are rare opportunities to focus on her specialty, and students' reactions to Marie de France's *Lais,* the chivalric exploits portrayed in *La Chanson de Roland,* and the comedic medieval farces are inspiring. She has had the good fortune of linking medieval art and literature in some of her courses and has taken students to art museums in her area to view medieval works. Survey courses allow her to introduce students to medieval music, manuscript culture, medieval art, and Old French. Because students are often unfamiliar with medieval society, Aubri relishes the chance to introduce them to the myriad elements of medieval culture through the lens of literature.

None of this is to suggest in either of our cases that a career consisting of general education is comparable to being a department's medieval specialist. Instead, it is to demonstrate that one can make opportunities to bring in specialized content in satisfying ways even when teaching almost exclusively general education courses.

Academic Skills in a Blended Career

Our emphasis above on teaching is not to say that the pursuits of our secondary careers have just been "side jobs." We have been able to translate academic skills into these careers naturally as well. Foremost has been the ability to make oral presentations. Mastery of material and presentation style proves very important because of the necessity of communicating with many people on a daily basis. We regularly engage groups and customers through asking and answering questions while making progress toward explaining a larger theme or greater issue. As curator of Flint Ridge, Tim's spoken portion of a tour can last anywhere from forty-five minutes to an hour-and-a-half: the same lengths of time as many college class sessions. Presentation and teaching skills are also applicable for Aubri because she would be aiding customers and teaching them technical details about their medical devices. Additionally, she would help them solve problems and would employ her verbal skills to convey, communicate and postulate about the suspected defect or malfunction.

Other academic skills than presentation ability also fit into each of our secondary career paths. Research strategies are another skill set that Tim has found applicable to interpretive work at Flint Ridge and the earthworks. One important application is as a complement to good presentation. As Native American scholars, historians, and archaeologists address new problems,

Tim's interpretation evolves by incorporating new material. Research skills are also vital for synthesizing academic material into mediums more accessible to the general public. One project Tim completed his first summer as site manager was setting up a display case at the Great Circle's museum explaining the importance of stone-chipped tools constructed at Flint Ridge in relation to the cultural expression represented by the Earthworks. His academic research and writing background has also helped him to write a collection of short essays for self-guided tours of the various sites.

Experience working with a historical period of literature also has given Tim what he calls a "contextualizing perspective" that is helpful to his interpretive work. By this, he means the ability to think in reference to the events and values of a time period other than our own. It is of course a skill necessary for any kind of academic work and one that is honed through graduate-level training. Although this perspective taking could apply generally to any culture and its time period, Tim's work with late medieval culture potentially provides a narrower connection as well. Specifically, fifteenth- and sixteenth-century worldviews represent the European values that collided with the pre-existing Native American cultures of the Western Hemisphere. Where there is overlap, great sensitivity in presenting European and Native perspectives that did and continue to conflict is necessary, but there is potential for cross-feed between the two content areas.

Aubri likewise has academic skills that transfer between her careers. In addition to presentation and communication, her fluency in French has been invaluable in her job search. Because it is sometimes difficult to find someone who has experience working in healthcare facilities and pharmaceuticals who also speaks French, Aubri's candidacy for a job in the medical device industry was a direct result of her ability to speak the language and engage French-Canadian customers effectively. Her years of communicative immersion training and teaching prepared her very well for industry specific training as well as acquiring specialized and technical vocabulary. Although she has no prior background working with medical devices, she was offered a package that was comparable to someone with at least two years of prior experience based on her language ability.

Furthermore, a natural extension of Aubri's French skills would be translation between a French-Canadian customer and other peers and supervisors who are primarily Anglophones. She would translate from French to English in order to document problems that customers encountered as well as to suggest or verify solutions she discovered during her interactions with customers. Thus, her previous experience in communicative language teaching has become an important aspect in her model of a blended career in the medical industry.

The transfer of skills and ideas also moves from our secondary careers to inform our research. Tim has learned that flint was a major construction material used throughout England and in East Anglia particularly. Indeed, this knowledge begins to color the lines from *Sir Gawain and the Green Knight* in which sparks fly from the hooves of the Green Knight's horse as it gallops out of Arthur's hall (line 459). What kinds of imagery are further associated with flint in Middle English literature may be an interesting avenue to explore. In Aubri's case, she sees the potential to investigate lines of inquiry combining her interests in the medical industry and medieval studies. Given her research experience in textual studies and manuscripts, she plans to focus future research on images of the body and depictions of medieval medical practices. She has also recently become a member of the Society for the Study of Disability in the Middle Ages.

Broader Applications and Observations

There admittedly are many aspects of our experiences that are highly particular to our situations. Not every community contains historical sites that are up for World Heritage nomination, nor does every community have a major medical industry. Nonetheless, the transferrable skills we found align well with those used by many people in similar situations. Teaching helps with making oral presentations. Research skills provide reliable information in a world in which the Internet is glutted with conflicting facts and opinions. The ability to think within different contexts builds empathy. In an increasingly globalized world, multilingualism is a major asset. We feel these points bear emphasizing, even if they're not original observations.

What we hope is a more insightful observation is that graduates on the job market should be attuned to the issues and opportunities within the communities where they live. By doing so, they can explore ways of tailoring their previous work experiences and academic abilities to unique and exciting career possibilities available to them locally. During the courses of our respective job searches, it was very easy to feel like the rest of our lives were on hold. Indeed, in many ways they were because the hope of being hired into a full-time position meant being prepared to move within a year's time and made us hesitant to take on challenges unrelated to our research and job searches. Although Tim's initial decision to begin working as an interpretive guide with Flint Ridge and the earthworks was geared chiefly toward supplementing his teaching income, it also provided an outlet through which he met new people and acquired new applications for his skills. Aubri is still in the process of trying to blend a career in the medical industry with a teaching career in the humanities. She hopes her search for a position in the medical industry will be fruitful and provide intriguing opportunities to use her knowledge of French language and culture. In both of our cases, there are dichotomies presented by the differences between the two halves of our respective career paths, but we find the differences interesting and complementary ways to continue developing our skill sets without abandoning our passions for teaching and medieval research.[12]

We would suggest that many who find themselves adjuncting "full-time" would benefit from a second job that provides a path for moving forward with their skills as a way to com-

---

12 We hope nothing in our discussion has implied that we have been dissatisfied with the students and colleagues with whom we most closely work. In fact, we have been fortunate in our roles as contingent faculty members because our tenured peers have always treated us with respect and appreciation as we have negotiated our blended career options.

bat frustration and burnout. In our situations, second jobs have also become opportunities for blended careers. Just as important as recognizing local opportunities for using one's skill set is the flexibility that the path of a blended career provides. Having the responsibilities and income from the second job provides Tim with a reason to limit the number of classes he teaches in a semester. These limits in turn leave him with more time for pursuing research and writing while at home. By limiting her teaching to a part-time position while continuing her job search, Aubri finds that she has time to return to medieval projects that she has wanted to complete and expand since graduate school and to focus upon her academic writing and conferencing. While she has yet to find a suitable solution for what she envisions as her blended career path, she appreciates the flexibility that her current position affords. Indeed, being able to find the time to complete our medieval research and participate in conferences allows us to remain fully engaged with our areas of specialization.

We do not wish to depict our emerging blended careers as perfect solutions. However, there's another type of flexibility in our situations: the ability to transition. After a few years of achieving publications and administrative experience, we could return to the academic job market. Alternatively, for Tim, the goal of achieving World Heritage status for the earthworks provides the possibility of movement toward greater involvement at the historical sites. Aubri would like to construct a model including teaching and using her language skills to benefit those outside of academe. She plans to find a balance between corporate and adjunct positions to achieve her goals in teaching and medieval studies while remaining on the job market. Neither of us intends to transition away completely from teaching and research, but that ability to move by degrees has proven to be important for maintaining optimism while finding blended careers that balance our academic passions with the necessities of daily and long-term living.

A Study of the Unexpected: The Advantages of Being the "Lone Medievalist"

Nikolas O. Hoel, Northeastern Illinois University

The challenges facing the academy are great and have in many ways been well documented in recent times. As a general trend, enrollments are slipping at many institutions and state legislatures are cutting funds to state universities in the name of reduced spending. Individual academics face mounting issues as well. Teaching loads continue to grow, while funding for research is dropping, not to mention the decrease in hiring. Particularly hard hit are the humanities, which are seen by many as unnecessary in a climate in which preparation for the job market is hailed as the paramount concern. The atmosphere is so hostile in many sectors that some writers have seen the need to present a "defense" of a liberal arts education.[1] While vocational training is an important tool for many, the liberal arts remain a cornerstone of the American educational system.

---

1 In particular see, Farreed Zakaria, *In Defense of a Liberal Education* (New York: W.W. Norton & Company, 2015); and Michael S. Roth, *Beyond the University: Why Liberal Education Matters* (New Haven: Yale University Press, 2015).

The medievalist faces all of these issues with their colleagues, but in many cases he or she confronts another challenge: isolation. At most colleges and universities, the medievalist is the "lone medievalist." A survey of websites from American institutions of higher learning reveals that, at most schools, departments in the humanities, such as history, English, the Romance languages, philosophy, and the like only have one medievalist each on the faculty. In many cases, there is only one medievalist in the whole university. This condition may appear to have dire consequences for the professor as well as for students. Discussions of issues that are specific to the time period cannot occur amongst scholars, who have similar training and academic backgrounds. Students may not get the diversity in course offerings that are present at larger schools that do have multiple medievalists on staff. In some cases, the medievalist is the only pre-modern Europeanist, which further limits course offerings, as he or she must teach everything from Greece and Rome through every medieval period and there are only so many slots in the course listings for a particular semester. The list of complications could go on. It would seem, then, that although the title of this volume is *The Ballad of the Lone Medievalist,* on the surface, it might as well be called the "Plight of the Lone Medievalist." Yet, as we examine the situation more closely, there may be advantages to being the "lone medievalist" whether in a department or at a school.

I would argue that the number one advantage of being a "lone medievalist" is that it allows one to truly be an interdisciplinarian. "Interdisciplinary" is one of those academic buzzwords that is in common parlance today. It seems that everyone is trying to achieve an interdisciplinary approach in their work, either on their own or in collaboration with other scholars. One needs only to look at recent academic job ads to realize that departments across the country are trying to find scholars who take an interdisciplinary approach to their work. Being the only medievalist at a school or in a department allows us to truly apply that approach to our teaching and to our research. To give students a full understanding of the Middle Ages, we stand alone and cannot rely on other medievalists to fill in the gaps we might leave out. We must cross fields, genres, and disciplines. In teaching a course on English History to 1688, when there is no medieval philosopher or specialist in Anglo-Saxon literature on staff, Bede must be taught alongside *Beowulf*. In the same course, the professor must look at the Bayeux Tapestry and the works of Anselm of Canterbury. It would be a disservice to the student not to teach as interdisciplinarians; we must assign letters, chronicles, pieces of art, and literature to give a fuller picture of the medieval world when we are the only one to teach about it. "Lone medievalists" reap the benefits of this approach. Their bookshelves are filled with primary sources of various types and from many periods. Eusebius sits next to Ockham; an anthology of Crusade sources abuts one of troubadour poetry. The secondary material can be just a diverse. Peter Brown's seminal work on Late Antiquity shares space with Tolkien's article on the monsters in *Beowulf*; for the "lone medievalist," it is not odd to teach Jane Schulenburg's studies of hagiography and Zachary S. Schiffman's *Birth of the Past* in the same semester.[2] The academy's interdisciplinary focus can truly play into the research and teaching of the "lone medievalist."

Although isolated from other medievalists, we should not feel isolated in general. Colleagues exist within our departments. Granted, they study different periods, topics, and may use different methodologies, but they are in fact there. I suggest that we can turn to them in order to enrich our teaching and our research. In talking with our Americanist friends, new ideas are bound to arise. We can ask new questions that we never would have thought of before. Talking to a scholar of pre-modern China may lead to a comparative project that would not have been possible if we limit ourselves to discussion with other medievalists.

---

2   Peter Brown, *The World of Late Antiquity AD 150–750*, (New York: W.W. Norton & Company, 1971); J.R.R. Tolkien, "*Beowulf*: The Monsters and the Critics," *Proceedings of the British Academy* 22 (1936): 245–95; Jane Tibbetts Schulenburg, *Forgetful of their Sex: Female Sanctity and Society, ca. 500–1100* (Chicago: University of Chicago Press, 1998); Zach Sayre Schiffman, *Birth of the Past* (Baltimore: John Hopkins University Press, 2011).

This leads to a more general point. The "lone medievalist" can ask new questions in our research and teaching. We are not pigeonholed as "early medievalists" or "late medievalists," as "Anglo-Saxonists" or "Chaucerians." We become medievalists in general. True, we have our specialties, but in many ways we are allowed to step outside traditional boundaries and explore a wider range of topics. Research need not be confined by narrow categories and neither should teaching. The same professor can teach both the Vikings and the Crusades. Most of us had to take field or preliminary exams in all areas of the Middle Ages in graduate school; being a "lone medievalist" allows us to use that knowledge and pass it on to our students.

The students may well be one of the greatest resources that the "lone medievalist" has. As "lone medievalists," professors must trust their undergraduates in a way that may not be found at institutions with multiple medievalists. Undergraduates, whom we inspire to take more of our courses and to study the Middle Ages, become the other medievalists at our institutions. There is nothing to say that advanced undergrads cannot participate in intellectual discourse that will intrigue us as faculty. Their thoughts can provoke new ideas and research projects. I do not exaggerate when I tell my students that I care more about what they have to say in class than about what I do. I stress that I cannot tell them how much I learn from them in exchange for the knowledge I teach. As a result, we as "lone medievalists" can learn so much from the classroom discussions we lead, from the research papers we read, and from the honors theses we direct. We may be perceived to have the training to be professors and instructors, but that training does not mean we have a monopoly on ideas and thinking. We must share the stage with our undergraduates and trust them to play their roles with great success.

In addition to the concepts they help the "lone medievalist" to explore, students can help the faculty member maintain his or her skills. Reading groups in Latin, Old Norse, or paleography can be formed in order to impart these proficiencies to the student. Although, in many cases, this means extra work for the professor leading these groups, it allows him or her to sharpen languages or skills that may otherwise fall into disrepair. The "lone medievalist" can indeed gain much from their students by trusting them and learning from them.

Finally, being "lone medievalists" means that we can train our students for better success. Our experience facing the realities of the field can be used to advise those who will come after us. We know that most of them, if they survive graduate school and are able to get a job, will become like us, that is, they will become "lone medievalists." We can shape our students to have greater success by having them study a wider range of topics, for example by encouraging them to be pre-modernists, instead of simply early medievalists.

In addition, we should not ignore technology. No longer is any scholar, no matter the field or discipline, truly isolated, given the nature of our interconnected, global world. The Internet is filled with resources that can open up the discussion of medieval studies. With chat rooms, Facebook groups, and the advent of the listserv, discussions of topics ranging from geometry in the Middle Ages to hagiography can occur in an instant and at any time of the day. Further, email allows for the connection of people in the field at a moment's notice. The world we live in ensures that the "lone medievalist" may be a faulty concept.

What I have said may well be true of all medievalists, maybe even all faculty in the humanities, but in the end it is particularly true of those of us who face the challenge of not having colleagues in our fields in the places at which we teach. It is clearly possible to lose all of the advantages that I have laid out amongst the issues that present themselves in our isolation. Yet, I want to be a cheerleader and show that being a "lone medievalist" is not necessarily a bad thing.

Saga Thing and the Benefits of Podcasting the Medieval

Andrew M. Pfrenger, Kent State University-Salem

For over a decade now, podcasting has become an increasingly popular form of entertainment and information sharing. An estimated 57 million Americans currently listen to one or more podcasts on a regular basis according to Edison Research's "The Infinite Dial 2016." It's a safe bet that many of our students already embrace this technology on a daily basis, using their phones to download or stream podcasts on a diverse range of subjects, from comedy to current events, from self-help to history. Though the medium is dominated by traditional broadcasters and entertainers, the podcast market is flooded with shows crafted by do-it-yourself hosts from nearly every walk of life speaking about their interests and opinions.

The number of non-professionals currently producing history podcasts with large audiences is indeed impressive, something university historians might do well to take advantage of. Many of these podcasts are either wholly devoted to medieval subjects or dabble in the medieval as part of their chronological or thematic survey. Among the standards any casual pursuer of medieval podcasts might encounter are *The British History Podcast, Rex Factor, The History of Philosophy Without Any Gaps, Medieval Archives,* the *English History Podcast,* the *Irish History*

Podcast, the *History of English Podcast* (a great supplement for HEL classes), *Norman Centuries,* and the fabulous but underappreciated *Medieval Death Trip.* What should impress both university professors and the departments that watch over their impact in the field is the fact that the audiences for each of these podcasts ranges from the thousands to the tens of thousands per episode. The true potential for podcasting as a medium for history enthusiasts can be seen in just a cursory glance at the top podcasts in the "Society and Culture" and "History" genres on iTunesCharts or Podbay. The giants of history and culture podcasting, like Dan Carlin's *Hardcore History, Stuff You Missed in History Class,* and Jamie Jeffers's *The British History Podcast* are heard by hundreds of thousands and sometimes millions of listeners. Whether in the upper or lower tiers of those rankings, podcasting clearly offers an impressive reach for audio narratives specifically designed to teach.

Despite the incredible popularity of the medium, podcasting in academia remains fairly new, especially in the humanities. It tends to be a genre of public scholarship commonly practiced by graduate students, most notably the *Footnoting History Podcast* and M*edieval Death Trip.* In my experience, active university professors rarely use podcasting as an outlet to express their academic inclinations in more creative and accessible ways. This is unfortunate, because men and women of all ages and from every walk of life increasingly turn to podcasts to quench their thirst for knowledge. One can certainly find the occasional professorial lecture or seminar series uploaded for mass consumption, like the excellent series of podcast lectures and talks from the University of Oxford, but these tend to be little more than a recording of a lecture with little to no production or awareness of the broader audience outside the speaker's room. Among some of the noteworthy examples of podcasts by active scholars are *History of Philosophy,* hosted by Peter Adamson, professor of Ancient and Medieval Philosophy at LMU in Munich and King' College London; *History Café,* hosted by Adam Franklin Lyons of Marlboro College; and *Podcasts on Medieval Texts* by Matthew Gabrielle of Virginia Tech. The number of academics doing podcasts of any kind is, however, quite limited. As far as I know, *Saga Thing* is the only active podcast on the market that is written and produced by professional medievalists. Again, this is unfortunate.

While there are a number of legitimate reasons for why this might be the case, I have found that podcasting provides some unexpected and potentially rewarding opportunities that could be especially advantageous for the Lone Medievalist. This brief essay shares my experience creating and producing a podcast in the hope that that others might follow the example. I want to encourage other professionals who share my enthusiasm for the Middle Ages to begin podcasting. First, because I believe it can invigorate your own experience as a medievalist. And second, because I'm eager for more great medieval podcasts to listen to.

The Origin Story

When I was hired as a tenure-track professor of English at Kent State University's Salem campus back in 2010, I quickly found myself in a situation familiar to many Lone Medievalists. I was teaching a 4/4 load, raising a young family, and adjusting to life in a new place where I was the only medievalist. To make matters worse, I was the only literature professor in a campus English department dominated by creative writers and composition specialists. While my training as a medievalist helped me to land the job, the position required me to regularly teach freshman composition courses as well as lower-level undergraduate surveys like "Great Books I." Because I love teaching and value my interactions with students, I accepted a professorship that would necessarily ask a lot of me in the classroom. I do not regret that decision, though at that moment I could not have anticipated just how difficult it would become to balance the demands of my everyday teaching responsibilities and campus service activities with my professional goals as an enthusiastic medievalist.

One of the repercussions of the position I chose was that I would not get to teach medieval literature as often as I had hoped when I hit the job market. I had pursued opportunities to teach a variety of courses, periods, and genres during graduate school in preparation for this likely outcome. Though I did not necessarily have a traditional medievalist's job, I still considered myself a medievalist above all else. But because I wasn't teaching medieval texts regularly, new experiences and ideas were getting fewer and farther between. I carved out extra time each week to engage with medieval texts on my own. I worked on my Old Norse and Old English. I hoped that the little time I could manage to devote to these tasks might help me hit a stride that would make up for the lack of contact. Nevertheless, as time went on and my various teaching responsibilities and campus service duties multiplied, the pace of independent study inevitably slowed. I began to feel increasingly distanced from the subject I loved and from the literature I was meant to be investigating for publication opportunities. I was left feeling frustrated, isolated from others like me and even from the self that I had come to know in graduate school. There was also a lot of guilt, because I believed that as a medievalist I should be able to make time to invest myself in medieval studies regardless of outside distractions.

In those first years of my tenure-track job, I was somewhat at a loss for how best to proceed in my studies of medieval literature and how to reignite that feeling of connectedness I had enjoyed throughout my years as a student. I reflected often on my graduate school days, where I could lose myself in conversation with peers about obscure topics related to medieval literature, history, and culture. The Icelandic sagas were always a favorite subject and my best days were the ones spent investigating the fascinating world of medieval Iceland with my good friend John Sexton. Those conversations stimulated my brain, helped me to make connections, and inspired me to take on new and ambitious projects. Like other Lone Medievalists, I looked forward to conferences where I could meet up with my graduate school friends who appreciated debates about kingship in *Beowulf* and the nuances of saints' lives. At conferences, I was with my people. I could meet other medievalists and feel a part of something, rediscover my passion for the field. But there are only so many conferences a regional campus budget will allow me to attend, typically one a year. If I was to maintain my involvement in medieval studies and recapture that feeling of belonging, I would need to seek alternative avenues beyond academic conferences.

In the summer of 2012, I began to explore podcasting as a viable outlet for my medieval interests and my desire to share those interests with more people than I could reasonably reach on my small campus. I saw podcasting as a welcome opportunity to dig deeper into medieval literature than my job allowed and to interact with other medievalists. As much as that prospect appealed to me, I was far more intrigued by the prospect of sharing my thoughts with an audience far larger than any I could ever hope to access in the classroom, through conference papers, or through journal articles. If done right, I could create a podcast that would reach thousands of people who either loved medieval literature like I did or perhaps didn't yet know just how much they could love it.

I should also note here that another motive behind the development of the podcast was my frustration at the lack of available podcasts on medieval subjects. Before embarking on the creation of my own podcast, I had been spending a lot of time listening to the popular British podcast, *Rex Factor,* which surveys the kings and queens of England from Alfred the Great to Queen Elizabeth II. As an Anglo-Saxonist, I was particularly drawn to the early episodes surveying the kings I knew best. Over time, I found myself voraciously listening to each episode, testing my knowledge of England's rich history against theirs, laughing at their jokes, and running to my computer to research topics that piqued my interest. At some point, I had made my way through the entire back catalog and had to endure the long wait between new episodes. I was eager for another good medieval podcast to fill the void, but there simply weren't many around at the time and certainly none with the level of entertainment value that Graham and Ali provided while discussing English monarchs. In this age of instant gratification that was a frustrating experience, but it got me thinking about the effect a good podcast can have on a listener.

As I thought about the way podcasts drew me in, exposed me to new information, and inspired me to think in new ways, I began to see many parallels to what I do in the classroom. Slowly, I started wondering whether or not I could do a podcast myself. There were a lot of questions that came with that. What medieval subject would I choose? I'm an Anglo-Saxonist by training, so it would make sense to share a bit of Old English literature and history with the world. Surely there was room out there for one more take on *Beowulf*! But the subject of the podcast was the least of my problems. There were more important questions to consider. What kind of equipment would I need? How much would it cost? How exactly does one record a podcast? And where do you put it once it's recorded so that people can access it? Who would listen? Should I even bother? Fortunately, the internet is full of quick and convenient answers. Over the course of the next few months, I began studying podcasts as a form of instruction, paying careful attention to what I thought worked and what didn't. I also endeavored to learn all that I could about recording and producing podcasts from home. I learned about microphones first and then about a program called Audacity, a free audio editor and recorder. In the end, I discovered that anyone with a vague sense of how computers work could figure out how to record, edit, and post a decent podcast without too much trouble. YouTube tutorials proved to be the most valuable tool in helping me gain a basic understanding of audio editing, though I would have benefited from talking with someone who had experience.

With a general sense of how to record and edit a podcast in hand, I turned to the subject next. In order for the podcast to work, I thought, I'd need to simulate the kinds of conversations about medieval literature I most enjoyed. While a lecture-style podcast would have allowed me a degree of scheduling independence and intellectual freedom, I felt that informal conversation would work best if I wanted to have any hope of maintaining listener interest. The dynamic exchanges of *Rex Factor*, which both informed and entertained in equal measure, served as a base model. I also hoped to recreate the kinds of energetic conversations my grad student friends and I would have in the Medieval Studies Library back at UConn. There was, I knew, only one man for the job.

The Plan

I approached my colleague and longtime friend, Dr. John Sexton of Bridgewater State University, about teaming up to produce a medieval themed podcast. After toying with the idea for a while, we finally met up in May of 2013 during the International Congress on Medieval Studies to begin planning the podcast's format and focus in earnest. We hadn't yet come up with a name, but we had a sense of what we wanted to do. Rather than do a general podcast on a variety of medieval topics, we decided to narrow the scope to a single genre and period that would offer a sense of consistency for our audience. The choice of genre was obvious. John and I had been working together since graduate school as co-directors of the New England Saga Society, now the Old Norse-Icelandic Saga Society. The mission of this academic society is to promote the study and appreciation of saga literature in North American universities. John and I have worked for over a decade now organizing panels and roundtables at conferences that explore a variety of saga related subjects and connecting medievalists who teach or hope to teach saga literature in the undergraduate classroom. The podcast could be, we hoped, an extension of the Old-Norse Icelandic Saga Society's mission.[1]

Of course, we knew that this choice would limit the potential size of our audience. Even among medievalists, the Sagas of the Icelanders remain a niche area of study and they are largely unknown by non-medievalists. The general public is aware of what "saga" means, but few have actually read one. Then again, the whole point of our endeavor would be to correct that prob-

---

[1] John was also teaching a course on the Icelandic sagas at his university and I was planning a special topics course on the subject myself. At the very least, our podcast experiment would serve as a "flipped classroom" supplement to our own classes.

lem. If we did our job well, listeners would be drawn into the sagas for the same reasons we were. We recalled that our best times in grad school were spent marveling over the action, wit, and substance of the sagas. In addition to being a lot of fun, we felt like the sagas could provide an excellent introduction to all that both early and late medieval literature has to offer. Each episode would review a single saga and offer discussion of its major themes, scholarly controversies, as well as lessons about the culture and history of medieval Iceland. Though the selected theme would certainly make it harder for us to break into the podcast market and grow our audience, we were so excited about digging back into the sagas that we were no longer terribly concerned about the size of the audience. If we did our job well, the right audience would come eventually.

We eventually came up with the name *Saga Thing*, which plays on the Old Norse word *þing* (government assembly). Just as disputes and legal cases were tried at þing sites in the sagas, our podcast would be a place for reviewing the sagas and putting them on trial. The format of the podcast would be simple and consistent, designed to offer a sense of familiarity as we approached each new text or subject. In each episode we would choose a saga, offer a brief summary with some close reading, and then we'd pass judgment in a series of categories that would allow us to both highlight the saga's more noteworthy scenes and expand on issues we were forced to pass over in the summary section.

Our episodes are intentionally scripted as a light-hearted and accessible, but hopefully substantive, conversation between two experts on saga literature. In the early stages of planning, before our first episode, we experimented with attempts at recreating our graduate school conversations by simply recording ourselves talking casually about a saga. While we could cover most of the material we had planned, the conversations were too long for what they managed to cover. We also noticed that the flow and structure of the conversations were less than ideal for holding a listener's attention, even if John and I were having a good time along the way. In order to balance our desire for a conversational tone with our hope of leaving the listeners with some critical awareness of the material, we decided to loosely script each episode. The script would provide us with a clear structure and direction while also allowing us to incorporate more of the critical contexts and scholarship that was too often left out of the unscripted conversations.

Because we planned to incorporate scholarship and higher level discourse in our coverage of the sagas, we chose to make the judgment section a place where audiences could relax and enjoy themselves. We would still engage in critical discussions where appropriate within each category, but the categories themselves were designed to draw the listener in. After much debate, we landed on the following topics for judgment:

1. Best Bloodshed — Because the sagas are full of action, we wanted to highlight those scenes featuring the most brilliantly described deaths or maimings. After a quick review of the most striking examples, we award one with the title of "Best Bloodshed."
2. Body Count — Any reader of the sagas knows that the bodies pile up quickly. We were curious which saga might have the most deaths and figured that our audience would appreciate a running tally of every unnatural/untimely death in each saga.[2]
3. Notable Witticisms — The wit and one-liners that come out of the mouths of saga characters can rival the best of what Hollywood has to offer. This category offers a review of the best.
4. Nicknames — The sagas are famous for the variety of nicknames attached to characters. John selects the most interesting of them and then researches their potential meanings and origins. This is a favorite category of many listeners.
5. Outlawry — Criminals and lawbreakers in medieval Icelandic society were subject to the penalty of outlawry. In this

---

[2] *Grettir's Saga* is currently in the lead for Body Count with a total of 147 deaths, most of them killings. Of course, this does not count the 5 supernatural creatures and 4 animals that also meet their ends in the saga.

category, we put the nastier characters in each saga on trial, review their crimes, and choose one to be outlawed.
6. Thingmen — John and I take on the role of Icelandic *goðar* or chieftains for this category. Whereas we highlight the worst men and women of the saga in Outlawry, we use the thingmen section to highlight the very best. In the end, John and I each choose a character to become our "thingman," a person who we'd want to have our back in a feud or at the Alþing. This category pits John and I against each other, which we hoped would provide for some lively exchanges. It quickly became our most contentious category.
7. Final Ratings — At the end of each Judgment section, John and I each take a moment to reflect on the saga under review and offer a score. While we attempt to be brief in our assessment, this is typically where John and I become most like our English Professor selves.

These judgment categories have proven to be quite popular with our audience, which suggests that the involved planning process we went through before recording our first episode was worth the effort. With every new episode, and often in anticipation of a new one, listeners contact us with their own opinions on the individual categories. The most rewarding part of those conversations with listeners is knowing that they are reading the sagas along with us and not only thinking about them but also making the effort to reach out to others to share their opinions.

Cost and Benefits

As we quickly discovered, putting an episode of *Saga Thing* together involves a lot of work. In addition to reading the saga selected for each episode, we also have to do research, write the script, revise the script, record the episode, edit the recording and add production, post the episode to our host site and then to our blog, and finally work on promotion. All of this takes time. This is one of the major obstacles any potential podcaster with a regular job and other responsibilities will have to contend with. While it might seem intimidating at first, I believe the rewards far outweigh the cost of time and energy lost.

Because I teach at a regional campus, few opportunities arise for me to teach in-depth upper-level courses on medieval literature. As anyone who has picked up this collection of essays already knows, teaching and scholarship intersect in some very important ways. There's a reciprocal relationship between what happens in the classroom and what happens in the mind of the researcher. While Lone Medievalists may seek to publish primarily, or only, on medieval topics, the bulk of our teaching load is not necessarily medieval. I tend to teach at least two College Writing courses and one early literature survey course each semester. I have a course release as the coordinator of the Honors program on my campus, which brings with it all manner of advising, course scheduling, event planning, fund raising, and other administrative duties. It is easy to get caught up in all of this.

The first thing podcasting offers the Lone Medievalist is the opportunity to explore texts and themes that we typically cannot cover in the undergraduate classrooms we inhabit. In the six years that I've been at Kent State University's Salem campus, I have taught only one course dedicated to saga literature. This was a special topics course that coincided with the birth of *Saga Thing*. I managed to convince my assistant dean to let me run the course even with low enrollment as a means of getting me in touch with the literature I hoped to publish on. I was fortunate that she understood that need. But that was only a one-time deal. Sure, I sneak a random saga into a literary survey now and again, but it's typically the same one or two every time. Given my busy schedule, if I am not actively teaching something, there's a good chance that I'm not going to have time to get to it. Podcasting, I find, is a useful way of engaging with material that I want to work on but lack the opportunity. In preparing for each episode, I am reading that material carefully, researching what others have said about it, developing my own understanding of its inner-workings, and then discussing my findings with others, which in turn stimulates further discovery.

Podcasting can also be a useful tool in the classroom. Both John and I have used the podcast as a supplemental text while teaching the sagas. Much to our surprise, we've heard from professors around the world that they too have begun assigning episodes of our podcast to their students. The students in my saga course were eager to download each new episode and even impatient for the next one to come out. The initial episodes of the podcast parallel the ordering and selection of sagas I chose to cover in that course. New episodes would come out not long after we had covered the saga in class and would sometimes incorporate elements of the conversations I had with the students. After listening, they would often comment on how they came away from their listening experience with a new perspective on the text. Because the information is delivered in an informal and conversational tone with plenty of bad jokes, they relax the barriers that they might have up in class. It is as if the podcast, which delivers material in a format and through a technology familiar to them, demystifies the text for them and removes the temporal distance in a way that we struggle to do in the classroom. As a result, they engage with the material differently. We frequently hear from our listeners that they have come to appreciate individual sagas as entertainment and art and philosophical discourses on society and the nature of man rather than as antiquated texts that have little relevance or value to them.

The greater impact, I think, is on how they discover their own potential as students of literature in the podcast. This is an unexpected, but welcome effect. Regardless of what John and I are talking about in a given episode, the students hear us enjoying what we do. They hear two professors discussing the intersection of history and literature, like 12th century Icelandic betrothal customs and the sources one might use to uncover them, while at the same time laughing as they discover their own understanding of the moment in the text where that information is relevant. John and I are genuinely excited about this material and we like to dive deep into it. We share that process sometimes on the podcast and quite unintentionally we end up modeling approaches to reading and research that can be beneficial to undergraduates. Students respond to the energy and methodologies they hear in the podcast and often bring it into the classroom.

Obviously, producing each episode has a profound effect on John and me as well. Over the years, we have learned a lot about medieval Iceland and its sagas while preparing material for the podcast. As we read each text and do our research, we inevitably stumble upon new ideas. Sometimes these ideas are even hashed out on the podcast in real time. If you listen to our episode on *Viglund's Saga,* you'll hear me discover a topic about which I am currently writing an article. The *Viglund's Saga* project is just one of many projects that John and I have uncovered while doing the podcast. In this way, the podcast has already met the most important of my expectations, which was to give me access to texts I wasn't able to teach regularly and to impact the way others view saga literature. The fact that the podcast put me back in touch with a good friend and brought us closer was just icing on the cake.

Saga Thing has also, much to my surprise, begun creeping into our professional lives, making the podcast more than just a hobby. Though we did not intend for *Saga Thing* to be a part of our academic portfolio, it has become a significant feature of how John and I now define ourselves as professionals in field of Medieval Studies. Podcasting falls under the umbrella of the digital humanities, which has really started to emerge as a legitimate and valuable approach over the past five years. One can see this, especially when surveying the work of innovative young graduate students and newly hired professors, in the diverse array of projects like online dictionaries, sophisticated tools for textual analysis, GIS mapping, and scholarly blogs. *Saga Thing* is currently the only medieval podcast being produced by professional academics, though hopefully not for long. One reason for the dearth of academics in podcasting would be the amount of time needed to produce each episode. This kind of commitment comes with a degree of risk for young scholars on the tenure clock uncertain how more established faculty will evaluate their less traditional efforts. More innovative departments will already recognize the potential value of projects like this, though in my experience those are still few and far between. I can at least say that each of the external reviewers for my recent tenure portfolio considered the podcast an important contribution to the field. One of them remarked that the podcast "benefit[s] the wider scholarly and student communities in a way that an article or book does not. In some ways, that should mean they count for more." Another noted that podcasts "are an invaluable resource for reaching wider audiences and, as an evolving facet of digital humanities, marks the changing nature of academia in many ways." This reviewer felt that the podcast would play a significant role in establishing my reputation in my academic discipline on a national level. Still another concluded that "*Saga Thing* provides a window into the academy at its best." As these comments from my external reviewers suggest, the field is becoming more open to digital humanities and the potential impact it can have. So, there is hope.[3]

Efforts to present and publish on podcasting can help to legitimize the work of the podcaster in the eyes of more traditional evaluators of academic portfolios. With the increased popularity of digital humanities projects, there are more opportunities every year to publish on them and to discuss their value at academic conferences. Shortly after I started working on *Saga Thing*, I began to seek opportunities to speak about the podcast with peers in academic forums. In 2014, I presented a paper about the intersection of podcasting and the spirit of the humanities at the International Congress on Medieval Studies. This presentation led to an invited lecture at Fitchburg State University later that October, where John and I lectured on the significance of genealogies in the sagas, a favorite subject for both of us, and then ran an interactive judgment section of the podcast for a saga the audience had been assigned. In November

---

[3] One important word of caution here. Before pursuing your podcast dreams, work with the appropriate authorities to make sure that digital humanities projects are included in your department's handbook language for what counts toward tenure. This is a problem that many young scholars in the digital humanities have encountered, including myself.

of 2016, John and I ran a two-day workshop called "Podcasting for Medievalists: An Introduction" at the innovative Seafaring Conference held at the University of Denver. Lastly, I am currently working on a pedagogical article about the value of podcasting with students. There are, in other words, plenty of conference and publishing opportunities for the academic podcaster to take advantage of.

The Audience

The response to this endeavor has been overwhelming. First and foremost, the podcast's audience has grown exponentially since we began. After roughly one year of recording, we had only 11,873 downloads. I was quite serious earlier when I said that John and I would still do the podcast even if no one was listening. That first year is proof. From 2014–2015, we began to attract an audience as the number of downloads increased sharply. By July of 2015, we had reached 58,550 downloads. Since then, the podcast has taken off as word of mouth has begun to spread and our social media campaigns attract new listeners. As of August 2016, we had surpassed 170,000 downloads, which is more than 100,000 new downloads for the year. We are currently averaging a minimum of 250 downloads a day and traffic is increasing on our rather roughly maintained website. While these are hardly the numbers that more established podcasts like *The British History Podcast* or even *The History of English Podcast* do, but it is a significant achievement for an academic podcast about the niche genre of Icelandic sagas that only puts out one or two episodes a month.

As the audience continues to grow, we find ourselves in contact with people from all over the world. We could not have anticipated the positive feedback and genuine enthusiasm our listeners have given us. *Saga Thing* has listeners on every inhabited continent on Earth, though English speaking countries like the United States, the United Kingdom, Canada, and Australia naturally make up roughly 85% of our audience. That said, the podcast has been downloaded in nearly every European, Asian, and South American country as well. We were particularly intrigued by the use tourists in Iceland have made of the podcast, integrating the auditory experience of saga scholarship with their experience of contemporary Icelandic geography in a way that both academics and perhaps even the original saga authors would recognize as faithful to the centrality of geography in the literature itself.

As noted above, our audience is mostly made up of medieval enthusiasts, especially lovers of the Viking Age, but we also have a large number of undergraduates, graduates, and professional academics. In June of 2014, for example, we received the following comment:

> I definitely will mention your podcasts for students who start up Scandinavian Studies as they (especially the first one) provide an excellent overview. Again many, many thanks for doing these and greetings from Northern Germany.

Another wrote:

> I like the fact that they bring what I suspect is their own academic research into their conversations. They talk about stuff like infanticide, disability, and the role of women in Icelandic society, and I feel like I'm getting something closer to what I'd get from a college class on the Sagas, which (for me) is great! I've actually used points they've made about Icelandic law and society in talking about social contract theory in my own philosophy classes. My only criticism is that their academic jobs slow down their pace in releasing episodes.

And more recently:

> I've always had that big thick book of Icelandic Sagas sitting on my shelf, but never was interested enough to pick it up. After listening to this podcast, I can't put it down. Intelligent, informative, with just the right amount of Monty Python references and silly accents, this podcast will teach you all about

feud culture, kennings (hope I spelled that right), and Icelandic literary motifs. Not to mention Scottish giants, French taunting, and underwater knife fights with bears that swim competitively and understand 13th century Icelandic...

Considering the response we've gotten and the intellectual stimulation I get from producing this podcast, I have long since put to rest any doubts I might have had about this pursuit and its relevance for my profession. As a teacher, I'm excited by the impact this endeavor has had on our listeners and their appreciation of medieval literature.

Conclusion

From the very beginning, we designed *Saga Thing* with the hope that we might provide a dynamic experience that both edifies and entertains, that famous balance of *sentence* and *solaas* we medievalists so deeply cherish. At all times we strive to teach something of the historical and literary contexts that make each saga special, while maintaining a strict awareness of the potential for our audience to become bored and drift away should our discussion become too esoteric. If they drift then the lesson, no matter how brilliant, is lost. If we can offer a listening experience that takes into account the needs of the different audiences who consume our podcast, with their varied tastes, interests, and levels of attention, we can achieve our goal of promoting a greater appreciation for saga literature.

This is why we put so much effort into the planning and writing of each episode, because the balance of close reading, lighthearted exchanges, scholarship, and humor is a delicate but necessary one. Through careful planning we are able to engage in those deeper conversations about literary production, authorial intent, cultural contexts, and all those big questions that make medieval studies such a fascinating field. As one listener wrote in an iTunes review of the podcast from February 11, 2016:

> As academics in the field, they provide deep observations about the characters, events, and even the forms of the sagas, and often go further to give historical and cultural context necessary for the listener to fully understand what all that means. Also, and this is important: they're totally fun goofballs. […] The two hosts have the chemistry of genuine friends and the show is loaded with them giving each other crap and BSing about the material as friends will do.

John and I take this as high praise, since this and the many comments that echo this sentiment confirm that we have managed to achieve the balance we sought.

What is truly remarkable about this delivery method is the fact that the initial conversation between John and myself extends beyond the individual episode. Listeners participate in the dialogue on our website, through email, and on our social media long after episodes are first uploaded. It often happens, as it does in the most successful classrooms, that the discussion evolves and takes on a shape of its own as the participants contribute their own perspectives and begin to feed off of one another. The relaxed format of each episode thus invites the listener, regardless of background, into conversations that are typically reserved for the university classroom or for specialists over lunch.

Our listeners are encouraged to approach the texts, the culture that produced them, and their historical moment with the same spirit of intellectual curiosity we encourage in our students, that same spirit that has always driven our own interaction with the Middle Ages. Whether through contemplative reflection or through social media exchanges, the podcasting audience is engaged in an interactive academic experience for the 21st century. We encourage listener participation in the hopes that with the contexts we've provided our listeners might begin to explore for themselves the variety of literary expression in Saga Age Iceland, how history and literature interconnect, and, most important, what these old texts might yet have to teach us about ourselves.

This is the single most attractive and important feature of the podcasting experience for me. As a Lone Medievalist on a regional campus, at a university with few colleagues who understand or appreciate the literature I study, and with few opportunities to teach the Icelandic sagas, the podcast provides me with an opportunity to reach beyond my campus and have an impact on the field I love. Likewise, those isolated individuals out there who share my passion for medieval Scandinavia find a community of like-minded individuals through the podcast and an avenue for self-expression that may not have otherwise been available to them. This is especially true for the non-academic, but also for the undergraduate and graduate students who find themselves falling in love with Vikings, as well as those Lone Medievalists out there who are looking for an outlet for their own passion.

Looking back on that Saturday night at Kalamazoo when John and I started this process, I don't believe we had any idea how deeply it would impact our pedagogy and our relationship to the literature our own friendship was founded upon. When we chose to podcast about the sagas, we honestly sought no reward beyond experiencing the literature for ourselves. The podcast would force us to pick up the books we loved every week, providing us with a much needed break from the rigors of our day-to-day work and the demands of life. There was no thought given to how much time the project would take, its potential value to our professional portfolios, to its influence on our own scholarship, or to the impact it might have on the lives and interests of our listeners. All of those things have indeed happened, but John and I simply wanted to play with the sagas and enjoy them as fans again. Along the way, our personal and professional lives have been enriched by this experience as the podcast has informed our teaching and our scholarship, expanded our network of professional contacts and put us in touch with new friends all around the globe. It has also given me a good reason to talk to my best friend on a regular basis despite the many miles between us and reinvigorated our friendship. For both of us, Saga Thing is first and foremost about friendship. I certainly struggled in the early days of my time as a Lone Medievalist to find a sense of belonging that I had lost, to find my people. Through podcasting I found it all.

The Lone Medievalist at Work

Or, How I Learned to Stop Worrying and Love the Job

Building Your Own Villa

Jane Chance, Rice University

The way I found to ease the many negatives of being both the lone medievalist and the first tenure-track woman in the English Department at a small private university (as Rice was at the time I arrived in 1973, with 2,300 undergraduates and 1,000 graduate students) was to learn to build on connections with others, whether students or colleagues. After finishing my Ph.D. at the University of Illinois in 1971, I had taught for two years at the snow-laden University of Saskatchewan-Saskatoon. Longing to return to an urban environment, I came to sunny Houston as a very young assistant professor, girded with a book contract in hand for a revised dissertation and boundless optimism. Two medievalists had taught in the department prior to my advent, but I was hired specifically to replace the Anglo-Saxonist.

As the only medievalist in a department dominated by modernists and the only tenure-track woman between 1973–1978 (when a second tenure-track woman in the Renaissance was added), I faced formidable obstacles. Among them was considerable resistance from graduate students and senior professors to the idea of having a woman replace two popular male medievalists. It was whispered I had been hired (like other new Rice women faculty that year and earlier) because of pressure from HEW (the federal Department of Health, Education, and Welfare). I was apparently a "token woman," meaning one that symbolized the Female Sex as a place-holder or talisman. Such a hire protected university officials from facing some dire penalty or other, yet because it was hard to find one who was qualified, much less very good, whomever they did hire was not expected to turn out very well.

Initially, I was asked to teach graduate-level Old English and *Beowulf* and service freshman courses in critical reading and writing. The latter were always full — twenty-five students was the maximum, although I had twenty-nine my second year there. In Old English I had nine students, but only four continued on for *Beowulf*. At a university where the average course numbered nine students (factoring in smaller graduate courses), creating a new course that attracted undergraduate students without a mandate from university distribution or department major requirements was always difficult. An additional problem in interesting students in medieval courses was the vacuum that existed after the departure of the medievalists. The relatively few graduate students in the department, primarily focused on the nineteenth and twentieth-centuries, were themselves often treated as second-class citizens by the faculty in comparison to the highly-valued, smart undergraduates.

At the time, departments often had to justify courses with low enrollments, especially when it came time to request new hires or more money — the familiar problem of accountability. As far as the faculty was concerned, it was necessary to become popular enough in this competitive environment to fill their classrooms. When student course evaluations were made public, survival for tenure, raises, promotions, and contract renewals necessitated not only healthy numbers of students but good ratings. So being a medievalist who wished to teach in her field but who was also vulnerable because of the lesser popularity of that field created another dilemma.

My field of specialization was in fact Middle English, for which I was tapped a year later to teach a junior-level Chaucer course. In addition, because I was the lone tenure-track woman in the department the chair asked me to teach a course on women's literature. I chose for the latter what was (at the time) the trendy topic among feminist academics of "Images of Women in Literature" (mostly twentieth-century). In the Chaucer course, I had eleven students, but twenty-nine in "Women in Literature." My claim to fame in the latter lay in teaching Erica Jong's *Fear of Flying*, a feminist 1970s novel which lauded the "zipless fuck." The novel landed my course a mention in *Time Magazine,* and I wrote an article about it in a collection of articles by other Rice women about women.[1] That spring in 1976, when only three students signed up for Chaucer but fifteen wanted me to teach an unscheduled J.R.R. Tolkien course, my department chair agreed to switch the two. And so I began a very different journey, one that allowed me to create a "villa of my own" at Rice.

This phrase I borrow from a colleague in the eighteenth-century who, envying my eventual success in overcoming the isolation we both initially but separately shared in our department, used it to describe what might be termed a "safe space." By "villa," he meant the creation of an intellectual space in which I built on and expanded the very fields which defined my isolation, one that became a comfortable respite from the power machinations of colleagues in more hegemonic fields within the department. Indeed, my villa represented the power I came to have in the more limited way academics can be said to have any at all by virtue of their specialization. Certainly my space centered on the courses and students I taught, but it also influenced my research and publication. One never knows where such opportunities will lead, no matter how much a failure one may feel at not having a course attracting students. Failure leads to your understanding of how to create success, or at least improvement.

I mean, by this, in case readers do not know to what I am referring, that I subsequently published a book based on my notes for the Tolkien course, which led to six other books and a number of articles on Tolkien's use of the medieval.[2] And, no doubt

---

[1] I also wrote an article about Jong's novel: see "'Isadora Icarus'": The Mythic Unity of Erica Jong's *Fear of Flying*," *Rice University Studies* 64 (Winter 1974): 89–100.

[2] See Jane Chance (Nitzsche), *Tolkien's Art: A "Mythology for England"* (London: Macmillan Ltd., 1979; rev. edn., Lexington: University of Kentucky

inspired and radicalized by the modern women we were reading in the "Images of Women in Literature" course, I published a book on *Woman as Hero in Old English Literature*. This led eventually to an editorship of a series now consisting of twenty-five translations of texts by or about medieval women, the Library of Medieval Women, and an edited collection, *Women Medievalists and the Academy*, with essays written by seventy contributors about the obstacles faced by women medievalists who pioneered in their fields.[3] But it was also the fact of my aloneness as a "token woman" that spurred my attempts to understand the climate of misogyny and patriarchy through feminist writing and literature by other women who suffered isolation in other facets of their lives.

What I realized early on was that a willingness to teach new courses or to innovatively construct freshman courses, even if outside your field, offered the bonus of filling your classrooms and, hence, adding to your attractiveness as an instructor when it came to those freshmen choosing upper-level courses later. Even when I was teaching obligatory first-year "Critical Reading and Writing Courses," I was allowed at Rice to create my own syllabus: no requirements as to what students would read except in the three genres of poetry, drama, and the novel, or the short story, and in the writing of the five five-page critical papers per semester. So I taught freshmen "The Heroic Quest" (thirty-three students in one section, thirty-one in the other), which might include Homer's *Odyssey, Sir Gawain and the Green Knight,* Cervantes' *Don Quixote,* Tolkien's *Fellowship of the Ring,* and Italo Calvino's *The Nonexistent Knight.* I also created the topic "Surreal and Absurd Literature," that included a field-trip to Houston's Menil Museum with its great Surrealist art collection; "Fantasy and Impossible Worlds;" and "Odd Couples" (trying to

---

Press, 2001).

3 See Jane Chance, *Woman as Hero in Old English Literature* (Syracuse: Syracuse University Press, 1986; rpt. Eugene: Wipf and Stock, 2005); The Library of Medieval Women, Boydell and Brewer, 1990–present, twenty-five titles; *Women Medievalists and the Academy,* ed. Jane Chance (Madison: University of Wisconsin Press, 2005).

work gender into the classroom). My goal always was to spark interest in what I taught to build a reputation among the students outside of medieval per se, especially given the lack of a departmental medieval requirement either at the undergraduate or graduate level. Undergraduate English majors at Rice needed to choose a Chaucer, Shakespeare, or Milton course, but it was always Shakespeare that attracted the largest number because of a certification requirement in Education for those wishing to become high school teachers. Majors also had to take several courses involving literature written before 1800, but these courses could count for either requirement. As time passed, the Chaucer class usually numbered twenty or twenty-five, and my evaluations were good to excellent.

None of this relates specifically to building a villa beyond securing my position as a popular teacher (and, as far as my own future was concerned, leading me down new paths where research and publication would help to better secure my future).[4] From the beginning, I learned about networking and sharing ideas with other medievalists by attending conferences, especially at Kalamazoo, which became my anchor. I attended annually, beginning in 1972, and rarely skipped—it is the best means of growing yourself as a medievalist and learning from what others are doing to overcome problems we all share. In addition, it served as a model from which I borrowed to obviate the loneliness of teaching a field for the most part regarded by my colleagues as directed by merely philological interests and defined as unimportant and uninteresting.

I laid the foundations for my villa through the creation of the Medieval Studies program at Rice, beginning humbly with a Medieval Club in my department that attracted graduate

---

4 I received tenure and promotion to associate professor in 1977 (and promotion to full professor in 1980). The two years at University of Saskatchewan did not officially count toward tenure, but the publication of three books did. I was so tickled with myself I wrote an article titled "How to Save Your Own Career: The Junior Professor's Dilemma," *Change Magazine* 10 (February 1978): 40–43. It was actually listed as an important resource in several bibliographies relating to faculty development.

students who were required to fill in gaps — medieval being a primary one — in their prior education. At the time I arrived at Rice, we had undergraduate junior-level courses for which graduate students could sign up under a higher course number to earn four credits in a "trailer seminar": that is, credit for an extra hour allocated for graduate-level issues (a separate discussion class, reading criticism, reviewing seminal books, writing a twenty-five page seminar paper, etc.). As time progressed and Rice became more flexible about offering less traditional courses, especially for the purposes of "Distribution" — that is, offered especially for non-majors who were required to take Humanities courses — I offered at the undergraduate level "Arthurian Literature," "Medieval Women Writers," "J.R.R. Tolkien," "Mythologies" (my top enrolled class, at eighty students), "Dante" (my next best, with forty-five, very popular with Space Physics and Religious Studies majors), "Medieval Cultures Through Film," "Christine de Pizan in Fifteenth-Century England," "Classical Mythology in Medieval Literature," "Gender and Power in Old English Literature," and so forth. But the same principle of innovation — and the same mission, to build an interest in the medieval — also held for any graduate-level courses I taught.[5]

The villa was built through professional training and mentoring for graduate students in English, particularly for the women, of which there were many. At the time, we did not offer many assistantships and no departmental fellowships; our best applicants were able to compete university-wide for stellar fellowships. For the Medieval Club, between 1981–1988 I invited graduate students in English (but especially those enrolled in my medieval course) once a month for a lecture by a fellow medievalist or a graduate student with an accepted conference paper, including wine and cheese or potluck contributions (food is important to community). Initially, after reserving a room — we had a big coffee room in our building — I mailed out and posted

---

5   Our department for decades was only able to accept six to eight graduate students per year, although we had a cohort of current graduate students who had not yet finished taking courses or earning a degree.

flyers (pre-email) and urged undergraduates to come for extra credit. I asked the dean for $30 for wine and cheese at the first lecture, but after the first year he granted us a small allowance of about $500 to cover the whole year. For the holidays, we had a potluck dinner along with several papers.

The Medieval Club eventually morphed into part of the Medieval Studies Workshop in the Center for Cultural Studies in the nineties, for which several medievalists in history, art, and music organized lectures and annual symposia. Seeing how beneficial this was to both students and faculty at departments at Rice and in Houston area universities, I gathered together the medievalists around campus to consider starting a Medieval Studies Program (not a workshop or a department — mostly a means of allowing undergraduates to earn credit in other relevant departments toward a major). It meant asking other department chairs to approve the idea of the major, designing it adequately, and then shepherding it through the Faculty Senate for approval. Because I was headed for a sabbatical year at the Institute for Advanced Study in 1987–1988, my colleague in history, Professor Katherine Drew, took over that year I was gone and succeeded in obtaining faculty approval.

Any such program takes years to build — we started with one major, just in medieval studies. Rice also encouraged double-majors, for which medieval studies was ideal (given the paucity of jobs available for undergraduates in the medieval); we might have, for example, a biology major doubling in medieval studies, the one field, giving her the possibility of a future job, and the other, the pursuit of humanistic interests. We had to create one introductory Medieval Cultures course, which, as director, I taught — a kind of sampler for students, with guest-lectures by as many university and local medievalists as I could supplicate, films scheduled at the Media Center, field trips such as paleography events at the library; and so forth. This sampler also helped build colleagues' courses outside the departmental rubric, or at least (I hope) made them feel they were a part of a community whose interests they shared in part.

The Medieval Studies Workshop at the Center for Cultural Studies in the nineties included a workshop I organized on "Imitation and Invention in the Middle Ages" (January 20, 1990) and an all-day symposium on "Writing Women/Women Writing: Gender and the Text in the Middle Ages" (January 26, 1991). For both I invited scholars from our own local universities and also some well-known out-of-town scholars whose deans were willing to spring for airfare and a hotel room because we offered an honorarium. I then sent out flyers to all the other Texas universities including English, French, German, Latin, and Italian departments, along with history, philosophy, religious studies, and so forth, and to those on the mailing list whose addresses I had acquired from sign-ins at all the prior monthly meetings. I also posted notices in the campus newspaper or humanities circular listing monthly/semester events. Colleagues from other departments sometimes attended. Because it happened that a philanthropically-minded visitor from Dallas appreciated some of the talks about religious women, he created a $25,000 fund so the interest could be used annually for the Medieval Studies Workshop, which pleased the Development Office and the dean. Thereafter the dean increased our allocation annually. Further, I edited a collection of papers in 1996 in part derived from the symposium on "Gender and Text in the Middle Ages."[6]

Creating such a professional forum worked for a number of reasons: because departments at my university did not mingle, for the most part, the graduate students from the languages, philosophy, history, and religious studies, like our department, relished having the intellectual stimulation and camaraderie it afforded, as did members of the larger community who attended. In addition, graduate students were delighted at being treated more frequently as colleagues and encouraged to submit conference papers and to publish chapters from their dissertations. Of the twenty-five graduate students whose MA theses and

---

6 *Gender and Text in the Later Middle Ages,* ed. Jane Chance (Gainesville: University Press of Florida, 1996).

PhD dissertations I directed, four have published books, some more than one.

After the Medieval Studies program was in place and other colleagues had spent time as directors of the Medieval Studies Seminar (or Workshop) — there was no extra salary or course release for any director, although there was a very part-time shared secretary eventually — I returned as director between 2005–2008 and created an undergraduate medieval committee to organize a medieval conference just for undergraduates, with a prize for the best paper (also judged by the undergraduates). This was enormously successful for everyone: participants invited their parents and the faculty member for whom they had written the paper, along with friends or roommates; they dressed for success, and they celebrated that evening with a banquet paid for by the Medieval Studies funding. For the student members of the committee, mostly A students solicited from my courses, past or present, but some from other universities in the Houston area, this was an invaluable lesson in organizing, judging, and putting it all together. At least one of these undergraduates went on for both a Master's degree and PhD.

To sum up, then: without departmental support, I elected to teach courses other than the standard Chaucer and Middle English literature to build interest in medieval studies and intended for students who wanted to take additional courses. To do so demanded an expenditure of energy that might seem daunting — this occurred at a time when I was a single parent and continued later on when I had remarried and started a second family. Whatever success I achieved was due, in addition to my own efforts, to those of others as well who wished to help. The private university environment became more flexible over time. The donor who stepped forward with financial backing for the Medieval Studies Workshop indirectly suggested to the administration that what medievalists do is important. And willing medievalists at the university and in the community participated. For myself, I no longer felt like a lone medievalist — a feeling likely shared by others at various levels in the university and at nearby institutions.

There are many other problems that exist for the lone medievalist that I might have discussed. First is convincing non-medievalists of the value of what success and excellence mean in the study of the medieval, especially in asking for financial support of projects, simply because colleagues and university administrators may not understand what being a medievalist involves. Second, a related problem exists in the selection of graduate student applicants or the hiring of colleagues by a committee in different fields that can readily ignore the lone voice. Third is making convincing cases for the award of fellowships or other prizes to worthy medieval graduate students during stiff competitions when so little is known of what research of the Middle Ages actually involves. Four could be evaluating you and your progress toward tenure and promotion given the general ignorance of what you have accomplished in your field.

Building this edifice, at the least, creates a network and support-system for you and others in an often adversarial environment. It also helps to publicize and build on the larger popular interest in the medieval that modernists like to ignore. Doing so certainly teaches you how you can build (sell?) almost anything if you are enterprising enough, energetic, patient, and willing to fail. To begin, you must love what you do, which is key to almost everything you undertake in life. Don't be discouraged. You are not alone.

The villa is a start.

Twice Marginal and Twice Invisible: On Being the Lone Medievalist Twice in One State

Michelle M. Sauer, University of North Dakota

In the classic Jacqueline Murray article, "Twice Marginal and Twice Invisible: Lesbians in the Middle Ages,"[1] she argues that lesbians are challenging to reclaim in history by virtue of being doubly excluded. I'm not exactly comparing myself to a medieval lesbian, although a good deal of my scholarship has focused on female same-sex desire in the Middle Ages; however, there have been several instances of intertwined marginalization like this in my career. I was, for example, the only medieval PhD student at my institution. That brought both good and bad, since I got plum teaching assignments (no composition), but lost out on a student community. As a woman of color, I am also sometimes on the outskirts of medieval studies (although that is changing in today's academic world), but have also been called a "race traitor" by other South Asians since I study "the whitest period in history" (a view also being challenged in today's aca-

---
1 Jacqueline Murray, "Twice Marginal and Twice Invisible," in *The Handbook of Medieval Sexuality,* eds. Vern L. Bullough and James Brundage, 191–222 (New York: Garland, 1996).

demic world). So I guess one could say that I pretty much began my career as a Lone Medievalist in my PhD program, and have continued as such to this very day.

My first job was at Minot State University in Minot, ND. North Dakota is my home state, by the way, so I was happy to have a job only five hours away from my hometown of Fargo. When I arrived on campus in August 2000, I officially became the only medievalist in any discipline on the entire campus. In fact, there was one early modern specialist in the history department; otherwise, I pretty much represented all early British everything. Minot State is a regional four-year university with a 4/4 load and all the accompanying standards (heavy service expectation, focus on teaching excellence over scholarship, etc.), including a requirement that all tenure track faculty members teach two composition classes a semester. That left only two other classes to teach. As the resident linguist, I also taught grammar each fall and History of the English Language each spring, leaving precisely one chance at a medieval-like course each semester. Imagine my surprise, then, when two colleagues in particular — a creative writing specialist and a modernist who specialized in Ezra Pound — fought me tooth and nail for those classes, including HEL. This was pretty unusual behavior, or so I thought. Their reasoning was also unusual, "I took a class in Chaucer once from somebody famous," and "but I really wanted to be a medievalist, so I should get to teach it." My response was, "Well, I really wanted to be a physicist, too, but I'm not asking to teach Thermodynamics!" Those colleagues both complained directly to me and to the chair that I wouldn't "come off" the early British classes, going so far as to say, "one little dissertation in anchoresses doesn't make you a medievalist," and "what gives you the right to teach those classes? Are degrees and publications really how we determine specialties?" (Seriously, these are direct quotes. I am not making this up.) Luckily the chair was just as confused by their comments as I was, and I was never forced to give up my early British courses.

I was amazed then, and continue to be amazed to some extent even now, at how many of my colleagues think that medieval literature is one of the subjects "everyone" should be able to teach. Sure, I'll grant you that a class taught by me on Edgar Allen Poe might be better than one taught by the Biology professor, but it wouldn't be as good as one taught by an Americanist. So that's one thing about being a Lone Medievalist, at least in my experience. I think as medievalists we're often "lone" because other people think they can somehow adequately cover our classes. (Similarly, I think those of us who specialize in Chaucer get hired more easily and quickly because search committees don't know what else to look for, but that is a different issue altogether.)

Aside from these odd colleagues, I found being the lone medievalist both lonely and freeing. It was lonely academically, since no one really did any scholarship even remotely similar to mine. I went to MLA every year since I was constantly job-hunting, but MLA isn't very medieval-friendly. My only true solace each year was Kalamazoo, where I could be all-medieval-all-the-time. To this day when I hear people say they want to skip Kalamazoo, I get defensive because where else would so many of us who are Lone Medievalists get to be, well, not alone? I would have enjoyed a writing group, but there wasn't even a general one — and I was too tired to start one. I was already overextended by advising two student organizations, serving on numerous committees, being diversity chair, and founding a gender/women's studies program.

You see, not only am I a medievalist, but also I am a feminist medievalist and a gender/queer theorist. I was, to paraphrase Murray, twice marginalized by profession. (I was also one of the very few persons of color on our faculty, hence the whole "diversity chair" thing.) But the bane of a small school can also be its blessing: a single individual can get more things done in a place like Minot State than at a larger institution. In Spring 2002, I began developing an interdisciplinary Gender/Women's Studies Program, the first such program at Minot State University and the first program in North Dakota to include Gender alongside Women's Studies. The program was approved by the State Board of Higher Education in 2003. I coordinated the program from its inception through my departure from Minot State in 2008.

The program had no money, no real tenure lines, no perks whatsoever, but I managed to get it done anyway. Because of this, I have the distinction of having taught the first course ever titled "Queer Theory" in North Dakota (or so the Registrar at Minot State told me then). I taught it at Minot State fall semester 2004. The reactions of people on campus were amazing, and of the 11 students in the class (eight women and three men), all but one lied to people about the title of the class. Several parents called me to complain (none were parents of my students, oddly enough). People in other departments on campus were horrified. Later, when I went up for promotion (and then for tenure the following year), I was asked by several people if I didn't consider my scholarship and teaching "obscene." And, because I am a medievalist as well as a gender theorist, I garnered the nickname "the Lesbian Goth Queen," which I took in stride despite how it was meant. These sorts of things did, however, mark me as firmly being even more alone than just a "lone medievalist." Ten years later, when I taught another Queer Theory course during the spring 2014 semester at UND and no one batted an eyelash, I felt like I had come full circle.

In August 2008, I accepted a position at the University of North Dakota in Grand Forks. It is the flagship university of the state and an RU/H: Research University (high research activity) in the Carnegie Classification of Institutions of Higher Education (formerly known as R1 classification). We have an MA and a PhD program, and I am lucky to have graduate students and to teach only medieval-related courses (and of course some linguistics). On the other hand, I am still in many ways, a "lone medievalist." I am the only medievalist in the English department. In fact, I am nearly the only medievalist on campus — there are, across all disciplines, only three other faculty members who would claim "medieval" as their specialty. Early Modernists fare better than that. Moreover, I am the only pure medievalist in an English department across the entire state, although there are a few in other disciplines.[2] That's 11 colleges and universities (excluding private and tribal institutions) all basically without a medievalist in their English department.[3] I am truly a "lone medievalist" in many ways.

I've found I've had to make some choices. In my first job, at MSU, I was happy to double up as English and Gender Studies. I founded the whole program. It was a way to make my job better and to better the university's environment. I was still the only medievalist on campus, but I was left more to my own devices. When I arrived at UND, however, I had to make a tougher choice. The Women Studies program[4] was in the middle of being revamped and was seeking a new director. I applied. I thought that an R1 school would have more money and more resources, and be more open to expansion. I was indeed offered the position — under pretty much the same conditions I had been working at Minot State. The budget was minuscule (under $3000). The program was marginalized. There was no pay increase for me, only a course release. There was no support staff, place in the curriculum, or ephemera of any kind except a shabby office across campus. Additionally, I would have had to sacrifice all my medieval classes to teach only Women Studies courses *and* supervise any and all independent projects and capstones (how this equaled a course release, I'm not sure). I'm sure my scholarly endeavors in medieval studies would also have taken a back seat to administrative concerns. I had to turn it down. The dean was surprised, but I told her why I made my choice: if I wasn't going to receive any visible support and was going to have to shoestring another program, it would be one in medieval studies. I actively chose to be a medievalist. That doesn't mean I am

---

2   There is technically one other, a Byzantine and Classics scholar who fills an official "medievalist" spot. Otherwise, there are none, or at least none that claim medieval.

3   When I arrived at Minot State in fall 2000, there were medievalists in the English departments at UND and NDSU, so I was one of three in the state.

4   Yes, the original name of the program was Women Studies, not Women's Studies. There has been many a debate over that apostrophe-s. Now it is Women/Gender Studies.

not part of the Women/Gender Studies program. I am an affiliate and teach cross-listed courses; however, I remain focused on medieval language and literature since I define myself as a medievalist and feel it owns my heart and is owed my loyalty.

When I was at Minot State, and really alone even more than I am now, I considered things like founding the Gender/Women's Studies program to be a "sanity saver." If I was going to live in that campus environment on a permanent basis, I had to make changes in order to survive. I also felt that if I was not only the medievalist, but also the early British specialist in general, not to mention the linguist, I needed to legitimize myself in those areas. Therefore, I sought out opportunities to publish on early modern subjects and on pedagogy in order to be more relevant to my home campus environment. I pursued other avenues of connection, and brought Minot State into them. A major accomplishment in this area was bringing the journal *Medieval Feminist Forum* to our campus. It was an amazing opportunity for a small regional university. I had student interns (who were excited about the opportunity to get work published), support from the library, and even a one-course load reduction. The journal really brought recognition to my institution, and allowed me to network with a wide number of medieval scholars, making me feel less alone. Back in 1992, a group of scholars from South Dakota founded the Northern Plains Conference on Early British Literature. I began attending in 1993 while I was an MA student (not in either Dakota), and, as such, have forged friendships through the years with that group of scholars. When I rejoined the conference group as a new professor in 2000 I felt it was an ideal opportunity to incorporate Minot State into that community — a relationship that continues to this day despite my departure from the campus. To this day, I continue to attend that conference almost every year, cherishing the network of early British scholars across the northern Great Plains.

Now, while at UND, I still find these local connections to be very important. I attend the NPC and other local conferences, lectures, and events and bring my students to many as well so that we can all raise our medievalist identities. The refinement of online writing tools has also allowed me to co-create a writing group with other medievalists in different areas of the country. The mere act of having these people in my life makes my "lone medievalist" status easier to bear. I know that even if I have no one on campus who is interested in reading my work, my group is — and they will be (virtually) available and be medieval. On the other hand, I now happily focus my own research primarily on medieval subjects. I no longer feel compelled to "beef up" my CV in other areas in order to legitimize my presence in the classroom. That isn't to say that I no longer dabble, but I no longer feel obliged to do so. Instead, I dabble for enjoyment.

It is nice, in some ways, to be the lone medievalist. I can teach pretty much whatever I want. Although I am a Middle English scholar, I have a solid background in Old English and some in Old Norse, so I teach the entirety of the Middle Ages. Any graduate student who is interested in medieval language or literature works with me. I escape teaching composition because I teach linguistics courses. (Although the desire to moonlight as a medievalist is still present in some fellow professors, it does not seem to extend to linguistics classes. I, of course, do my own moonlighting as a linguist.) I have also found that by expanding my teaching into the realm of medievalism, I can capture a larger student presence, and subsequently interest them in "real" medieval courses. I still feel the strain of having to defend my profession and my choices. I approach scholarship and coursework differently than many colleagues. Medievalists aren't afraid of footnotes. I allow and encourage use of Chicago style citations. I prefer secondary research over personal reflection in formal assignments. Overall, however, although it is sometimes a lonely position to be in, I have made peace with being the lone (English literature) medievalist of North Dakota.

Pushing Boundaries: Making the Medieval Relevant through Public History and Engagement On and Off Campus

Amber Handy, Mississippi University for Women

When I arrived on the campus of this small regional public university fresh out of graduate school, I felt like I had won the lottery. Not only had I secured a tenure-track job in a terrible market, but I had done so at an institution with small class sizes, a liberal-arts based teaching mission, and a long history of supporting women's education, which was precisely the type of university at which I had always wanted to teach. I soon discovered that leaving behind a well-supported medieval community comprised of a diverse and thriving scholarly body, phenomenal library, and financial support for teaching and research had its challenges. While my new university valued my teaching skills, its library resources were far more limited than I had anticipated, and the student body, comprised largely of first-generation college students, did not immediately understand the relevance of medieval history to their course of study or future career goals. Despite the warm welcome I received from my new colleagues, I soon began to wonder if some of them harbored similar questions about the wisdom of using one of their few tenure-track lines on a premodernist. As the lone medievalist in a department of only four historians, and one of only two medievalists on the entire campus, I have found that the best way to ensure that medieval history is taken seriously by my colleagues is by actively seeking ways to professionally engage both with my departmental colleagues outside of the medieval period and as a medievalist across and beyond campus. In my experience, the following six areas have been key in demonstrating how my training in medieval history can be an asset in program and curricular development, undergraduate education in core history skills, student recruitment, and public outreach.

Apply your skills to the task at hand: Saving the archives and creating undergraduate research opportunities

Through my co-leadership, our department successfully lobbied the university to reopen the shuttered university archives that had lain dormant for nearly twenty years after a tornado damaged the building housing the collection. Working closely with colleagues in history and women's studies whose research agendas could make far better use of the materials in this collection than my own, I used my training as a medievalist to make an argument for the value of archival research in undergraduate education. I reached out to contacts at similar college archives for advice and was also able to use my previous experience with grant writing to help us locate and eventually win a small disaster-relief grant to begin the rebuilding process. We recruited a local volunteer with degrees in library science and history to help us with the more technical portions of our task and over the course of a few years were able to get him hired on a part-time and, eventually, full-time basis as the new university archivist.

Along with presenting the archives as an exciting tool for hands-on undergraduate research[1] and student engagement,[2] we also explained to our administration how a functional university archives would be a boon for institutional history projects, reaccreditation documentation, and long-term university record-keeping. It took us several years, but I am pleased to note that the university archives is now a thriving program that employs multiple student workers and interns each semester, many of whom collected oral histories, conducted original archival research, and produced a public website and published anthology as the core of our campus-wide celebration of the fiftieth anniversary of the university's desegregation.[3] The archives has also proven valuable to the university's public relations and alumni offices, providing them with historical information, images, and the occasional magazine or website article to stir interest in the university and its history. While the materials in this collection are still irrelevant to my own research agenda, I make use of them in my classes and work regularly with our archivist and my history colleagues to help promote history and original undergraduate research across the university.

---

1 See Sandra Roff, "Archives, Documents, and Hidden History: A Course to Teach Undergraduates the Thrill of Historical Discovery Real and Virtual," *The History Teacher* 40, no. 4 (2007): 551–58; and James Gerenscer and Malinda Triller, "Hands-on Instruction in the Archives: Using Group Activities as an Engaging Way to Teach Undergraduates about Primary Sources," *Journal for the Society of North Carolina Archivists* 6, no. 2 (2009): 55–66.
2 Keith A. Erekson, "From Archive to Awards Ceremony: An Approach for Engaging Students in Historical Research," *Arts and Humanities in Higher Education* 10, no. 4 (2011): 388–400.
3 Derek Spencer Webb, ed., *The Price We Paid: An Anthology of the Desegregation of Mississippi State College for Women* (Columbus: Mississippi University for Women, 2016). See also "Those Who Dared Student Research" (last modified 2016), http://www.muw.edu/pioneers/student-research.

Build the program: A medievalist's role in creating a public history major

As we worked to reopen the university archives, my colleagues and I decided to use the opportunity to launch a new undergraduate program in public history. Now offered as a concentration option within the larger history major, this program combines traditional history courses with classes like archives management, oral history, public budgeting, and internships and is unique as an undergraduate major within our region. Here again, my background as a medievalist meant that I did not have any obvious contributions to make to a program focused by practical necessity on the history of the United States. However, I saw the value of the new major track to our overall department and looked for ways that I could contribute. While I leave courses like archival management and oral history to my colleagues, I am more than capable of guiding students as they seek out internships at regional and national archives, museums, and history centers and then coordinating with their supervisors to manage their academic internship credits and ensure that they get the most out of the program. I also collaborate in preparing our advanced students to present their research at academic conferences and at public forums such as the local library's lecture series or semi-annual research events on campus. Although I may not be as familiar as some of my colleagues with the students' source material or the immediate historical context of their research, my years of experience presenting my own research in public means that I can offer suggestions about structure, pacing, and public speaking skills. Beyond that, I provide a sympathetic audience for an initial read through and a supportive presence in the crowd at the event itself. The new public history program has led to a significant increase of these "archives to podium" student projects, and we are becoming recognized in our region for the enthusiasm and skill our undergraduates show in both research and presentation. I am proud to contribute as I can to those presentations, even if the material is not medieval, and I know that my students and colleagues appreciate my help.

Adapting modern history techniques for a medieval classroom: An oral history collection project

After working so closely with my modernist colleagues, I began to wonder if there was a way that I could incorporate some of the techniques I was learning from them into my own classes. In particular, I was intrigued by the idea of an oral history project. Normally oral histories are quite impossible for medievalists, at least without the use of a séance and a very active imagination. However, I realized that an oral history project might be just the solution I needed to solve a challenge in my course on the early Islamic world. When I had initially developed the course I had access to the library resources of a much larger research university. The library at my new institution had a much smaller operating budget, which meant that purchasing deeply on the topic of the medieval Middle East was understandably not near the top of their annual acquisitions list. That made it very difficult for students to complete an independent research paper successfully. The first time I taught the course I relied on a combination of lending out my personal resource collection and attempting to guide my students through the pre-planning and coordination required for interlibrary loans and trips to other, larger university libraries in our vicinity. Although it was not a total disaster, I certainly would not call it a successful approach. When the time came for me to teach the course again, I decided to scrap the research paper and replace it with an oral history project. With the generous help of an Americanist colleague and our local county public archivist, I designed a project where teams of my students contacted local Muslims and conducted oral histories about their experience living as a minority religious group in a relatively rural, deep southern community in the early twenty-first century. I introduced my students to oral history best practices, guided their proposal through the Institutional Review Board, helped them hone their interview questions, and assisted them with developing phone and email scripts to invite area Muslims to participate in the process.[4] We practiced interview techniques and recorder use in the classroom and had regular team progress reports nestled between discussions and lectures about the medieval Islamic world. The interviews were conducted by small teams and the resulting digital recordings and student-generated transcripts were donated to the county archives where they are housed in the permanent collection.

On the surface, this project sounds like an interesting alternative to the traditional research project but looks completely disconnected from the medieval subject matter of the course. However, the completion of the oral history project actually helped my students to better understand the nature of the medieval source base and to better appreciate the importance of the historian's work. Too often, the voices of the "average" person from the medieval era are lost to the modern student. When previous classes had questioned the imbalance of elite voices to those of the comparatively silent majority in this course, I engaged them in a discussion about how literacy rates, perceived value of texts for preservation over the intervening centuries, and bias in modern source translation to English have resulted in a lack of accessible source materials about the common person's experience. That conversation took on an entirely different tone in the semester when I introduced the oral history project. The students quickly realized that, due to the small nature of the Muslim community in our region, their stories were equally hidden from the larger historical narrative. Those who had already conducted interviews spoke about how some area Muslims were hesitant to speak about their faith in public out of concern for their safety or the success of their family businesses. The majority of interview subjects tried to keep a low public profile and often socialized within circles that rarely overlapped those who

---

4   The Oral History Association offers many helpful resources when starting a class project like this, including *Principles and Best Practices for Oral History,* Oral History Association (2009), http://www.oralhistory.org/about/principles-and-practices/.

wrote the news, advocated for public policy, ran for local office, or otherwise had their stories told in places that might wind up in the region's historical record. The students connected the experience and worries of this modern religious minority community to how the earliest Muslim community may have felt in and around seventh-century Mecca where they were similarly viewed by some as a disruptive and potentially dangerous religious and political threat.

Further, my students recognized that without the work they were doing to collect these oral histories these modern "average" Muslims might face the same fate as their medieval brethren and be lost to the historical record, not through deliberate omission but rather through simple oversight. The occasional failure to connect with an interview subject or refusal by some potential interviewees to participate in the project caused frustration among my students, but it also led to a deeper understanding about the challenges inherent in oral history collection and the generation and preservation of historical source material. More than one student mentioned that they would never again take the existence of primary source materials for granted. This project gave my students a deeper understanding of the nature of the medieval source base and a way to access the emotional repercussions of living as a minority religious group in a larger community that is sometimes uncomfortable, or at least perceived to be uncomfortable, with their presence. These realizations substantially increased their pride in recording the oral histories and several students have told me in the semesters that followed what an impact the project had on their understanding of the medieval world and their appreciation of the importance and difficulty involved in historical research.

The opportunities of departmental curricular review: Service courses with a medieval twist

When the time came to reassess the core major courses of historical methods and capstone, I worked closely with my modernist colleagues to create a more skills-driven sequence that has greatly improved our student outcomes. Along with my upper-level medieval and world civilization survey classes, I now regularly teach the department's historical methods and research course. As it would for any of my colleagues, my training as a historian allows me to teach students the skills required to plan a research project, utilize local archives and libraries, organize a research paper, and convert a written paper into a compelling oral presentation. While I recognize that some historians find teaching the methods course to be a chore best avoided whenever possible, I have come to see it as an opportunity to show students how medievalists and medieval source materials are relevant to modern historical understanding. Previous experience had shown me that it is sometimes easier for students to discuss difficult topics like racism, sexism, and institutional violence in the relative safety of the distant past than it is to do so in a course focused on a more modern period. The same proves to be true of discussions about historical ethics, source use, or methods for uncovering authorial bias, where beginning with a medieval example and moving to more modern ones led to lively student discussions. I also ask my students to read Judith Bennett's article "Forgetting the Past" and to consider what might be lost if we ignore the distant past in favor of the more popular recent periods of history.[5] Thankfully the debate about whether or not research on premodern topics is still relevant in the modern age generally results in the conclusion that it is, in fact, still important, and I'm fairly certain that they are not all just pandering to their professor in saying so.

Beyond making a case for the importance of the medieval world to contemporary students of history, teaching the methods course has helped me to develop connections with my colleagues. I cannot teach this course without engaging with the materials, sources, and techniques used by my modernist peers, which has caused me to have a better understanding of their research practices. Asking them for reading suggestions has helped

---

5   Judith M. Bennett, "Forgetting the Past," *Gender & History* 20, no. 3 (2008): 669–77.

to broaden my own education and has led to some fascinating professional conversations which I otherwise might have missed. After several years I think that my colleagues all recognize that, while the medieval material I teach may remain foreign to them, I can use it to impart the same vital skills for academic or public history and that our students are able to successfully transfer those skills into their other courses within the department.

Student outreach: Build the minor and grow your program

While gaining the respect of my students and colleagues for the relevance of medieval coursework and research has helped them to see me as valuable member of our department, it is also important to show administrators how a medievalist can be an asset to the contemporary university. The public history major appealed greatly to them since it is more clearly tied to job opportunities than a traditional history degree and provides many opportunities for our students to actively engage in hands-on learning, which is an important part of our university's teaching mission. My work in developing that program, along with the curriculum work in my department and my extensive service work on university committees, proved that I was willing and able to work outside of my immediate field to benefit our students and institution. To make my case for the relevance of medieval studies to the modern student, however, I had to push further. Capitalizing on public enthusiasm for the Middle Ages, I created an interdisciplinary Medieval and Renaissance Studies minor on campus which is now housed in our department.

Despite clear student enthusiasm for the subject, I was wary of creating a medieval studies minor on a campus where the only medievalists were a professor in the English department and myself. However, with a little flexible thinking the program came together quite easily and did not require the creation of a single new course or teaching line. After poring over our course catalog I decided to expand the temporal range to include the Renaissance. I compiled a list of thirty courses from nine different disciplines which had a substantial medieval or Renaissance component that formed the core of the minor's elective course offerings. By initiating several discussions with the faculty who regularly taught those courses, I generated both the structure for the minor and a faculty advisory board. The minor was easily approved by the university's undergraduate curriculum committee, where the provost happily noted that the minor was both unique among our regional peers and would cost the university nothing to create since the required courses were already regularly taught by existing faculty.

While the minor is certainly a niche program, it attracts an enthusiastic group of students and is growing steadily. The minor has helped to steer students into medieval courses which had suffered from low enrollment in the recent past, thus keeping the premodern period regularly on the academic schedule and earning the gratitude of my colleagues and their department chairs. Programming like medieval movie nights and a fencing demonstration have generated student interest beyond our small core of existing minors, which has also helped to draw students into medieval and Renaissance courses to fulfill their general education or elective requirements. Enthusiasm has in fact been so high that this year saw the reemergence of Latin language courses, which had been discontinued some ten years ago when the previous Latin instructor retired and the subject area was not deemed important enough for a replacement. While the current Latin course offerings are few and the instructor was already an employee of the university rather than a new hire, the growth of this program in just a few short years has proven that student interest in the Middle Ages can help to raise enrollment in existing courses and revive previously suspended ones.

Public outreach: Using popular interest in the Middle Ages to build the university's local profile

A second way I have found to show campus administrators how a medievalist can be an asset to a small university is by performing community outreach through public speaking engagements. Broad interest in the Middle Ages provides the lone medievalist with a built-in method for public outreach. For an institution of our size, appearances in the local media and public lectures are a great way to garner regional recognition and appreciation for the university. They are also a good way to gain the respect of the public relations staff and administrators inside the campus gates. I have been able to use media appearances and public lectures to good effect in this way. In my first year at the university I was contacted by a local news outlet and asked to record a short interview for a segment on the history of Valentine's Day. That interview went well enough that I have now been invited back to do brief live segments about the history of other holidays with medieval roots, such as St. Patrick's Day, and to advertise community outreach programs, such as the free event I coordinated to assist area high school students and their parents in preparing to apply for college. I have also presented public lectures on topics like the "real" history of St. Patrick and medieval interactions between Muslims, Jews, and Christians on our campus and at the local public library. I will soon give another public lecture explaining how medieval subject matter is not only relevant, but important, to contemporary undergraduate education. All of these engagements have helped to raise my university's local profile. Each one has generated interest, and usually a press release, from our public relations department, which in turn has shown the university administration how a medievalist can contribute to the university's larger mission and regional reputation.

While I stumbled into most of these opportunities without much planning or forethought, in retrospect the key was letting it be known that I was willing to speak. Most small communities are desperate for public speakers on interesting topics, and as the recent spate of medieval-themed movies and television series demonstrates the Middle Ages are a very trendy topic. Our university public relations office keeps a list of resident subject experts which they use when the media calls to request someone to speak on a given topic. I recommend that you find out who keeps that list at your university and ask to be added to it. I was not on the list when I received my initial interview request, and I certainly would not have listed the history of early Christian saints as an area of expertise if I had been, but someone in the public relations office knew that I was the "historian of really old stuff" on campus and routed the call to my office. Similarly, my first offer to speak at the public library came from helping the public archivist employed in that library with an NEH grant she won to bring the Muslim Journeys bookshelf program to our community. Because we worked together in developing my department's public history program and I regularly took my majors to visit her archives, she knew that I occasionally taught a course on medieval Islamic history. She therefore invited me to join the grant programming committee which led to me giving a presentation and introducing a film screening for the series. It was also part of the genesis for the student oral history project in my course, the results of which are now housed in her archives. That lecture led to an invitation to submit my name and further public lecture proposals to the state humanities council, which offers programming across the state. My public lectures on campus have been the result of similar collaborations and discussions. What I learned is that if you let your colleagues know what you do and are enthusiastic when explaining to them why it interests you, it can lead to interesting invitations. Being willing to say "yes," even if the requested speaking topic takes you slightly outside of your comfort zone, is also an important part of the equation. Although I would never claim to be an expert in some of these topic areas and would certainly never present on them at an academic conference, I know that my understanding of the material through teaching and reading widely in my field is deep enough to help clear up common public misconceptions about the medieval period and to offer a new perspective on a familiar topic to an interested lay audience.

These six items have helped me to show my colleagues and administrators that medieval history can teach the same vital historical skills as more modern subject material while also proving to be a great tool for outreach and student recruitment. Though most of these programs have led me outside of my temporal field, my familiarity with grant writing, the vital nature of archival research, my broad training as a medieval historian, and my interest in engaging with the public meant that I was at the forefront of all aspects of these departmental developments. By stepping outside of my comfort zone, I have shown myself willing to engage with my colleagues, students, and community members where their interests abut my own, and I have proven that a medievalist can be relevant in a twenty-first century university.

Brought to You by Your Friendly Campus Medievalist

Lee Templeton, North Carolina Wesleyan College

I have been a lone medievalist for eight years—longer than some, but not nearly as long as many in our profession. Sometimes, when I am introducing myself to new faculty members or participating in one of the countless academic rituals that require an introduction and declaration of specialty, I am tempted to acknowledge my lone medievalist status after stating my name. As a way of giving an account of myself, I think this would be highly effective. Not only does it provide the necessary identifying information, but its similarity to the ritualized language of some twelve-step programs would alert my colleagues to the nature of my situation. "Ah," they would whisper to each other. "That explains quite a bit. At least he can admit he needs help." Of course, being a lone medievalist is not a condition for which one needs to seek treatment, despite what our colleagues may sometimes think. Yet, many of us who are lone medievalists have, at one time in our career or another, felt as if we are suffering from some sort of affliction that isolates us from the rest of our colleagues and causes us to be misunderstood by those with whom we share our academic lives. Such was certainly my experience as I began my tenure-track position at a small, private, liberal arts college, and, I must say, it initially threw me for quite a loop.

While my colleagues in the English department understood and supported my work as a scholar and teacher, none were specialists in medieval literature or had any experience teaching medieval texts. The rest of my colleagues knew very little about the Middle Ages or the work I did with medieval British literature. This was in stark contrast to the community of medieval scholars and fellow graduate students I was immersed in during my time in graduate school. As I endeavored to find my footing as the lone medievalist at my institution, I came to understand that not only did I need to educate my students about the Middle Ages, I needed to educate my colleagues as well.

From my current vantage point, it is easy to see how fortunate I was to complete my graduate work at a midsize research university whose English department housed, on average, three medieval scholars during my time there. In addition, I was part of a small cohort of graduate students who were also specializing in medieval literature. Given this level of contact and collaboration with established and emerging medievalists, I assumed — with the naiveté of the newly-minted PhD — that I would enter a similar environment when I began a tenure-track job. After accepting a position at a small liberal arts college, whose student enrollment was between six hundred and seven hundred and whose number of full-time faculty hovered around fifty, my expectations naturally shifted. Hired to teach classes in British literature before 1800, I knew I would be the only medievalist in the English department. When I learned that the college had a History department consisting of only two full-time faculty members, who specialized in American and modern European history, no Philosophy department, no foreign languages, no archaeology courses, and a part-time Religious Studies instructor who did not specialize in the Middle Ages, I realized I would be it — I would be the lone medievalist. Despite this, I was confident that my new colleagues, like those in the English department, would possess at least a basic understanding of the nature and value of what I did. After all, these were intelligent, well-educated individuals who surely were exposed to the Middle Ages in some form over the course of their education.

I began to be disabused of this belief almost as soon as I arrived on campus. The first opportunity to introduce myself to my colleagues came at a faculty convocation that opened the academic year. As we all mingled before the beginning of the program, I was approached by a member of the biology faculty. The usual pleasantries were exchanged, and then she inquired about my area of specialty and my research. I explained that I worked primarily in medieval British literature and focused on issues of masculinity and grief in medieval romance. As I warmed to the subject, I saw a glazed look enter her eyes and noticed that she was looking over my head, into the crowd of faculty behind me, searching for someone to rescue her from my enthusiastic discourse on medieval literature. Identifying her out, she politely excused herself and slipped away to join some colleagues from the Math and Science division. Hers was the panic of coming face to face with the medieval, and I admit I was sympathetic; it can be overwhelming for those with little experience. For many, the Middle Ages are disconcertingly foreign, offering little in the way of connection to modern lived experience. I imagine part of the biologist's reaction was rooted in her belief that there was no common ground between my work and her own, between her experiences, interests, and understanding of the world and the distant, and therefore "other," past. In contrast, I noticed that the other new faculty present at the convocation, whose fields included criminal justice and political science, did not face the same challenges when speaking about their areas of expertise. Indeed, their areas proved easily relatable to other faculty, who could discuss the local correctional facility or the current political landscape. Such easily identifiable points of connection, however, proved elusive to my colleagues when it came to my own area, and the biologist's response set the tone for most of my interactions with my colleagues that day. While few were as extreme as that, they were all characterized by a lack of awareness of the nature of medieval studies, as well as a certain benign dismissiveness. One colleague asked if I owned any armor and seemed genuinely surprised and disappointed when I replied that I did not (I decided not to reveal that I did, however, own a sword). Another suggested that, apart from *The Canterbury Tales*, there were not many medieval British texts, so my job should be relatively easy.

I do not believe these comments were made with intentional malice, but they were common, especially during my first few years. It was as if all but a few of my colleagues simply could not wrap their heads around the idea that someone would choose to spend so much time reading and thinking about the past, attempting to better understand an era so far removed from our own. Many assumed it is impossible to get students to read texts that posed so many challenges, particularly in terms of language and context, and, despite my arguments to the contrary, offered their deepest sympathies for the frustration I must experience every day in the classroom. The tenuous nature of my colleagues' understanding of my work reached its absurd pinnacle during my pre-tenure review. At a meeting to review my pre-tenure dossier, attended by my division chair and several members of the personnel committee, my division chair noticed one of the personnel committee members growing increasingly perplexed as he read through my dossier. After several minutes, he asked why, if I was a member of the English faculty, I was attending and presenting at so many medical conferences. My division chair was naturally confused by the question, but after a brief exchange realized that the member of the personnel committee had been reading the word "medieval" as "medical." It was as if "medieval" was such a foreign concept for him that, in order to make any sense of it, he had to translate it into a more recognizable word. Once his error was pointed out to him, however, he seemed to be even more perplexed than before, unable to envision what a medieval conference would even look like or what one would do there. I like to imagine his mind was filled with images of otherwise staid and respectable scholars giving in to their bloodlust during the mêlée portion of the Saturday evening banquet, but this would require knowledge of medieval tournaments which he probably does not possess. And while this story almost certainly benefitted from some embellishment when my division chair shared it with me, it nevertheless illustrates just how perplexed many of my colleagues were by a medievalist in their midst.

Long before I learned about the incident at my pre-tenure review meeting, I realized that I needed to help my colleagues better understand my work as a medievalist. Some of these people would be sitting on the personnel committee when I came up for tenure, so it was vital for them to be able to knowledgeably evaluate my teaching and scholarship. Beyond this, though, it was important to me that my colleagues understood how the study of the Middle Ages fit into the larger mission of a liberal-arts education, that they viewed the study of the Middle Ages as just as valuable and necessary as the study of biology, history, mathematics, or psychology. I do not fault my students for their lack of knowledge when it comes to medieval literature or history; it is my job, after all, to teach them about this. I decided that if my colleagues were similarly uninformed, I would teach them as well. One of the ways I approached this was through informal conversations with my colleagues. My aim in these conversations was to present the Middle Ages not as a long-past, "dead" time period, but rather one that laid the foundations for many of the ideas that we consider to be "modern," one that is still very much alive in its influence on the world in which we live. I sought to build connections with my colleagues working in political science, history, art, theater, the social sciences, and the sciences, to help them see the traces of the medieval in their own fields. In doing so, I often returned to Umberto Eco's expertly articulated explanation of the connections between the medieval and modern:

[A]ll the problems of the Western world emerged in the Middle Ages: Modern languages, merchant cities, capitalistic economy (along with banks, checks, and prime rate) are inventions of medieval society. In the Middle Ages we witness the rise of modern armies, of the modern concept of the national state [...] the struggle between the poor and the rich, the concept of heresy or ideological deviation, even our contemporary notion of love as a devastating unhappy happiness. I could add the conflict between church and state, trade unions (albeit in a corporative mode), the technological transformation of labor.[1]

Almost all of the issues we face and the questions we ask as modern scholars originated in the Middle Ages, and it is this point I wished to make to my colleagues.

In addition to these informal interactions, I engaged my colleagues, and the local community, with my work as a medievalist in more formal ways. In my first few years, I took advantage of my institution's monthly faculty colloquium to present my own research, giving a talk on the construction of chivalric masculinity in medieval literature, as well as a talk on Harry Bailey and marginal space in *The Canterbury Tales*. These presentations introduced my colleagues to the practice of literary criticism as it applies to medieval texts. More importantly, perhaps, they forced me to consider the best way to present this material to, and engage with, an audience of non-specialists. As in my informal conversations with colleagues, I highlighted in these talks the various ways my work intersects with disciplines such as history, gender studies, art history, and sociology. I sought to reinforce the idea that my work as a medievalist, like medieval studies as a whole, does not exist in a vacuum, that it engages issues addressed by scholars in a variety of fields. The presentations were well received and accomplished what I set out to achieve — my colleagues gained a better understanding of my work and began to view the Middle Ages as less foreign than they previously imagined. I broadened this type of outreach by taking part, in my second year, in an academic seminar organized by the college for members of the community. Examining the questions of human origins before and after Darwin, the seminar featured several members of the college faculty exploring the topic from the vantage point of their individual disciplines. My portion of the proceedings introduced the semi-

---

1 Umberto Eco, "Dreaming of the Middle Ages," in *Travels in Hyperreality*, trans. William Weaver, 61–72 (San Diego: Harcourt, Inc., 1986), 64.

nar attendees to several ancient Greek cosmogonies and their influence on and connection to medieval European thoughts about human origins, and how those, in turn, influenced more modern conceptions of humankind and its place within the universe. Once again, I wanted to both introduce the audience to the practice of medieval scholarship and reveal the connections between past and present. Like the presentations to my colleagues, this engagement with the larger community proved successful in exposing a wider audience to the medieval.

I also enlisted the help of my students in reaching out to the wider community and teaching them about what it means to be a medieval scholar. One of the assignments in an honors course I teach, which explores the ways the Middle Ages influence our modern imagination, particularly through popular culture, requires the students to organize a "medieval" film festival open to faculty, staff, and students. The students are responsible for choosing the films, which must be set in the "Middle Ages" or otherwise explore medieval themes, promoting the event, introducing each film, and leading a discussion of each film after its screening. The discussions focus on a number of issues, including the ways the Middle Ages are portrayed in the film, what this reveals about our modern understanding of the past, and how the medieval past offers a lens through which modern issues are addressed. These have been well attended, both by faculty and students, and have provided wonderful opportunities to discuss not only how we continually reinvent the Middle Ages, but also why the medieval exerts such a powerful influence over modern thought.

Eight and a half years after that faculty convocation where I was confronted with the reality of being the only medievalist at my institution, I think my efforts to educate my colleagues about the Middle Ages have been successful. I am no longer asked if I own armor, nor is my area of study casually dismissed as too far removed from contemporary concerns and, therefore, irrelevant. Over time, my colleagues have gained a better understanding of how the study of the Middle Ages contributes to a liberal arts education; they have come to see that in order to understand our present, we must ask questions about our origins. In order to get to this point, however, I needed to perform a kind of public service for my colleagues and institution. I had to become what Richard Utz has recently described as a "public medievalist," relating "the Middle Ages to postmedieval times," connecting the medieval to students, colleagues, and the general public.[2] The difficulty, distance, and strangeness of the Middle Ages is often what separates our students, colleagues, and the general public from a better understanding of the time and of what we, as medievalists, do. But it is also what is so attractive about the medieval, as those of us who work in the field already know. Indeed, the current bloom of popular medievalism — from recent television shows such as *Game of Thrones, The Last Kingdom,* and *Beowulf* to the enduring popularity of *The Lord of the Rings* — attests to the allure of the medieval. Helping others uncover the medieval foundations of these works of the modern imagination will lead, perhaps, to a greater appreciation of the continuing relevance of the Middle Ages and of the work we do as medieval scholars. My efforts as a public medievalist at my institution have allowed me to reveal to my students, colleagues, and the community that, yes, the Middle Ages are difficult, distant, and strange but they are also pleasurable, provocative, and relevant. In doing so, I found a way to avoid the sense of isolation and frustration that undoubtedly plagues many lone medievalists. Now, when I am asked to give an account of myself, I am no longer tempted to respond in the language of a twelve-step program. Instead, before driving my sword deep into the conference table, I confidently proclaim that I am a Lone Medievalist.

---

[2] Richard Utz, "Don't Be Snobs, Medievalists," *The Chronicle of Higher Education* (24 August 2015), http://chronicle.com/article/Dont-Be-Snobs-Medievalists/232539/.

Down with Dante and Chaucer? Navigating a Great Books Curriculum as a Medievalist

Sarah Harlan-Haughey, University of Maine

When I accepted my job as a joint hire between an English department and an Honors College that used a fairly conventional Great Books curriculum, I was excited to have a job and to be teaching the classics as well as my own research interests. But I quickly learned that there are some dangers and stressors in being the only person who works on anything remotely premodern in a four-semester curriculum that dwells a year on ancient Roman and Greek classics, hurtles over the Middle Ages after two or three short weeks with Dante and Chaucer, and comes to rest heavily in the Renaissance and the Enlightenment. I quickly found myself saying things that surprised and even scared my colleagues as we discussed our curriculum and book lists every year with hopes of improving or innovating the hundred years' culture war that is a Great Books curriculum.[1] "Why not teach a

---

1 The Great Books system was introduced by John Erskine at Columbia after the First World War. For a succinct overview, see Joan Shelley Rubin's *Cultural Considerations: Essays on Readers, Writers, and Musicians in Postwar America* (Amherst: University of Massachusetts Press, 2013), 150–52. Rubin notes: "The Great Books curriculum consisted of a systematic, text-based

saga instead of Dante?" I might say. Or: "Can we replace Chaucer with *Sir Gawain and the Green Knight,* or even *Piers Plowman*?" "No, I do not feel comfortable lecturing on the political climate that led to the creation of Virgil's *Aeneid*—that's why we need a *classicist*." "Can't we add another medieval text and remove *The Golden Ass*? Marie de France can cover a lot of the same ground." And so on. My colleagues have come to look upon my perpetual war for a non-standardized view of the Middle Ages, for readings from saints, weirdos, and outliers with exasperated good humor and a quick vote to maintain the status quo: a week of the *Inferno,* a week of Chaucer's greatest hits. Done, and done. I never thought I'd argue the things I have in this job as strongly as I have argued them.

The following is an autobiographical sketch that I hope may amuse and ring true for other medievalists caught in traditional Great Books curricula (or other traditionally organized or canonical curricula) and ask some perennial questions: why is it so hard to get colleagues to think outside the box about the Middle Ages? Why do Americans want a prepackaged, easy view of the past? How can we lone medievalists help each other fight the good fight when reality can be so inert and seemingly unchangeable? I hope to share some of my winning strategies as well as some of my more spectacular failures. I conclude with an argument that we lone medievalists must fight to reposition ourselves not as guardians of "cultural literacy," but as participants in a post-colonial dialogue that explores the web of interconnectedness of all human (and non-human) ontologies. We can help modern students think outside of their post-Cartesian,

---

approach to the 'best' Western literature and nonfiction. The idea that good reading could be sorted from bad was not in question. Another central premise of the Great Books ideology was that the best books were older texts that had survived generations of rereading because they addressed large questions about the human condition" (150). This basic argument continues to justify Great Books curricula—and sustain humanities departments—worldwide. See also Thomas J. Tomcho, John C. Norcross, and Christopher J. Correia, "Great Books Curricula: What Is Being Read?" *The Journal of General Education* 43, no. 2 (1994): 90–101, esp. 90–91.

post-industrial worldview and can offer access to medieval systems of being that are analogous to other non-dominant ontologies like those of indigenous and non-western peoples.² For this we are valuable, not just because we might know more about Dante than other people.³

So why'd you hire me?

In the current academic crisis in the United States, honors colleges and programs have cannily positioned themselves as the

---

2   It is perhaps important to note that the dominant interpretation of the Enlightenment as a polar opposite to the "Dark Ages" is not historically accurate: while part of the Enlightenment paradigm did valorize "historical progress, the rational, the universal, the male," Enlightenment thinkers, particularly Rousseau, who "saw in the 'first age of mankind', equated with the medieval, a powerful antidote for the ills of modern, corrupted society." Thus, as Alice Montoya argues, Enlightenment thinkers maintained the medieval. "In the foundational rhetorics of modernity, the medieval stood in for the superseded, the irrational, for the bodily and the emotive, and for the female," that is, as an alternate form of modern reality. See her *Medievalist Enlightenment: From Charles Perrault to Jean-Jacques Rousseau* (Martlesham: Boydell and Brewer, 2013), 222. Thus, in their focus on the paradigm shifts of the Enlightenment, survey courses, including our four-semester Civilizations course at UMaine, underemphasize the Enlightenment thinkers' interest in the medieval.

3   But see Arthur Krystal's editorial in the *Chronicle of Higher Education* for a recent defense of the classics. He argues: "[T]he prevailing mood welcomes fiction and poetry of every stripe, as long as the reading public champions it. And this I think is a huge mistake. Literature has never just been about the public (even when the public has embraced such canonical authors as Hugo, Dickens, and Tolstoy). Literature has always been a conversation among writers who borrow, build upon, and deviate from each other's words. Forgetting this, we forget that aesthetics is not a social invention, that democracy is not an aesthetic category; and that the dismantling of hierarchies is tantamount to an erasure of history" (Arthur Krystal, "What we Lose if we Lose the Canon," *The Chronicle of Higher Education* [5 January 2015], https://www.chronicle.com/article/What-We-Lose-if-We-Lose-the/150991). For a sense of the vitriol that is still generated by this issue, check out the comments thread… if you dare! See also Kevin J.H. Dettmar's "What's so Great about the Great Books?" in *The Chronicle Review* (11 September 1998), https://www.chronicle.com/article/whats-so-great-about-great/11135.

last bastions of the liberal arts, using the rhetoric of medieval warfare. The honors college becomes a little city-state within the heterogeneous landscape and balkanization of the American University. It defends the quadrivium and trivium. It champions the values of the liberal arts, held hostage by the accelerating instrumentalization and vocationalization of post-secondary education. It preserves ancient forms of tutelage — preceptorials, tutorials, and seminars abound. It teaches the same authorities that medieval scholars encountered, either in digest versions or in whole cloth — the Old and New Testament, Virgil, Aristotle, Ovid, Augustine, Apuleius, Homer. It advocates rumination, isolation — cloistering? — from the more frenetic specializations of the worldly modern academy and promises revelation. And — against its will, I hope — it has been a bastion of class privilege, as, historically, scions of families in the wealthier echelons of American life were the ones recruited to honors programs.

This championship for the past can make honors colleges a great refuge for people trained as medievalists, as jobs dry up elsewhere. And, in fact, medievalists have often become invaluable members of honors colleges.[4] Their skills as interdisciplinarians, linguistic knowledge, wide-ranging historical expertise, and ability to make connections between the ancient world and the early modern one are all useful resources for a Great Books community. Such was the justification for the creation of my job as a joint hire between the English department at the University of Maine and the 88-year-old Honors College.[5] I have often been called upon to aid in the defense of a Great Books

---

4 Susan Yager organized a panel discussion on the phenomenon of many medievalist becoming members or leaders of their universities' honors programs at the National Collegiate Honors Conference, entitled "Why Honors Programs Need Medieval Studies" (13 November 2015). While Susan Yager, Tara Williams, Mickey Sweeney, and I came prepared to defend Medieval Studies as an important component of any honors program, we found we were preaching to the choir; a surprising number of the audience self-identified as medievalists.

5 A detailed description of the rationale behind the creation of my joint appointment can be found in Robert W. Glover et al., "The Genesis of an

Curriculum — when I often find the rationale for the curriculum unconvincing. This false position is, I suspect, a common one for medievalists hired in such positions, who may be happy to hold jobs with such promise, but may not be willing to embark on quests as defenders of the western canon as it was understood by advocates of the "Great Books." This short essay will be an anecdotal account of my own experiences teaching in a Great Books curriculum and my struggles as a representative of the past that can often be too narrowly-defined by entrenched college traditions. I believe it will strike a chord with others in similar positions.

Why do you hate Chaucer?

In a *National Review* article, conservative journalist John Zmirak identified University of Maine as a "Blue collar Ivy" for various reasons including that the "humanities programs are less ideological than at most state schools" (whatever that means) and that students have "very good options" for their Western Tradition gen-eds, including "History of Ancient philosophy" and an "Introduction to the Jewish Bible."[6] Zmirak notes that the "pickings are slimmer" in the "required Cultural Diversity and Population and Environment subcategories," which he disapprovingly notes include "Sex and Gender in Cross-Cultural Perspective." He does crow elsewhere in his list of the "strong points" of the university that the "women's studies department may close for lack of student interest."[7] One of the foremost reasons for Yale-educated Zmirak's inclusion of UMaine in his list

---

Honors Faculty: Collective Reflections on a Process of Change," *Honors in Practice* (2012): 193–212, http://digitalcommons.unl.edu/nchchip/157.

6 Zmirak, John, "Meet the Blue Collar Ivies," *The National Review* (17 October 2014), http://www.nationalreview.com/education-week/361456/meet-blue-collar-ivies-john-zmirak.

7 It is unclear where Zmirak got some of his information. His description of courses offered seems to rely on out-of-date course catalogs, and the Women's, Gender, and Sexuality Studies Program (never a department) is going strong under the joint leadership of Elizabeth Neiman and Maisie Hough.

of "Ivies" was the Great Books curriculum offered by the Honors College, the "jewel in the crown" of the university. Zmirak argues that "The thesis project, a well-chosen adviser, and some of the excellent course material offered (the *Odyssey,* the *Republic,* Greek dramas, the *Aeneid,* Augustine's *Confessions,* Dante's *Inferno,* Renaissance art, the Bible, *The Prince,* Shakespeare's plays, *The Social Contract,* the works of John Locke, Darwin, Freud, Nietzsche, and much more) make the honors sequence the best choice for an undergraduate at UMaine."

This kind of good press troubles me. I do believe it is important for students to learn about the past and to read classics, yet I am uncomfortable that these great works are all written by men, are pressed into service as bulwarks of political conservatism, and are seen as somehow better than other options. I am happy to teach Chaucer, Dante, and Shakespeare, but I would like to see a curriculum that includes more voices and works that have not come to stand for the values of a single political philosophy. Moreover, I am troubled that these works have been forced into such a static position and that we promise our students a "rigorous and unified approach to the liberal arts core."[8] A unified approach to a core seems a monolithic way to think about a body of temporally and philosophically diverse texts.

For these reasons, I have been arguing rather vociferously for a review of the entire curriculum, and horror of horrors, to eliminate famous authors in favor of lesser known — or even (gasp!) anonymous ones. This stance has surprised some of my colleagues, who had assumed that I would be grateful just to have medieval texts on the docket. One of my colleagues, horrified at my suggestion that we read *Sir Gawain and the Green Knight* and Julian of Norwich instead of the *Canterbury Tales,* said: "Why do you hate Chaucer?" He then went on to argue, quite passionately and with great eloquence, that to deprive students of the privilege of hearing the poetry of the "Father of the

---

8   This is a quotation from current honors dean François Amar's welcome letter to prospective students in his "Dean's Welcome," http://honors.umaine.edu/deans-welcome/.

English Language" in the original was to deny them part of their inalienable right to "their Honors Journey." I backed down at that curriculum meeting, and I have not suggested that particular sacrilege again.

Fighting the Hundred Years War, again

The University of Maine Honors College has been using a Great Books curriculum for many years. Our curriculum centers on the Western tradition and spans millennia. Our decisions about readings are a result of conscious choice and yearly deliberation, taking into account the charges leveled against Great Books curricula in the academic battles of the 1970s, '80s, and '90s. While we do include some subaltern voices, the bulk of our curriculum consists of famous, dead, named, white males. Concerns with such underrepresentation of diverse voices have been hashed and rehashed in the academy, and we do it every year in our faculty meeting about the Great Books curriculum. We academics are all familiar with "the intensely serious and frequently quite wearing debates" about curriculum into which faculties "fling themselves, generation after generation, with seemingly undiminished ardor"; and we all know it's better to steer clear of such debates if possible, if only for the sake of our personal sanity — curriculum reform is a Sisyphean labor.[9] But, as the Great Author Shakespeare so memorably noted, "this all the world knows, but none knows well" — generation after generation of well-meaning academics like me get pulled into the debate.

In spite of my deep desire to stay out of campus politics as much as possible, I find myself wound up in the same old endless fight: what and how should we teach? And as I am uncomfortably aware, "Opinionated champions of a particular curriculum are often advocating the importance of knowing what they know. All curriculum champions bring profoundly subjective

---

9 This is a quote from Francis Oakely, a former Williams College president, included in Victor Ferrall's discussion of curricular reform in his book *Liberal Arts at the Brink* (Cambridge: Harvard University Press, 2011), 148.

judgments to their cause, no matter how artfully they cloak them in claimed fundamental, albeit perhaps ineffable, truths."[10] But in spite of all this self-knowledge and cynicism about the possibility for real improvement or change, my sense of unease is not generated simply by the representative texts we have (carefully) chosen; my deeper concern is the much less explored, and thus more insidious. Such a curriculum leads students to see the past as a series of graded steps leading to the present.

Dante and Chaucer are made to stand as either pillars of humanism in a dark age or, conversely, illustrations of the darkness of said age. In our "long view" of western cultural history, Chaucer's social satire is (erroneously) presented as the first secularism or the first anti-fraternal, proto-protestant literature, in an age that was so oppressively Catholic (read: superstitious). Dante's *Inferno* — read in isolation from the rest of the *Divina Commedia* — often stands in for orthodox Catholicism, and Dante's *Inferno* is interpreted by students to be an accurate representation of the hell that all medieval Europeans imagined and believed in. The vision of the Middle Ages preserved here in our honors college is one that has been out of style in our disciplinary circles for over seventy years. It pains me to see these authors boiled down to talking points: medieval religion=oppressive and superstitious; medieval people and characters=wooden; medieval science=backwards. This sort of packaging of medieval material proves that Régine Pernoud was right when she noted that the "Middle Ages is privileged material: one can say what one wants about it with the quasi-certitude of never being contradicted."[11]

I love Dante and Chaucer, and like many literary medievalists, was led to become what I am by my first shocking encounters with the miraculous richness and complexity, the alterity and intense aesthetic beauty of these great works.[12] Thus I find

---

10 Ibid., 149.

11 Regine Pernoud, *Those Terrible Middle Ages: Debunking the Myths* (San Francisco: Ignatius Press, 2000), 142.

12 For this first inspiration to set off on our dubious and delightful career path, I am most indebted to another "lone medievalist," my mentor and friend Ashby Kinch at the University of Montana, my undergraduate institution.

myself constantly arguing for my students to have the chance to see what I saw when I was in their position: for them to have a richer, more meaningful encounter with these artifacts. I'd like the medieval readings not to be placed in explicit (and unfavorable) contrast to the "breath of fresh air" that is the Renaissance as presented by our old-fashioned curriculum.

I argue often for different texts. When my honors colleagues claim that there are no women who wrote in the Middle Ages (our curricular discussions often hand-wring over the marked lack of diversity in our readings — and someone always asserts as a justification for maintaining the status quo, "well, that's just the way things were back then; women didn't have a voice until recently"), I cite Marie de France, Christine de Pizan, Julian of Norwich, Teresa de Ávila, Hildegard von Bingen, Héloise, Margery Kempe, and many, many others.[13] I also note that greatest medieval poet of all, Anonymous, who must have been a woman, at least sometimes. When my honors colleagues claim that medieval writing is overpoweringly moralistic and religious, I argue that the sagas, the early Irish and Welsh material, the fabliaux, the travel narratives, the romances, the framed narratives of Boccaccio, Manuel, and Chaucer, and many lyric poems can be remarkably secular. When my honors colleagues claim that there was no science in the Middle Ages (and we must always appeal to our greatest demographic, STEM students, at least seventy percent of our current honors population), I point out that Aquinas refined the science of deductive reasoning, that medieval logicians built the framework for critical thought that is still such a prominent learning objective today, that medieval scientists and scribes in North Africa and Spain preserved and refined ancient mathematics, that Grosseteste's and Bacon's optics provided the groundwork for modern physics, and that medieval medicine was a holistic system similar to Ayurveda and

---

13 Tomcho et al. note that "the composition of these GB lists contains very few women, racial minorities, or non-Western contributors. For example, only 2 of the 55 most common authors (Virginia Woolf and Jane Austen) were women" ("What Is Being Read," 99).

traditional Chinese medicine, which westerners revere as alternatives to western medical approaches today.[14] When my honors colleagues claim that the classical and early modern periods are simply better, because they are more in line with our modern world and our priorities of progress and innovation, I throw up my hands in despair.[15]

Swimming Upstream: Strategies that (sometimes) work

Change happens slowly and is often a matter of gradually introducing new literature and concepts to non-specialists. I haven't succeeded in eliminating the two "greats" from the curriculum, but I have eased them into a richer context. I have argued for a unit on Chaucer that contextualizes his work within the broader tradition of European storytelling so that he becomes less of an anomaly in a "dark age" — we read Apuleius's *Golden Ass* earlier

---

14 I also, now, cite the Anglo-Saxon charms, thanks to the wonderful collaborative effort led by Christina Lee, as examples of successful medieval medicine — a combination of religious ritual, folk magic, and medicinal applications. See Sarah Knapton, "Anglo-Saxon Cow Bile and Garlic Potion Kills MRSA," *The Telegraph* (30 March 2015), http://www.telegraph.co.uk/news/science/science-news/11504166/Anglo-Saxon-cow-bile-and-garlic-potion-kills-MRSA.html.

15 Milton McC. Gatch has an eloquent rebuttal to such a claim, however: "Perhaps at the core of many of the social, economic, educational, and intellectual problems that face us today is our deep, nearly unconscious commitment to the notion that history is progress, that the human community moves inexorably and endlessly towards betterment, sophistication, wisdom, happiness, and that the future will be preferable to the past. With progress, we have committed ourselves to its illegitimate children: the notion that technological change is evidence of progress and the belief that growth (not only macroeconomic growth but also the growth of my university, my department, my program, my grant, and my salary) should be infinite if we are not to be plunged backwards beyond even the darkness of prehistory. Those of us involved in historical studies need to be introducing cautions about the doctrines of progress. It should be stressed that past cultures were sophisticated in ways that often outstrip us. It might even be appropriate to dwell on the apocalyptic assumption of times past: the deep belief that things must get far worse before the world is turned to right" ("The Medievalist and Cultural Literacy," *Speculum* 66, no. 3 [1991]: 591–604, at 595).

in the term, and I added several *lais* by Marie de France. Both of these earlier raconteurs offer stories of complexity, ambiguity, satire, and humor arguably equal to Chaucer's, and, moreover, one is one of those nonexistent female medieval writers!

I argued vociferously that if we must read the *Divina Commedia* in a week (or, if we're lucky and the breakneck pace of the curriculum allows it) we should at least read selected cantos from all three canticles — then, hopefully, the students' impression of Dante will not be all hellfire and damnation.[16] It's not an ideal situation, and I will continue to strive to try to amplify the medieval curriculum, developing a more diverse set of readings, but each change will need to be piloted, and only one text can reasonably be piloted in a given year. When I take my own long view, I can imagine a transformed curriculum in ten years or so.

One-offs are also a strategy; though our curriculum is at times hidebound and traditional, we have some open spaces from time to time for experimentation.[17] After we lost our classicist to retirement (due to the budget constraints of a state school, she will not be replaced), I and others argued that the space that used to be devoted to Greek drama, the last reading of the first semester, might become a forum for exploring new texts, but specifically ones that offered students an alternative to a package tour of the past. I started this new "tradition" with readings from Old Irish narratives — in particular selections from the *Táin* cycle. My rationale was that the warrior society

---

16 At time of press, I must note that the during the most recent curriculum meeting on May 18, 2016, the honors faculty were leaning towards returning to a reading of the *Inferno* alone. I stalled, but the writing's on the wall for next year.

17 Ours is not the only hidebound Great Books curriculum. In their nationwide survey of Great Books curricula, Tomcho et al. find that "for better or worse, the canon has evidenced little change since 1952" ("What Is Being Read?" 93). The most read books (between 60% and 40% representation across the board in Great Books programs) have all been included in our curriculum in the last four years: "*Bible* 69% *Iliad* (Homer) 62% *Divine Comedy* (Dante) 59% *Aeneid* (Virgil) 49% *Odyssey* (Homer) 46% *Confessions* 44% (St. Augustine) *The Prince* (Machiavelli) 44% *Canterbury Tales* 41% (Chaucer) *The Republic* (Plato) 41%" (96).

portrayed in these narratives looks a lot like the world of the *Iliad* and the *Odyssey* — warbands with tribal kings, chariots, a gift economy, and iconic women as plot catalysts (just compare Dierdriu of the Irish tale with Helen of Troy, and you'll see what I mean). I used my lecture on the Irish material to talk about all the cultures that existed on the margins of the Roman Empire — and grew into the cultures we know today.[18] I discussed the ways in which the Roman attitude towards Gauls and other Celtic peoples (as exemplified in the famous sculpture of the dying Gaul) modeled later colonial British attitudes towards the Irish, Welsh, and Scots in both the medieval and modern periods. Instead of allowing the new readings to become part of the curriculum, I argued that the space should turn over to another experimental text, and this year, we are reading the Bhagavad Gita — another eye-opening perspective on the ancient world, different from the centralized authorities of Greco-Roman classicism and Mediterranean basin monotheism.

Other strategies I've tried are offering talks and workshops to faculty to let them know about the diversity and complexity of medieval literary culture, providing different and unique lectures every year within the curriculum so faculty are exposed to new ideas and approaches to medieval literature and do not fall into a rote approach to the material, and sharing news and journal articles on the medieval world that challenge conventional wisdom on the subject.

One of the most successful ways I have found to counteract a gross misunderstanding of medieval culture is to focus on student learning. There are currently more than 600 honors students in UMaine's program. If I can find a way to speak directly to them, and draw them in, they become agents of curricular change. This happened, for example, when I first introduced the

---

18 A note on the idiosyncrasies of UMaine's honors curriculum: we offer small seminar-style classes of under 13 students, but we supplement these with weekly lectures on the current reading delivered by an expert in the field — if we can find one at UMaine, Bowdoin, Colby, or Bates — before an auditorium filled with honors students. Classicists are even harder to find than medievalists.

Marie de France readings to the preexisting Chaucer unit. Several of my colleagues were not sure what to make of the overt romanticism and supernaturalism of the stories, but many enthusiastic students did get it — and argued that it should remain in our curriculum to their preceptors. I offer a Medieval Reading Group, which meets once a week in the academic year and allows anyone to dabble in medieval language and read wild new things. Students gravitate to the medieval — its alterity, familiarity (a result of the pop medievalism that suffuses our culture), and its challenges — and enjoy coming to the weekly meetings. Currently, long-term medieval enthusiasts and I are forming a new club on campus — the UMaine Medieval Club — and plan to host at least five events a year that raise awareness of the past. We will have a celebration of medieval readings in December, a movie night in February, a historical ball in March, and a Maying in the first week of May.

The past in the future

I have tried all these aforementioned strategies, with mixed results, as you can see. I have come to believe that as long as we teach medieval texts in this Great Books curriculum (or any traditionally "canonical" curriculum) as part of a chronological long view of western culture, faculty — and many students — will never be able to see the Middle Ages as anything but a benighted pit-stop in between the great periods of the Renaissance and the classical world.[19] I believe the only real solution would be to start again and create a Great Books curriculum that is thematically, not temporally, oriented.[20] If we had four-semester modules that

---

19 David Matthews discusses the common misconceptions about the Middle Ages, as well as how the era serves as a repository for any perceived "barbarism" of the western world, even when many of the perceived barbarisms were more a feature of the ancient or early modern world than the medieval one, in his *Medievalism: A Critical History* (Martlesham: Boydell and Brewer, 2015), 13–17.
20 I made a lengthier argument for a non-teleological curriculum in my article, "Against Teleology in an Honors Great Books Curriculum," in *Honors in*

explored topics like "science, technology, and magic," "nature and society," "religion and ritual," and "what is the good life," to pick four viable examples at random, medieval texts could be placed in conversation with works from many places and times, without an overwhelming sense of "progress." Faculty would be more open to curriculum modifications, and students would not be searching for "takeaways" from each text, quickly separating the wheat from the chaff, and applying all lessons learned to their mental map of progress in the western world.[21]

I believe medievalists — especially medievalists who are not surrounded by like-minded humanists and scholars of premodern culture, but rather those who might not immediately see the relevance of what we know to the modern academy — are in a unique position as we continue to rethink "the canon." I believe that we can help break the iron grip of universalism. We no longer think of ourselves as defenders of patriarchal knowledge and outmoded western ideals; we know ourselves to be stewards of a valuable, and increasingly rare, alterity that is enlightening for everyone. As Gatch puts it, "the world we study can be made forbidding, distant, deplorable, or it can be presented as an intriguing place and state of being, different from our own but also clarifying our sense of the present by putting forth contrasts."[22] But the outer world still sees us as gatekeepers to privileged, prestigious western ideals, and we must fight tirelessly to change that old-fashioned view of our work or face

---

Practice (2014): 95–108, http://digitalcommons.unl.edu/nchchip/207.

21 In order for this to work, a sense of history must be preserved by selection of texts within each thematic semester that span more than a few centuries' time — and more than one continent. For I agree wholeheartedly that there is "one curriculum content imperative: history. None of us can live safely in the world without the ability to identify the risks and dangers a course of conduct poses. To take only one example, before one assumes that an invading army from the West will be greeted in Iraq or Afghanistan as liberators, the safety of the world demands that leaders have some understanding of the thousand- year history of such invasions. Global security is put at risk by leaders ignorant of, or who chose to ignore, history." Ferrall, *Liberal Arts at the Brink*, 153.

22 Gatch, "Cultural Literacy," 597.

obsolescence. And that would be a great loss to the academy. In his impassioned manifesto for a development of a post-colonial curriculum that allows for multiple ontologies in dialogue with one another, Kinchaloe says it best:

> In a counter-colonial move critical ontologists raise questions about any knowledges and ways of knowing that claim universal status. In this context they make use of this suspicion of universalism in combination with global, subjugated, and indigenous knowledges [here I also read "traditional," more broadly defined] to understand how they have been positioned in the world. Almost all of us from Western backgrounds or non-Western-colonized backgrounds have been implicated in some way in the web of universalism. The inevitable conflicts that arise from this implication do not have to be resolved immediately. At the base of these conflicts rest the future of global culture as well as the future of research and pedagogy. Recognizing that these are generative issues that engage us in a productive process of analyzing self and world is in itself a powerful recognition. The value of both this recognition and the process of working through the complicated conceptual problems are treasured by critical ontologists.[23]

We medievalists, I am convinced, need to resituate our field for other academics — especially when we are alone in an institution, as our positions are seen at times as luxurious or irrelevant to current academic exigencies. We are not valuable because we represent a single pearl on the teleological thread of "Western Civilization" or because we hold the keys to "cultural literacy"; we are valuable because we can strengthen the web of knowledge that transcends discipline and can help students make connections between past and present, self and other, and become

---

23 Joe Kincheloe, "Critical Ontology and Indigenous Ways of Being: Forging a Postcolonial Curriculum," *Curriculum as Cultural Practice: Postcolonial Imaginations,* ed. Yatta Kanu, 181–202 (Toronto: University of Toronto Press, 2006), 187.

more empathetic, thoughtful members of the modern world because they better understand the alterity of the medieval world (and other premodern or traditional worlds like it) as a thing valuable in itself. My experiences in this Great Books curriculum have convinced me that becoming part of a less monolithic interdisciplinary conversation is not only a way to preserve our own (inter)discipline, but radically to transform it. We lone medievalists, often the lone voice for a thousand-year period of art, culture, and history on our college campuses, have a long hard battle ahead of us, but it's worth the fight.

Of sondry folk: What I Learned After My First Year as the Lone Medievalist on Campus

Ann M. Martinez, Kent State University at Stark

August: *"So, like Chaucer?"*

My first month as an assistant professor was a whirlwind. There were new people everywhere. Faculty, staff, administrators… everyone was very welcoming, and they all wanted to get to know me, so they asked: "What do you work on?" And my I-just-finished-my-dissertation-and-still-have-a-lot-to-say-about-it brain kicked in. I responded: "With a formalist methodology regarding textual analysis, a historicist approach to literature's and to society's attitudes about nature, and an ecocritical lens, I examine the periodization that sets the Middle Ages against other eras. This allows me to trace the extent to which attitudes toward land use, landscape beautification, and woodland delineation developed within Middle English literature. These medieval perspectives are a crucially important pre-history to our modern views regarding the use, exploitation, and sustainability of the environment."

Fail. Sometimes their eyes would narrow a little, sometimes they smiled, sometimes they nodded, sometimes there was a glint of recognition: "So, Middle English. Like Chaucer?"

Success? No. I failed in the simple act of communicating. Examples. I needed to give examples. Titles. Authors' names. My colleagues were more likely to relate to what I do if I gave them a foundation. It is not about "dumbing down" — it is about translation. It's about communicating with people outside of my field and situating my work within a larger academic world. This, it seems, was harder than I thought.

September: *"Yes, like Chaucer."*

My stock answer changed. "I mostly focus on Chaucer and Arthurian literature. I examine representations of nature to show that environmental awareness isn't that new." As a doctoral student I lived far too long cocooned within an English Department, speaking in code. Now I belong to a state university, and I also belong to a regional campus where I am the lone medievalist. There are others of my kind, sprinkled among eight different campuses. I know they are there, but I seldom see them. Once in a while we are lucky enough to congregate and talk the medieval talk. But on a day-to-day basis, I work amongst my very own *sondry folk,* my diverse colleagues within English and without.

October–November: *"Beowulf was the original superhero."*

My students come from different backgrounds. All are from working-class families, and many are first-generation college students. In my surveys of English literature, only some are English majors.

"So why are we reading *Beowulf*... *Sir Gawain and the Green Knight*... *The Canterbury Tales*?" I've yet to have a student ask me this question directly, but I know that some students wonder about the viability of reading these works as we make our way through the centuries of literature. The survey class is a requirement for the English major and an elective for non-majors.

Their advisor made them do it — that is why some are there. However, it is also my chance to lure them in to this wonderful world of warriors and dragons and pilgrims and mystics. And so, as we advance through the readings I tell them why.

I explain why older literature is important; I talk about being informed readers, about finding and making connections, and about understanding where our literature comes from. I deliberately bring the question of relevancy to the forefront of discussion. We consider the medieval texts in isolation and in context as foundational for their study of later literature, but at times the distance in time and place is hard for them to bridge. It is not my place to be offended if a student is dismissive of medieval literature. It is my place to engage him/her and get that student to think critically about such an assessment.

At the beginning of the Fall semester, some students were enthusiastic while others skeptical about reading "really old stuff." Routinely, I found myself giving some light history lessons, as well as language instruction, sprinkled with a bevy of Tolkien and *Game of Thrones* references — I use what I can. Visuals help this generation, and after uttering things like, "The Rohirrim are modeled on the Anglo-Saxons," and "Think of what it was like to travel long distances while wearing armor like Jaime Lannister's," heads began to nod more often. After they became more comfortable with Middle English, after we talked about the history, after we started connecting the old with the new, the raised hands in class no longer indicated basic questions about *who/what/where,* but instead contributed statements addressing the *why*. I found that when students discussed this last point, they often bridged the time and space divide that existed at the start of the semester: "The reason *why* we have _____ nowadays is *because* of _____ back then," they now often said. Students found the echoes and, I believe, garnered a stronger understanding of the literary and cultural past and present. When a student said, "So, if Beowulf was the original superhero, then he's a literary ancestor to Captain America," I was totally fine with it.

December–January: *"Sorry, but I'm busy for Summer 2022."*

As my first semester ended and a second one started, finally, there was time for ~~rest and relaxation~~… catching up with research. Teaching a 4/4 load is challenging. As a doctoral student, I was lucky enough to teach a 2/2 load. This change has led to some adjustment. New preps + More students = Full-time teaching. However, as a tenure-track faculty member, my publication record matters. Because of the nature of my research (there's the language to translate, there's the paleography to decipher, there's the decades-of-previous-research to read up on), I have to plan ahead — a lot.

What can I (realistically) accomplish during Winter break? During Spring break? During Summer? I've set research/writing goals for each break to keep me productive and focused as well as smaller monthly goals that will keep me headed in the right direction. Some of these goals are not very detailed (e.g., "SGGK's Morgan – Summer 2016"), but it helps me know what project I intend to tackle.

I have to feed my medieval brain with new material, and research is great nourishment.

February–March: *"Are you the one who teaches Shakespeare?"*

I have a confession to make: I moonlight as a Shakespearean… or, should I say, "daylight"? My position covers pre-1800 British literature. So, obviously, Shakespeare is included in the package.

In my doctoral program one of my mentors was a Shakespearean. Because of him, a lot of my research (including part of my dissertation) and my conference attendance was and still is related to Shakespeare. While I delight in teaching the Bard, as a regional campus faculty member I feel like I serve two masters: Chaucer and Shakespeare are perpetually battling over my soul.

For me, this means proficiency in both areas. "More to read, more to research, more to teach" has become my mantra. That, however, is not a complaint but rather a depiction of reality. Many universities are doing away with medieval-only positions and blending these with the early modern period, and sometimes even beyond. I have the opportunity to teach a diversity of classes, but at the same time I have to make sure I stay balanced and up-to-date on the scholarship, both for my own research and for my courses.

April: *"Even the Lone Ranger had a companion — to whom can the lone medievalist turn?"*

The answer: Social media.

During my first year at my regional campus I felt a gap. No longer could I simply walk down the hall at work and chat with a few folk who would immediately share the excitement (mixed with dread, of course) for the premier of *The Last Kingdom*. The medieval-colleague-gap might seem trivial, but it is not. This sense of loss isn't just for a missing like-minded colleague with whom to chat about new period shows, but for someone to talk with specifically about teaching and about research in the field. From ordinary questions — like, "I'm reviewing different *Le Morte D'Arthur* editions to use in class. Which is your favorite?" — to the ever-important pair of expert eyes to review a draft of an article. Missing.

So I turned to social media.

I have met many medievalists in my life, and they are all over the globe. But while these friends and mentors are miles and miles away in person, virtually they are right here, just a click away. The distance between me and Kansas, Colorado, Texas, or New York is measured in computer screens, not miles. Questions. Advice. Jokes. Drafts. Everything can be shared in an instant.

I might be the only medievalist on my campus, but I am not alone. I just have to be willing to reach out and stay connected via email or social media. It can be difficult, though; with teaching responsibilities and research looming over me, I initially thought about social media as a vortex that might suck away my negligible amount of free time. However, both reading the feeds of my medievalist friends and checking in on online groups I have joined has kept me informed of new editions to anticipate, new shows to problematize, and, more importantly, about upcoming CFPs.

May: *"Than longen folk to goon on pilgrimages"*

In May, everyone goes to the Zoo. Kalamazoo, that is.

Attending conferences was important when I was a doctoral student because it helped me see academia in action, get to know new people, and learn about new research. As an Assistant Professor, attending conferences is important because it helps me see old friends, get to know new people, and learn about new research. Some things don't change much.

Or do they? One key difference: attending conferences is even more important now than ever before. Conferences are like spa holidays for lone medievalists — we leave recharged. It's the opportunity we have to talk the talk, see and be seen, listen and be heard. It's total immersion: a reminder that there are others like us out there and that new ideas on teaching and researching the Middle Ages are blossoming constantly.

Sometimes travel to conferences is uncomfortable — the room is too hot, too cold, or there's a shared bathroom with a door that won't fully close. Sometimes travel to conferences is expensive — maybe there are no travel funds, maybe flights are pricier than ever. But, always, travel to conferences is worth the investment in time and money because the ideas I take away with me from the sessions, from the plenaries, from conversations in the hall will stay with me and fuel me for a whole year.

June–July: *"The lyf so short, the craft so longe to lerne"*

Summer. Finally, there is time for ~~rest and relaxation~~… catching up with research.

The Collaborative Medievalist

Courtney Rydel, Washington College

My colleagues who work in theatre have taught me my new favorite word: collaboration. Being the lone medievalist in my field at a small liberal arts college, I've learned to work on active collaborations with friends in fields outside medieval studies. We can meld our approaches into a process that works for both of us, since collaboration primarily requires working together closely to create a finished product. Starting from the same background knowledge does not matter. Coming together over shared materials — while appreciating my colleagues' distinct approaches and methodologies — has reinvigorated my teaching and research, making possible different class projects, better class discussions, new research initiatives, and new classes and co-curricular opportunities.

Three main strategies have helped me in these collaborations: working with those in adjacent fields, building connections to active artists and practitioners, and offering historical perspective. While a smaller school certainly facilitates these kinds of close connections I have enjoyed with my colleagues, hopefully my reflections will help others consider how they can build collaborative endeavors with their colleagues. Some of these thoughts may also be relevant to adjunct and contingent medievalists who desire to stay intellectually engaged, but are receiving less institutional support and resources for research.

The first strategy, working with fellow faculty in adjacent fields, came the most naturally to me. In graduate school at the University of Pennsylvania, a host of formal groups — the Medieval/Renaissance Seminar, the Medievalists@Penn reading group and the Gender, Sexuality, and Women's Studies reading group — made those connections easy for me. At a small liberal arts college, however, I don't have the luxury of specialized working groups with their formal structure to develop ideas, or dozens of colleagues with similar backgrounds and methodologies. At a small liberal arts college, I find myself fighting the constant temptation with colleagues to revert back to discussing teaching, what we have in common, instead of stretching myself to discuss our very different research agendas, which involves a lot of explanation. Planning to get lunch or coffee to specifically discuss our current research, or making a conscious effort to ask about a friend's work, is a stretch but has helped me understand their work better and often yielded new ideas for me as well.

Conversations with colleagues have given me a fresh perspective on existing research interests that can also cycle back into teaching. At present, I do not teach the material that forms the basis of my scholarly writing and research. Without that really direct, obvious link between classroom praxis and research agenda, I've found that leveraging my colleagues' expertise to rethink the foundational ideas about my research helps me sustain the "teacher-scholar" balance. Chatting with friends about my current teaching and writing helps me narrow the gap between my on-campus commitments and my long-term research interests. Casual conversations with our resident classicist Philip Walsh, for example, led to us holding a one-time special event that brought together students from his Elementary Greek class, my general education course on the Bible as Literature, and my upper-level English majors seminar on Anglo-Saxon Language and Literature. We worked together to create the symposium, in which students from each class read aloud and discussed the account of the nativity from Luke's gospel in Greek and Anglo-Saxon. Since both Phil and I work on translation and reception, this exchange was a chance to integrate our teaching and research, with some exciting discoveries about etymology and cultural inheritance happening in the moment with the students. The students enjoyed the program and brought those ideas back to subsequent classes. Phil and I have been able to continue that conversation about translation with more knowledge of each other's research and background, which keeps those ideas fresher in my mind. In the course of lunches with my medievalist colleague in the history department, Janet Sorrentino, she brought up her own recent research on Muslim travel writing. Janet inspired me to teach some Arab travel writers alongside Mandeville in a Medieval Literature survey course. Instead of having to research the genre and its context from scratch, I could leverage her background to help me prepare to teach those new texts. I'm constantly talking with colleagues to glean ideas, questions, and expertise from them, whether it's the poet who talks about reworking history as metaphor, the business professor enthused about revision and rhetorical precision in writing, or the philosopher excited about feminist theory developments. Some of their ideas have led to better teaching strategies, and other times just having the conversation about common interests keeps me motivated to carve out time for my own writing.

Being immersed in the work of teaching can make encounters with colleagues' research newly vital and transformative because the stakes can be so much higher. My friend Jonathan Hsy visited campus last spring and presented his current research on the history of eyeglasses in the Middle Ages. Before Jon's visit, I prepared my Arthurian Literature students by discussing the burgeoning field of disability studies. A student then decided she wanted to bring that perspective to bear on Chrétien de Troyes' *Perceval*. Her sharp and insightful essay on Perceval as an autistic character completely transformed my understanding of the text. Those new insights led to me rethinking my Attendance and Participation syllabus policy, with help from Andrea Vassar, director of the Disability Services and the Office of Academic Skills on campus. This more precise and explicit policy, structured like a "social script" that spells out expectations in a particular scenario, has actually resulted in a better classroom environment since expectations are now more clear for all students. Talking about research as a regular activity with colleagues and students can yield these kinds of fortuitous benefits, and can help us bridge the divide between the teaching that ties us to our home institutions and the research that nurtures us.

Building connections to active artists and practitioners, a second and very different form of collaboration, has required me to think more critically about how what I teach connects with the present. I try to attend as many presentations and craft talks by visiting artists as I can. The presence on campus of the Rose O'Neill Literary House and its attached Print Shop, with hundred-year-old antique letterpress, offers unique opportunities to ground my students in material texts, such as when I could bring Medieval Literature students in to handle lead type and see letterpress for themselves as we discussed early printing. Then a visiting typography designer, Cyrus Highsmith, helped students connect unfamiliar manuscript culture with their daily experiences with electronic and print typeface. By explaining his process and showing finished typefaces he had designed, Cyrus attuned students to the importance of empty space and legibility as key elements in designing lettering and the look of a page. Students returned to studying the mise-en-page of online images of the Auchinleck Manuscript with new attention to line breaks and empty space as actively creating meaning. Instead of just talking about the content, students looked at manuscript images and discussed, for example, how rhyming couplets reinforced line breaks, and how stanza organization in Middle English romances seemed more significant units of meaning in the edited versions than the manuscript, where they were not as visually prominent, changing how they read the text. The modern artist's perspective helped us deepen the literary sophistication of our class discussion.

In classes I have taught to date, we've enjoyed visits by several other working artists: a dramaturge, a director, a lighting designer, a playwright, and a poet. These artists will note elements of craft I did not initially see, as when an actor physically shows us all a staging problem in Hrotsvit of Gandersheim's plays, or a published poet discusses an adaptation of alliterative meter in modernist poetry influenced by Anglo-Saxon traditions. Such insights always deepen and enrich the conversation. In turn, that often encourages students to ask more questions and try to connect our literary, historical material to their own experiences in the creative and performing arts. Seeing advanced practitioners offer those connections models for how students to connect their own avocations to medieval literature and culture. Those connections make my potentially marginalized position — working on historically distant and little-known material — more clearly central to the humanities and arts as whole on campus, both for me and for my students.

Finally, the third strategy I've used in forging collaborations has been in exchanges with other subject matter experts, which often takes me beyond the humanities, and means I'm offering a literary historical perspective to others. The temptation will always be to talk about teaching, the easiest common denominator, but there's validation in discussing research with a friend who hears your ideas develop, even if they don't know the context. When I was researching torture, I visited my colleague Rachel Durso's class on the sociology of punishment. I walked students through medieval and early modern methods of judicial torture, incarceration, and punishment to give a historical context to how systems of punishment reflect cultural values. In turn I learned from Rachel about post-1800 American penal systems, which often were presented as enlightened in contrast to "medieval" models. Asking our ornithology expert Jennie Carr about bird behavior in poems by Anne Bradstreet arose from a student question in a class on premodern women writers: "To what extent is the bird behavior described in a poem merely a metaphor, or does it describe how real birds behave?" In answering that question, Jennie and I discovered many cases of birds in poetry imitating the behavior of birds in real life. We are now collaborating together on an NEH-funded project contrasting how birds are depicted in Chaucer's "Parliament of Fowls" against actual bird behavior and modern day classification systems. We will be working with both my own students from Chaucer and Medieval Literature and Jennie's Evolutionary Biology class to explore these questions, bringing together biology and English majors. That joint research will form the basis of a talk in Fall 2016, as well as an interactive gallery exhibit open to the public in downtown Chestertown. All of this work will be incorporated into a website to serve as a teaching resource for others interested in teaching "Parliament of Fowls," which I will be piloting myself by teaching the poem in a British literature survey course in Fall 2016. Hopefully, just as English and poetry fans will glean some better understanding of birds and the natural world from this project, science students and colleagues will learn about the historical roots of observing the natural world and what medieval studies has to teach them.

When I say "subject matter experts," I include collaborations with my faculty-librarian colleagues, who constantly help me and my students to engage more deeply with primary sources. My most recent completed digital humanities project with students came about because a colleague in Environmental Studies mentioned his work with the MIT Annotation Studio, a collaborative web-based annotation tool that enables students to annotate texts with video, pictures, web links, and comments. Specialists in Academic Technology helped me implement the technology side so that I could focus on helping students create these multimedia annotations. In their pop-up annotations, students considered how the research they did changed their understanding of Middle English romances — as when some students developed more sympathy for the mother in *Lay le Freine,* for example, after reading articles about medieval childhood, and they noted their reactions on the specific lines they now read differently. Another set of students became more disturbed by the Saracen/Christian conflict in King of Tars once they learned about coexisting communities in medieval Spain. They linked the text to images of historical maps they found online to illustrate the proximity and interconnections among members of these religious groups, demonstrating that these conflicts were not inevitable in the medieval world. Densely annotating these texts in this way would not be possible without this technology that enabled multiple students to work simultaneously and collectively with a variety of media. The students gained greater historical perspective because they were working with modern technology that enabled them to connect everything they were learning back to the text in a visual, interactive way.

My biggest future gambit in bringing historical perspective will be a planned summer course in England for summer 2018, co-taught with Laura Eckelman. As a professor and professional practitioner of theatrical design and productions, Laura will be able guide our students' exploration of performative and contemporary elements of the medieval mystery cycle plays performed that summer in their original towns of Chester and York. Her expertise on space and place, and more recent theatrical history, will be invaluable. Our hope is that students will become deeply versed in our main theme, "Ways we relate to the past in present locations." Whereas I'm firmly rooted in (relatively) stable texts and a past that has always already happened, Laura brings an entirely different perspective as someone who works in the present. Whatever happens in that class, I suspect I will probably come back more changed than the students.

Developing these collaborative strategies has taken time. When I started at Washington College, I thought about intellectual community primarily in terms of shared research interests. Graduate school training, our major conferences like Kalamazoo and Leeds, and our professional organizations all prepare medievalists to flit across disciplinary boundaries. But we don't always cultivate cross-period connections — or going beyond the humanities — with the same assiduity. On the advice of a friend I joined Twitter to stay connected with the larger medievalist community when I took this job. That helps to motivate my own research and makes conferences livelier events as I meet up with other medievalist Twitterati, and live-tweet panels. But to my surprise, the real transformation has been expanding my own sense of what it means to be a *collaborative medievalist,* going beyond my discipline to work actively with others here at Washington College. I don't think I've felt this excited about learning new things, without even knowing where they might lead, since I started my own undergraduate education.

Make Yourself At Home

John P. Sexton, Bridgewater State University

When I landed my job in the Department of English at Bridgewater State University, I was undeniably a bit of a naïf. This wasn't the fault of my graduate program, my dissertation directors, or the many other people who tried to help me find my way to professional readiness. And yet, when I received the all-important call from the then-Dean of Humanities offering me a position, I responded (as I'd been trained to do) by saying firmly, "Thank you so much for the offer. I'll need to talk it over with my wife, of course…" and then continued, "Then I can call you back tomorrow to accept the offer." I was, to put it mildly, not in a dominant bargaining position when I called back.

Nine years and a successful run at tenure later, I still have a great deal to learn. And as anyone who knows or works with me can attest, I'm still jamming my foot in my mouth on a regular basis. But nearly a decade working as an isolated medievalist with research and teaching interests all over the map has bought me a certain degree of professional confidence. Some of it is even deserved. As I've built a small corner of medieval studies for myself (with the help of colleagues, friends, students, and the occasional administrator), I've picked up bits of wisdom I wish I'd known when I was starting on my professional path. What follows is an attempt to organize those scattered bits of knowledge into a set of suggestions to help medievalists — whether newly-minted or mid-career — make themselves at home in their jobs.

1. Get on the scheduling committee for your department, or at least befriend the person/people who are in charge of scheduling, and pay attention to the scheduling needs of your students.

This isn't to say that you should be overly mercenary about the best course slots. You *definitely* shouldn't make yourself obnoxious, wheedling, or overly demanding when dealing with the *éminences grises* in charge of your scheduling. But the fact is that Medieval courses, often elective and often well outside of our students' comfort zones, need all the help they can get in presenting an appealing option to our students — especially at commuter-heavy schools or colleges with high percentages of so-called "non-traditional students." Getting those courses on the books is one challenge. Getting them filled is another. There's nothing wrong with a bit of careful and polite self-advocacy to get those courses scheduled at times when students are more likely to be looking for a course to fit their schedule. At my university, many students commute via a rail system that, several times a day, drops them off or picks them up right on campus. Convenient for them — and for me, since a quick check of the train schedule tells me when those students are likely to be arriving on and leaving campus in large numbers. A few minutes' work with my school's course time grid and I know exactly when the largest numbers of students are likely to be on campus and can build my offerings to suit those patterns.

You may find that this strategy means that you will have to be more flexible in your teaching times or your course offerings than you would like. Well, yes. You will. Your courses will need to make minimum enrollment numbers in order for you to teach within your own area. But in order to prove your worth as an expert in your field to your colleagues, your administration, and the committees who oversee tenure and promotion review, you want those numbers to be as close to the course maximum as they can be. Ideally, your specialist course in Monastic Life, Byzantine Art, Continental Church Architecture 1000–1500, or Outlaws and Exiles of Anglo-Scandinavian Literature should be bursting at the seams — a student complaint that there isn't *enough* seat availability in your Material Culture in the Middle Ages course will certainly get your chair's attention, and opportunities to teach those courses will come along more often as a result.

2. Teach entry-level and non-majors courses as often as you can, and make those courses an advertisement for you as a teacher/scholar.

These include any first-year or introductory courses your department teaches to most or all new students, but also courses that fulfill non-major requirements for your institution. My circumstance in an English department means that I have regular opportunities to teach first-year composition courses, but also the writing-intensive literature surveys and theme courses that draw students from all majors. You may or may not have much control over which courses you teach, especially if you are contingent faculty or early in your career (though you should absolutely be working to gain whatever control you can; see step 1 above). But often, disadvantaged scheduling means you are more likely to be teaching the types of courses I'm describing. And when you bring your top work to those courses (with the occasional unit or even mere reference to medieval subjects), you are an advertisement for yourself as well as your subject.

As a lone medievalist, you are, for better or worse, the face of medieval studies in your department or institution. And when students make registration decisions about electives, area requirements, or future requirement-filling courses, they look at a number of criteria. While it's difficult to quantify any one motive force behind students' course selection decisions in the aggregate, previous familiarity and comfort with the instructor is almost certainly a factor.[1] Providing students with impressive, creative, engaging lessons in these early courses will build demand for your showpiece courses when you have the opportunity to teach them. And whether or not your lower-level or campus-service courses are able to heavily feature medieval studies, the goodwill created may be the deciding factor in students signing up for those medieval courses when they're offered. Under ideal circumstances, students may begin to advocate for those courses on your behalf as they become interested in returning to your classroom and learning about the subject that fires your interest.

3. Take shameless advantage of open-topic and wide-reaching courses to create "funnels" for your medieval courses and to produce trial-runs of courses that you might eventually want to introduce as permanent courses.

In the decade I've spent at Bridgewater State University, a combination of First- and Second-Year Seminars (required of all students) and Writing-Intensive courses (Core requirements across the board) have allowed me to offer several courses introducing individual medieval texts or medieval-adjacent works and approaches to the general student population. Permutations

---

[1] Without delving into the complexities inherent in student course evaluation and self-reporting, both common sense and a survey of the literature make clear that, while students' ratings of professors may not be valid as a means of assessing the quality of their received education, they can predict the likelihood of a return to a specific professor in later semesters. See Wendy Bryce Wilhelm and Charles Comegys, "Course selection decisions by students on campuses with and without published teaching evaluations," *Practical Assessment, Research & Evaluation* 9 (2004), http://PAREonline.net/getvn.asp?v=9&n=16; and Anthony G. Greenwald and Gerald M. Gillmore, "No Pain, No Gain? The Importance of Measuring Course Workload in Student Ratings of Instruction," *Journal of Educational Psychology* 89, no. 4 (1997): 743–51. A less formal but still clear-eyed assessment is offered by Cat Reynolds, "Factors Affecting the Choice of Courses in College," http://classroom.synonym.com/factors-affecting-choice-courses-college-2817.html. Reynolds lists "Who's the Professor?" as the second factor students consider during registration.

have included courses on the Oxford Inklings, Hero's Journey, Apocalyptic Literature, and Outlaw Literature, each with its own ways to tie in to my more traditional medieval courses. A student who spends a semester reading J.R.R. Tolkien and C.S. Lewis through the lens of their dedication to and immersion in medieval studies comes to my Medieval British Literature or Sagas course with a great deal to contribute in peer discussion. Moreover, that student already begins the course primed to study the medieval as a meaningful field with clear links to more recent and familiar post-medieval traditions. A student who takes an Outlaws course with me and reads Grettir's saga or the Saga of Án Bow-Bender will (with any luck) actively seek out the Sagas course as an extension of their newly-kindled enthusiasm for Icelandic medieval literature.

Also, there's a logical extension here of the earlier point about scheduling. Many of the freshman-level or non-majors courses at your school, regardless of the type of institution you work at, are likely to be much more open-ended in their subject requirements than the courses for majors. That lack of specificity might exist due to focus elsewhere (an emphasis on course outcomes, a compromise among several departments offering the course, etc.), but it also may be a hook baited to entice faculty to offer those courses. Take the bait. Even if the medieval only shows up in small ways, it can still provide opportunities to build projects, reading units, or entire courses around medieval studies, and your enthusiasm and energy level for that material will serve as an advertisement all by itself.

4. If your course assignment doesn't offer an obvious way to foreground medieval studies, find a place for "five minutes of medieval studies." Get creative about this.

No matter the course you're teaching, there are hopefully ample opportunities to draw student interest to your own subject. Very few courses offer *no* chance to incorporate an element of medieval studies. Courses on film, philosophy, literature, art, history, etc. will likely all offer fairly straightforward ways to engage with your interest in the medieval. Nearly all courses, obviously, are generally designed with room for at least *some* creativity on the instructor's part. Even if you are teaching a rigidly-organized course with no room for deviation, the occasional quick aside during a discussion on some other point, if done well and often, can build interest.

If the course you're teaching offers little or no chance to incorporate medieval studies directly, you may have to think outside the course limits. Recommend to promising students that they read an epic poem, take in a nearby museum (with a medieval component, of course), read a book of popular history on a medieval topic, or consider an independent study (preferably on a subject of research interest to you as well).

If that doesn't seem likely or practical either, or if you're doing all that but want to try something more, there's another solution — something I've come to think of as "five-minute medievalism." When we dissertate and prepare for the job market, most of us are drilled on the importance of an "elevator talk" — a two-minute explanation of our research that "hooks" a listener without drowning them in the minutiae of our work. It's great advice, but too many of us jettison it once we find teaching positions — failing to recognize that each generation of students needs that same introduction to our subjects, and that same listener-friendly introduction. Five-minute medievalism is a version of that elevator talk, and it's easily done. Just show up early to class or hang around for a few minutes after the meeting ends. In the course of a few minutes' conversation, make a point of casually mentioning how well your medieval course is going or some great bit of material you're covering later that day. Ask students how their papers are going, and offer advice using the material you're currently working on. Quote from the Benedictine Rule, Marie de France, or Geoffrey Chaucer. Ask about a tee-shirt that seems promising for your purposes.[2]

---

[2] I once ended up in a semester-long conversation with a trio of students in two separate class sections because of a stray question about a shirt advertising a metal band named Týr. Two of those students later took my Icelan-

My favorite tactic is to find an excuse — no matter how flimsy — to break into Middle English or Anglo-Saxon at least a couple of times over the semester in my non-medieval courses. I then offer to spend a couple of minutes teaching students to "get the hang of" pronunciation "in case you decide to take a course on that." It goes without saying that the bits of poetry I teach them are calibrated to intrigue or delight students. Spending an office hour teaching a business major to recite the "hot coulter" scene from "The Miller's Tale" or helping a sports medicine major to design a tattoo of Byrhtwold's *The Battle of Maldon* speech may bring an elective-seeking student to one of my medieval courses a year or two later — or it may just result in a student in sports medicine wandering around my campus showing off a new tattoo, knowing a bit about the honor code of an Anglo-Saxon warrior, and maybe telling a friend or two where and how she learned it.

5. Teach — or create — one or two flexible courses that will allow you to showcase your scholarly profile.

In an ideal world, we would all be allowed to bring teaching to our departments that showcase our expertise and enthusiasm for medieval studies. Since very few of us will find life so congenial to our dreams, it's important to build and safeguard a couple of "showpiece" courses that will allow you to demonstrate the value of having a medievalist around the place.

As you develop a set of courses that you teach regularly, seek a balance of general-appeal courses, open-topic courses, and "signature" courses. Ideally, you want to offer a cross-section of the breadth of your field of knowledge, the depth of your knowledge in your areas of focus, and your capacity for creativity within medieval studies. My own current set of courses includes (in addition to Composition courses and several campus-wide courses for non-majors): single-author courses on Chaucer and

---

dic Sagas course, and I learned a tremendous amount of ephemera about Viking metal.

Shakespeare; surveys of medieval British literature and literature of the European Middle Ages; The History of the English Language; seminars on Law and Literature, Dream Visions, and Medieval Outlaw literature; and a course I created for Sagas of the Icelanders. Obviously, the range and number of your own courses will be determined in part by professional circumstance and field. If one or more medieval courses *do* already exist, your job is so much the easier. Your chief concern then should be to seek out any programs, minors, or cross-department partnerships that might drive students into your courses.

In either case, it's important to mix showcase moments for your areas of greatest expertise with flexibility about your area of teaching. As you undoubtedly know, one of the less tangible advantages a medievalist brings to his or her department is the ability to cover wide swathes of material in various forms. Our boundaries tend to be wide — your colleague who teaches only early nineteenth century literature or Fauvist Post-Impressionist art, resisting all offers and pressure to expand into apparently related areas of focus, is not the model you want to follow. Look instead to the teaching CVs of medievalists at peer institutions to your own. Get a sense of what they're offering, think about how to translate that to your own situation, and show the fruits of that research in your teaching. And when in discussion with your colleagues about course offerings and coverage, take full advantage of the breadth of your knowledge to offer to teach a wide range of materials. That flexibility is a selling point for medievalists, and you should make it work for you. And a course designed around ideas, questions, or topics carries the further advantage of growing with your scholarly agenda, allowing your teaching to reflect your intellectual growth and shifting focus over the years. Remember — you're in this for the long haul.

At the same time, that "showpiece" course is something you want to have up and running as soon as possible. Your circumstances may place some limitations on the choice of subject — a regional campus without a dedicated major in your area may barely offer scope for even a survey course, while a more comprehensive institution may offer plenty of majors but no requirements that would drive those students to a premodern course. Regardless of the challenge offered by your situation, make your mark on your department's course offerings. Build a course that pushes the envelope slightly, while also working to make incremental changes to your institutional circumstances. Not enough students? Look for a partner institution in your area and seek a cross-listed course. Departmental (or administrative) resistance to medieval courses? Use (or create) a repeatable "special topics" course that you and your colleagues can fashion into what you want — and use that to make a case for your subject's popularity (see item 3 above). No requirements? Look for a course-outcome "hook" (Writing-Intensive, STEM, Teaching-Certification, etc.) that will allow students to fulfill existing requirements while taking your dream course. No matter what it takes, you want that course up and running before you go up for tenure — ideally to help your portfolio, but in any case to build a future full of desirable teaching for yourself.

6. Use pop culture, current events, intersections with areas of student interest or administrative concern, and your critical apparatus to reflect attention to your medieval interests.

This may seem an obvious statement, given that many medievalists are already answering the bell and bringing attention to public misapprehension of the medieval. Early-stage politicking during the 2016 Presidential election cycle in the US offered multiple opportunities for high-profile scholarly intervention from our medievalist colleagues. In the fall of 2015, American business executive-turned-presidential aspirant Carly Fiorina claimed that her degree in medieval history and philosophy qualified her to deal with ISIS. David M. Perry offered a reasoned intellectual response to refute Fiorina's claim that the organization was trying to "drive us back to the middle ages, literally."³ Perry (like fellow medievalist John Terry⁴) noted that ISIS's ideology is a function of its modernist reinvention of the past, and crumbles in the face of actual medieval inquiry. Soon after this, another American would-be candidate, Ben Carson, confirmed his previously-stated opinion that the pyramids of Egypt were built and used as granaries, bringing scorn from all corners — and a number of astute responses noting that Carson's error has its roots in the writing of Gregory of Tours, the Irish monk Dicuil, and "John Mandeville," among others (while the myth was originally exploded more than 500 years ago by Bernhard von Breidenbach, who wrote in his 1486 *Peregrinatio in terram sanctam* that the pyramids were tombs and that the granary theory, held by only "the vulgar," was "clearly false").

Obviously, not every political season offers quite the low-hanging fruit described above. But popular entertainment's perpetual fascination with medieval themes provides "teaching moment" points of entry for any medievalist. As I write this essay, a debate is taking place in the public sphere of social media about whether medievalists ought to be offering public commentary on the HBO fantasy series *Game of Thrones*.⁵ Regardless of one's position on the subject, the fact is that the debate itself raises the profile of medievalists as public intellectuals.⁶ Our field remains

---

3   Perry, David M. "No, Carly Fiorina, A Degree in Medieval History Doesn't Qualify You to Fight ISIS," *The Guardian* (6 October 2015), http://www.theguardian.com/commentisfree/2015/oct/06/carly-fiorina-medieval-history-degree-fight-isis.

4   Terry, John. "Why ISIS Isn't Medieval," *Slate* (19 February 2015), http://www.slate.com/articles/news_and_politics/history/2015/02/isis_isn_t_medieval_its_revisionist_history_only_claims_to_be_rooted_in.html.

5   Philippa Byrne, "Why Medievalists Should Stop Talking About *Game of Thrones*," *The Conversation* (15 June 2016), http://theconversation.com/why-medievalists-should-stop-talking-about-game-of-thrones-61044; James Palmer, "Medievalists Should Talk About *Game of Thrones*," https://merovingianworld.wordpress.com/2016/06/17/medievalists-should-talk-about-game-of-thrones/.

6   For purposes of full disclosure: I should add that as someone who has spent the last three years live-tweeting commentary during episodes of the History Channel's program *Vikings* in my capacity as one half of the *Saga Thing* podcast team, I am unable to pretend to neutrality in this argument.

a (much-misunderstood) cultural touchstone for film, television, comic books, video games, board games, and other entertainments and art forms. Allowing students a few minutes to examine the History Channel's *Vikings* series alongside *Ragnars saga Loðbrókar* or taking to the internet to discuss medieval and modern iterations of Robin Hood needn't be a dilution of scholarly investigation. It's an acknowledgement that gateways into the discipline come in all forms, and that our students, our audiences, and even we ourselves come to the medieval through intellectual connections. Every time we enter into a conversation about the links (or lack thereof) between our subject and the world around us, we increase the visibility of our discipline while making a case to our students and colleagues for the necessity and relevance of our courses.

7. Look for and support promising students, and offer to sponsor or mentor them through independent studies, honor projects, capstone or portfolio projects, or any other introductory research.

About how much of your day's work is spent on actual medieval studies? Unless you're very fortunate in your professional situation, the answer is probably some variation of "not enough." Realistically, that means that some fairly large percentage of the criteria upon which decisions about your reappointment, tenure, or continued employment are made will not be based in a detailed appreciation of your scholarly profile as a medievalist. Mentoring students through investigatory work in medieval studies addresses this problem in two ways simultaneously. First, finding ways to link the medieval to your work with students is a low-risk, high-reward way to increase the amount of medieval studies you get to *do* in a day. Second, it's also an easy way to make sure that "medieval" remains an integral part of your campus profile and is a part of conversations about your work that go on when you're not around.

In this, our students are our best allies. For institutions that offer them, we can encourage promising students to conduct independent studies and other honors projects. One student writing a senior thesis on the disabled figure in the *Canterbury Tales* will do as much as a full course for the profile of your discipline, your position, and yourself. Depending on the visibility of undergraduate research at your institution, it may even do more to bring medieval studies to the attention of administrators and department chairs than your course offerings, since campus leaders often attend research celebrations and undergraduate presentations. Harnessing the enthusiasm of the most involved, capable members of your student population keeps medieval studies active and visible on your campus at times and in places where you are not the star of the show — and that's a powerful argument that you're doing your job well.

Even if the intersection of a student's interest and your work falls outside medieval studies, the reflected glory will be only to the good. This is particularly true if you can clearly articulate the role of your medieval work in guiding a student's academic success. Some years ago, I was a committee member for a graduate thesis on disability theory and *Dr. Jekyll and Mr. Hyde*. The student gave portions of his paper at a regional conference, and then won a campus "Distinguished Graduate Thesis Award" for his work. When I mentioned my own work on medieval disability in my tenure portfolio, this student's work was mentioned alongside it, along with a few leading points about connections to other "monstrous" figures in medieval literature.

8. Be available, whenever and wherever possible, to serve as a living advertisement for what you do.

Look for intersections that would allow you to work with outreach groups on campus, scholarly initiatives, speaker series, or book clubs in your capacity as a medievalist. Accept invitations to share your work on campus, particularly if those opportunities can be made to overlap with your teaching or scholarly plans — and learn to take the temperature of your campus to determine what sorts of work might be most appreciated or even expected of you. Don't be afraid to let your institution's motive forces and *raisons d'être* help shape your professional direction. Muhammad Ali's adage that "a man who views the world the same at fifty as he did at twenty has wasted thirty years of his life" might well be adapted to scholars who spend a career holding their scholarly lives aloof from their institutions. By all means, pursue the work that invigorates you. But don't spend all your energy arbitrarily fighting to preserve a scholarly agenda you brought with you if it means ignoring opportunities that current situation and your campus community open up.

A few years ago, I was invited to speak to the honors society at Bridgewater for their "Pizza with a Prof" series. I spoke about Campbell's Hero's Journey, a topic chosen because I was scheduled to teach two sections of a sophomore-level writing-intensive course on Heroes' Journeys (Campbell's and others) the following semester. I presented in part by inviting students to show off their knowledge of a set of texts by pairing them with various texts and taking them through the process of a Campbellian reading. Those texts, of course, were an even mix of modern cultural touchstones and medieval literature "greatest hits." Thus, an hour's work spent discussing the synchronicities of Gilgamesh, Luke Skywalker, Grettir Asmundarson, Harry Potter, Katniss Everdeen, and Sir Gawain produced unparalleled advertising for a specific course as well as general exposure for material from my upper-level medieval offerings, all directed to some of the University's most capable students, many of whom signed up and enlivened my courses over the next couple of years. *And* I got free pizza.

9. Forge an identity as a teacher/scholar.

Use your best students as you would colleagues in grad school. Think about what they have to say about the literature, and build your course structure around a combination of their interests and your own. To whatever extent your teaching assignments and project advisement make it feasible, bring your students into the intellectual world you inhabit in ways that will make sense to them, will mirror your time spent in scholarly endeavors, and create a sense of community for you all. An organized student group can create a well of on-campus enthusiasm for broad-based medieval studies. But even if that's too much to contemplate in the early going (or if your campus culture or employment situation makes creating a student organization unfeasible), a well-crafted course or two can build student interest in deeper and more intellectually rigorous engagement with medieval subjects. And though obvious, it bears pointing out that, if you're a lone medievalist, the students in your classes are *the only people you're likely to interact with face-to-face that day who are thinking about the same things you care about.* Learn to treat them like colleagues, like potential intellectual collaborators, and let them amaze you.

Build your assignments around the sort of work you'd like to be doing yourself, so that your assignment modeling doubles as prep for a conference paper, article, or book review you'd be doing anyway. I once found myself teaching a senior capstone course on Literature and the Law (obviously, pursuant to points 1, 3, and 5, this became Medieval Literature and the Law on my syllabus and in the electronic catalog for that semester). My students were building their research projects toward a final paper, and several planned to present their papers at local undergraduate conferences in addition to the in-class conference-style presentations I require of all my seminars. Over the course of the semester, I shared with my students various stages of a conference paper I was preparing on Anglo-Norman land law and the Northumbrian cult of St. Cuthbert. Eventually, because it seemed obvious to do so, I began to workshop the paper with my students alongside their own. A certain shaky fearlessness is required to bring your own first draft of an idea to your students, studded with unnecessary adjectives, forced parallelism, and mangled footnotes. But students were able to learn from my ongoing revision of the paper the importance of drafting and redrafting an idea for felicity of expression as well as for rigor, and I was able to prepare my teaching in part by eking out valuable hours for scholarly research and writing. And all along the way, we were building, together, a small community of medievalists bonding over the challenges of our work.

10. Use whatever knowledge of technology you might possess to build connections between yourself and other medievalists — and among the different parts of your professional identity.

This might be as simple as contributing to or starting a blog (*In The Middle,*[7] remember, began as a sandbox for a group of like-minded medievalists), participating in collaborative projects through social media (e.g., Elaine Treharne's *Beowulf By All* translation project[8]), getting yourself and your students involved with one of the ongoing wiki-type projects going on in all corners of academia (such as the *Medieval Disability Glossary,* which benefits from Cameron Hunt McNabb's students' research into word origins[9]), or even creating your own podcast or video channel for a "flipped classroom" model that can double as an outreach project.

This last has proved particularly successful for me. Dr. Andrew Pfrenger and I have spent the last couple of years devoting time to a podcast, *Saga Thing,* in which we discuss the plot, themes, and literary and critical contexts of each of the Icelandic Sagas in turn.[10] The show began as a flipped classroom experiment, providing us with a repository of preparation lectures for our students to access (I key my syllabus to specific assigned episodes of the podcast). Two of us speaking together provided a better dynamic for these discussions, and in collaborating we've both continued to learn from one another. But interest-

---

7   *In The Middle,* http://www.inthemedievalmiddle.com/.
8   This project is currently ongoing and is not yet available to the public.
9   *Medieval Disability Glossary,* http://medievaldisabilityglossary.wikispaces.com/Terms+Working+Page.
10 *Saga Thing,* http://sagathingpodcast.wordpress.com/. In the interest of promoting collaboration with other medievalists, it may be worth noting that Andy and I live and work over 600 miles apart; our recordings are facilitated by the use of social media and less than $300 worth of total equipment.

ingly, the podcast has also developed a small following outside of our students — several episodes have been downloaded over 7,000 times, and a group of listeners, expert in everything from mead production to historical archery, have begun contributing to our social media pages.[11] The podcast links my teaching, scholarship, professional collaborations, and public intellectual work and has become a part of my professional profile. It's also tremendous fun to do and gives me a reason to continue in-depth conversations with a colleague and friend.

11. Use everything and anything at your disposal to create interest in your subject — on and off your campus.

Generate a general-audience friendly version of a paper you're preparing, and offer to deliver it at a local library or as an on-campus open lecture. Write an introductory essay about your research area to be published in your faculty or alumni magazine (the alumni magazine option works particularly well if you can include some aspect of your teaching in the article). Unless it's actively frowned upon by your department, put up interesting-looking posters promoting your courses in the weeks leading up to student registration. Find out about local antiquarian societies in your area and offer to host a "research day" at the campus library (if locals aren't automatically provided with access to all library holdings and collections), including a short talk about your own archival work as part of the after-lunch remarks. Speak to students, especially, whenever an opportunity crops up — and work in intriguing anecdotes about the materials you teach.

If you're meeting resistance or a lack of funding to bringing a speaker to campus, you may have to get creative. Are there travel funds to defray *your* travel costs, but no money to bring a speaker to campus? Find another scholar at a peer institution

---

[11] Andy and I are also scheduled to offer our first workshop on podcasting for medievalists at the University of Denver's Seafaring Conference in November of 2016.

and offer a home-and-away swap: each of you visits the other's campus, delivers a paper and/or guest-teaches courses, and generally does things that will contribute to the campus profile of medieval studies. No money at all? Stay at each other's houses and travel and eat cheaply while you visit, or use Skype or Googlechat to bring a guest speaker to your classroom.

Reach out to other groups, fields, offices, and specialists on your own campus. When you're done with that, reach out to people on *other* campuses. Seek regional support — within a year of taking your job, you should know the three nearest museums or collections relevant to medieval studies, and within three years, you should be on a name basis with the people who provide access to them. Look for opportunities to collaborate with fellow medievalists (you're going to want and need the support), but also look for ways to collaborate with colleagues who have a reputation for good teaching at your institution. Find out about the possibility of shared courses, mirrored courses, patterns of student transfer, etc.

In other words: Get creative. Get active. Get noticed.

12. In the middle of all this, stay connected to your friends and mentors from graduate school. I cannot emphasize this enough.

Never underestimate the power of those grad-school bonds — collaboration with your former coevals is a tremendous source of support, and can be a powerful way to build a network in your discipline. A case in point: the Lone Medievalist is a product of grad-student friendship. The organization grew out of a 2015 roundtable at the International Congress on Medieval Studies in Kalamazoo sponsored by a blog (*MassMedieval*) which Dr. Kisha Tracy and I started when we both landed jobs in the same university system in Massachusetts. The point of that panel was to think about how other medievalists could create the same sense of community that Kisha and I have enjoyed with our fellow alumni from the University of Connecticut Medieval Studies program. Kisha is one of several UConn alum with whom I actively collaborate (Andrew Pfrenger, co-host of *Saga Thing*, is another — see point 11 above). My career has been shaped in large part by those friendships, through shared syllabi, conference panel collaboration, co-written articles, co-edited volumes (including this one), invitations to guest-lecture on campuses, and more.

While you're at it, continue to take an interest in and be available to the next generations of grad students making their way through the program you came from — if there's already a way for you to connect with them, get involved. If not, maybe all that's needed is that you reach out to a gifted organizer among the current generation of grad students or to your old dissertation director. Think about what you learned, or wish you could have learned, from those who walked the same path before you. Have a cup of coffee with a current grad student at a conference. Take an interest in their careers. Share what you know, and learn what they can teach you.

If you don't have that sense of connection to your alma mater, or if your grad school didn't surround you with other dedicated medievalists, use professional societies and social media to build that network of support and collegiality. The Lone Medievalist exists, in large part, as a way for otherwise unsupported medievalists to meet, gather (in real and virtual spaces), share ideas, and generally feel less alone and more connected in our work. By all means, take advantage of the organization for that purpose — but any scholarly society should offer a starting point for the sharing of ideas, for potential collaborators to meet, and for resources to be shared or distributed. Again, if it doesn't, maybe it needs to — and you're as likely a candidate as any to make that happen.

Ultimately, all this advice boils down to two directives:

1. Your job is not perfect. For that matter, neither are you. But you have something to offer any institution. And no matter where you work or how overstretched you are, you can still be a professional, productive medievalist. The key is to stop thinking of teaching, scholarship, service, advising, and

all the other parts of your job as separate demands on your time. The more you can integrate the parts of your professional self, the more productive you will be. Learn to think of students as collaborators, co-workers as colleagues, and institutional situations as relevant and valid shaping forces on the focus and venue of your work, and your productivity and satisfaction will increase.

2. Stop thinking of yourself as being limited to being a *lone* anything. You are probably surrounded by students, colleagues, personal acquaintances, and local communities, all of them potential collaborators. You may well have administrators, campus programs, or nearby institutions hungry for the expertise, energy, and enthusiasm you can bring to a field so often shrouded in mystery and misunderstanding for the uninitiated. And you have professional societies, social media, and your friends in the field from which to seek collaboration and support, and to which you can offer your own perspectives and knowledge. You may be lonely, but you are not alone.

This Eremitic Life

Notes from the North

Laura Saetveit Miles, University of Bergen

LETTER I
November, year 0

Dear ———

We have arrived in Norway. On the trip I began Mary Wollstonecraft's 1796 *Letters Written during a Short Residence in Sweden, Norway, and Denmark* (Broadwell, excellent edition) and have been inspired to write you real letters on real paper about our big adventure moving abroad and my new (first, real, permanent) job. I am now officially associate (!!!) professor or the much more delicious title "førsteamanuensis" of English literature in the Institute for Foreign Languages at the University of Bergen, Norway. The other languages in our department include French, Spanish, German, Arabic, Chinese, Japanese, Russian… both literature and linguistic sides. I have five other colleagues in English literature: total three for British, three for American (picture a buoy right in the middle of the Atlantic, demarcating the fields). No one has mentioned if medieval English literature was ever taught here before. Either it never was — or the institutional memory has been lost — or they want to forget — or they haven't thought to mention whose shoes I am stepping into. Well, they are mine now.

First advantage is that I can teach basically any medieval course I dream up. Or, any medieval-early modern-onward course, for that matter. Lots of flexibility before 1800 if it's not a pure Shakespeare course (covered by a colleague). I am excited to teach as an upper-level seminar the Visions and Madness in Medieval Literature course I developed at University of ———. *Pearl,* Hoccleve, *Yvain,* Julian, Margery, *Hamlet,* with some Barthes, Foucault, Gilbert & Gubar, and this great chapter by Littau on affective reading, just recommended to me by someone here.

Tomorrow I begin working hard on the lectures I will give in January for the team-taught Introduction to British Literature and Culture survey course: eight lectures, each 90 minutes long with a 15-minute break, over three weeks. All English program bachelors students and other students as well, about 140 total, take the course. My colleague who works on Shakespeare and things after usually does some of those pre-1800 lectures but he has teaching relief this year, so in future years we will share. Then other faculty and PhD students take care of the remaining 200 years of British literature.

The survey syllabus from last year starts in 1550. Guess where it starts now: Cædmon's "Hymn." Then I've added Chaucer's *Miller's Tale,* a few Middle English lyrics, a bit of Julian of Norwich, and also added Elizabeth I to the so-called "Renaissance poetry" lecture (someday, someday, it will be early modern, so everyone doesn't get confused with the twelfth-century renaissance). Previously the earliest female author had been Mary Shelley. I've also replaced *The Man of Feeling* with Eliza Haywood's *Fantomina,* which I know from orals, and is so fantastic: masquerade, gender, power, ruinous birth, exile to French monastery. Other lectures I've inherited include the "metaphysicals," eighteenth-century poetry, and a bunch of Swift. So I basically cover 800–1800. No problem.

Our generalist oral exams: I'm not sure it ever occurred to me in graduate school, studying furiously over that long short summer all those years ago, that such broad reading was basically an investment in a very real future where I have to teach anything. At the time it seemed like a distraction from learning

Latin and reading twelfth-century anchoritic guides. I mostly recall thinking that we had to cover other periods in order to be good conversationalists at academic cocktail parties (which has in fact been true). And also obviously because *literature*. But did anyone ever tell us we had to learn this stuff because we would actually have to lecture for two hours on the rise of the novel to 140 students? *My God, but I'm a medievalist!* Don't get me wrong, it is invigorating and challenging and stretching me to be a better teacher. But when I was actually given the luxury of time to study outside my field I really don't think that it occurred to me I would be quite so responsible for teaching so much of that material (and more). Did you think about that? Do you think that now? But you are one of many medievalists…

So far it is as rainy as we were warned — Bergen is the rainiest city in Europe — and we quickly upgraded our raingear to Norwegian brands. So far my distant relatives and our new neighbors are lovely and more welcoming than we could have hoped, just as Wollstonecraft describes her Scandinavian hosts, greeting her with "so much overflowing of heart, and fellow feeling, that only benevolence, and the honest sympathy of nature, diffused smiles over my countenance." Though perhaps that will not be the case with all our new acquaintances, whose politeness somehow leaves me feeling lonely; "for the politeness of the north seems to partake of the coldness of the climate, and the rigidity of its iron-sinewed rocks" (56).

xoL

LETTER II
March, year 1

Dear ———

I have finally reached the top of the mountain we live on, Ulriken. I've never really known mountains, much less run up them — never lived among them, much less on one. Our house is at about 170 meters over sea level (moh, *metre over havet,* på norsk) and the top of Ulriken is 643 moh. I suppose it's not really that high in terms of all mountains everywhere but when you're up this far north on the earth, it is high enough that there are no trees above about 550 moh, where the thin soil cannot hold them, and it can be a completely different climate. A month ago: somewhat terrifying Arctic winter. Ice, rocks, wind-scraped snow. Now: still snow in the shadows and lees, most rocks reborn. Lichen, neon green and bright white, grey and brown. "Before I came here, I could scarcely have imagined that a simple object, rocks, could have admitted of so many interesting combinations — always grand, and often sublime" (119). From the top of Ulriken you can see over a huge jagged wilderness surrounding the city, and beyond to snowier higher mountains, and fjords, and the North Sea, and on clear days across the fjords to even higher mountains with white glaciers touching clouds. Even though it is something like under 2 km to the top it takes me 45 minutes hard work and I now have to carry a backpack with food and water. It is a new kind of wonderful exhaustion running up a mountain.

I have begun Norwegian classes: Norskkurs. Having survived seven years of graduate school and Latin etc. and orals and MLA interviews and job talks I really want to wallow in expertise, just roll around and luxuriate in the authority of a real job, but no, I have to be a student again and learn this new language from scratch. Old English will help: *Jeg heter Laura*. As in: *hatan! Wæs se grimma gæst Grendel haten / mære mearcstapa!*

Work is going fine. Sometimes I feel a bit intellectually lonely. And not just because everyone works with their office doors closed (though the quiet can be lovely). After so many years in medieval-rich institutions with an embarrassment of lectures and seminars, I have yet to hear of any lectures I want to go to. I think I am not on the right mailing lists. This is literally true as I just became aware of a Medieval Philology research group, mostly Old Norse and Latin faculty, and now that I'm on their list they have some interesting lectures. But many are in Norwegian. I can't really drop by someone's office and air a new idea for my chapter because no one on campus has read *Ancrene Wisse* or the two ME versions of Aelred's *Institutione Inclusorum* or *Love's Mirror* or *Speculum Devotorum* (so great). My colleagues sometimes ask me how my work is going, which is nice, and maybe someday I will actually answer honestly because I will not be afraid of alienating or boring them.

Next month brings Kalamazoo, and then New Chaucer Society even more north in Reykjavik. "My thoughts fly from this wilderness to the polished circles of the world, till recollecting its vices and follies, I bury myself in the woods, but find it necessary to emerge again, that I may not lose sight of the wisdom and virtue which exalts my nature" (108), Mary writes. There are only some woods around me as they soon give way to brush and scrub. But twenty minutes' run straight up from the end of my street and the hum of the city is gone and I can hear the wind across the rocks, the little mountain birds tittering — I think of clever ways to teach things and clever ways to write things. And soon for a moment I'll be back in my natural habitat surrounded by people who like to dish about the Wife of Bath and queer theory.

Send news!

xoL

LETTER III
June, year 1

Dear ———

How is everything? I am immersed in grading at the moment and taking a break to write you. Have you ever noticed that in the US we give out A, B, C, D, F — but no E? Well, I have found it: hiding in the snowy mountains of Norway. We give out E grades like Halloween candy — that is, like the Halloween candy nobody wants. There is almost no grade inflation in Norway: the C really means average, and there will be more D and E grades than A and B grades, and there will be F grades. A lot of them.

Then that makes the A grades much more like the full-size Snicker bars they really should be.

In Norwegian universities undergraduate and graduate classes are almost always assessed by one of three formats: a final "school" exam, between 4 and 6 hours long; a take-home exam of one or two weeks; or a slightly longer term paper with the teacher providing some feedback during the drafting process. Sometimes there is also a follow-up oral exam for the term paper. No other parts of the course contribute to the final grade: no smaller assignments, no participation, etc etc. These final assessments are graded completely anonymously (or in the case of supervised term papers, as much as possible) and now after we have submitted grades we are not even allowed to find out which student got what grade. I think the anonymity is very important for avoiding biases of all kinds, especially gender, yet I do miss the final reveal of names after blind grading in giving some sense of understanding about how students succeeded or didn't, and being able to apply that knowledge to the improvement of my teaching.

Beyond being graded completely anonymously, every final assessment is also graded *twice*: by *two faculty members* who agree on each final grade together. Most of the time there is an internal and an external examiner: the internal examiner is the faculty member in charge of the course (or involved with it, as in team-taught courses) and the external examiner is another faculty member from a different Norwegian university. Each examiner independently considers what grade each exam deserves, and then they chat on the phone or via Skype or occasionally in person, to come to an agreement for each and every grade. The external examiner is paid money. The idea is that this double grading helps to standardize grades across the whole country, to prevent grade inflation, and to give fair and balanced evaluations of students' work. By and large, the system is effective (though expensive).

But what if no one in the country has read the texts you teach except your students and you? Because I'm realizing now that there are actually no other Middle English literature professors in Norway. In the whole country. Well, I met one in Oslo, but she has just retired, and technically she was in linguistics though she researches the same literature and culture I do. There are lots of linguists who teach History of the English Language and Old and Middle English, and they are about as comfortable with literary approaches to the material as I am to advanced linguistic approaches, or as any of us would be with deep cave diving: it would make us very very nervous (read: terrified) — so they cannot help. To be sure, I've been put in touch with excellent external examiners — other English literature faculty in Norway — who have past experience with Chaucer and a few other medieval texts. But these are specialists from other fields peering back into the Middle Ages. So it looks like I am the lone medievalist for English literature in the country of Norway. Fortunately the population is only about 5 million (i.e. equivalent to the population of Brooklyn and Queens).

So now it's just me and my 15 upper-level undergraduates who have all read *Pearl,* Hoccleve's *Complaint,* Chrétien's *Yvain,* Margery, Julian, and *Hamlet* to top it off — us bound together by this syllabus on madness and visions. I tell them they are each in a unique position of actually having become, in just a semester, a kind of national authority on their paper topic — that they must inhabit the essayist's "I" with confidence and gusto, to persuade the external reader not only of their argument, but also of the excitement, complexity, and value of these early texts. They are gospellers going forth with the word of pre-modern literature: green converts, but convinced (most of them, anyways).

In this situation the grading experience becomes an even more explicit balancing between what the students are writing about (my evaluative expertise) and *how* they write it (shared evaluative expertise with the external). After the paper there is a *muntlig eksamen* — a short oral exam for each student with me and the external examiner, covering both the paper and the rest of the texts in the course. I am actually looking forward to making those oral exams positive learning experiences for the students, in a small step towards recuperating some of the lame guidance and questions I received for the only oral exam I ever took… (Will my whole career be in comparison to those graduate school years, sometimes better, sometimes worse, but never again with the same extraordinary time, mentorship, and library resources? Is it normal, some days, to miss my dissertation advisors more than my parents?)

Another peculiarly Norwegian system I feel I have begun to understand is hiking etiquette. While *ut på tur* in the mountains, when is it appropriate to greet those people you pass? The default answer is "never," since ideally you have the mountain to yourself or you must pretend that is the case. For the few other scenarios I have worked up this handy guide to help you evaluate when it is safe to nod, say *hei,* or even have a short conversation.

- Is it sunny out (or just Sunday) and there are trees around?
- Are there more than five people on the trail?
- Is it raining normally and not unusually early or late in the day?

→ Avoid eye contact at all costs (all altitudes).

- Is the weather really terrible (hail, etc) and you are above the tree line?
- Is it so foggy out (or you're just up in a cloud) that you suddenly come upon them?
- Is the weather really lovely and you are on a very obscure trail?
- Is it the first human you see after over an hour on the trails?

→ Nod or say *hei.*

- Do you both have small children with you of approximately the same ages, and you are on a less-traveled trail *or* the weather is very bad?
- Do you both have camping backpacks on, clearly on a *telt tur,* and it is getting late?
- Is it very snowy, nearly a white-out, and you are some distance from the trailhead?

- Is it exceptionally beautiful out, very early in the morning, and you are engaged in the same activity — running, skiing, walking a dog (i.e., not regular hiking)?

→ Try for a brief chat in Norwegian.

- Is the weather bad, and they are wearing jeans *or* regular sneakers *or* a normal coat?

→ They are tourists. Make sure they know how to get off the mountain so they don't have to be rescued by the Red Cross later that night.

- Are you both snowshoeing?

→ This is very unusual, so chat in a friendly manner, and they might even invite you to their mountain *hytte* at the end of a perilous icy ridge. But beware *Hansel and Gretel* scenarios.

Above all, don't take it personally if the Norwegian doesn't respond. And if you see them approaching while they assiduously avoid eye contact, don't be an American and say hi — obviously they need the mountain to themselves. Alone is not the same as lonely.

These guidelines generally translate to my department hallways. Maybe someday I will learn the names of all these people I pass several times a day; maybe some *julebord* when we accidentally sit with people outside our discipline. Of course say *hei* to colleagues by the copier, or even chat innocuously; but try not to make eye contact with others, and only dare a smile after at least six months.

The days are long here. Only vaguely dark around 12:30 am; quite light by 3:00. During the slow dusk bats flit in front of our living room windows, silhouetted against the darkening valley and the mountain far on the other side. The sunsets astound. "Nothing, in fact, can equal the beauty of the northern summer's evening and night; if night it may be called that only wants the glare of day, the full light which frequently seems so impertinent; for I could write at midnight very well without a candle"

(59). I like staying up late to write too, Mary. Especially with that cool air sliding off the mountain and into the bedroom.

Come and visit soon…

xoL

LETTER IV
November, year 1

Dear ———

We have been here a year now. I am teaching a master's course (think senior seminar) on Chaucer After Theory. Powered by Dinshaw's *Chaucer's Sexual Poetics* as some kind of immortal churning diesel engine, the course pairs tales with feminist/gender critics like Gayle Rubin, Cixous, Irigaray, Butler, Sedgwick, Halberstam. I dreamt up a syllabus that would challenge me too and give the students some theoretical frameworks to move forward with even if they never touch Chaucer again.

I am advising three MA theses: one on Hardy's *The Return of the Native* and another on Elizabeth Gaskell's *Cranford* (so I read those two for the first time this summer) and one on *The Great Gatsby* and *The House of Mirth*. Those were covered in orals, but now I wish I had not just the eighteenth-century novel but also the Victorian novel for an orals field. Well, I am sure learning a lot now. I have to say I do know how to ask much better questions of strange texts than I did back then. *Cranford* was a surprise winner — a kind of secret feminist utopia, more complex and moving than you might first assume. ("Have you any red silk umbrellas in London?" The narrator is marvelous.) For these students I just try to help them develop sharp close readings, strong arguments, engaging what critics they find, since I can do less about recommending specific critics and necessary historical angles. But fortunately there is an MA thesis Work-in-Progress weekly seminar where all the faculty and students give feedback on draft material for each student — crucial for getting fresh criticism and theory tips and catching oversights — plus one of those faculty will be the internal examiner for these theses (I won't be involved in grading at all). I learn a lot from my colleagues' feedback. They are kind, and sharp, and smart.

My Norsk is getting *ganske bra.* They have two main forms of the language: *bokmål,* most closely related to the Danish language that ruled for recent centuries, and *nynorsk,* a kind of "authentic" Norwegian the way it was before Swedish and Danish influence — basically a reconstructed language by this linguist guy who traveled around the country recording dialects (and whose gruff face graces the bottles of Kinn, a Norwegian craft beer you would love). In addition, at least in spoken form, each micro-region has its own strong dialect and accent, with the high mountains and equally deep fjords isolating people and their languages over millennia. We only learn bokmål in class. Nynorsk kind of looks like everything is spelled wrong, with lots of random words thrown in. So in parallel to the feel of reading Middle English. In fact my working theory is that Norwegian speakers are perfectly set up to read Middle English for two reasons: they have both the modern English cognates ready, as well as a whole set of Norse/Germanic cognates to pull from; and they are experienced in accommodating great variation in spelling and dialect already, from their experience with bokmål and nynorsk and all the huge range of dialects spoken today. They also read ME aloud beautifully by just importing their Norwegian accent. It warms the cockles of my heart to hear these students recite Chaucer for the first time.

I use the historical connections between medieval English and Norwegian to help justify the inclusion of original texts in the entry-level survey and upper-level classes: Look! They can do Middle English because they have great linguistic competency! The cognates jump right out at them! Also, the students in the English program take both literature and linguistics simultaneously, so they get a lot of History of the English language, etc., which makes my job a lot easier in terms of actually teaching Middle English.

In other news I have been doing a lot of mountain running. I ran a crazy race in August, 800 m (2624 ft) straight up a mountain for 3.7 kilometers, one hour of pain and misery and muscle cramps. Really not fun. I was not prepared. How could I have been? Twice as tall as my usual mountain. While it was blue skies and lovely views at the top, I was achingly lonely with no one including me in their celebrations (why would they? they don't know me, no reason to include me, Welcome to Norway) and I chose a long wild lonesome path back down, which ended up being another six miles across a ridge and following a river back into the valley through farms and finally meeting the fjord and my ferry home. Just as in 1796: "Arrived at the ferry, we were still detained; for the people who attend at ferries have a stupid kind of sluggishness in their manner, which is very provoking when you are in haste. At present I did not feel it; for scrambling up the cliffs, my eye followed the river as it rolled between the rocky banks; and to complete the scenery, they were covered with firs and pines, through which the wind rustled, as if it were lulling itself to sleep with the declining sun" (80).

xoL

LETTER V
August, year 2

Dear ———

I got tired of not having any lectures I wanted to go to, or ever meeting any researchers outside my department, so I started the UiB Literature and Religion Research Group. Really a PhD student gave me the idea — she works on Blake and mysticism and she too felt like she fell through the cracks of other research groups, no common minds with which to rave about poetry and exegesis. Through the research group I have met lots of new interesting researchers at UiB, including a professor in a neighboring department — basically comp lit but also Norwegian literature and digital culture — who works on medieval devotional culture and perception and memory and all kinds of interesting things, and sometimes he stops by my office and he recognizes the books on my shelf and we talk about how great Aquinas is.

So now the research group has a program of lectures and writing workshops for the semester and it is exciting. At the opening event I was part of a panel that gave mini-talks exploring literature and religion, and I was pleased to have some of my English literature colleagues (modernists, Americanists, etc) in the audience so I could give them a taste of some of the best medieval stuff out there. I talked about how the *Pearl*-poet uses the very *form* of poetry, and the semantic flexibility upon which poetry hinges, to probe theological quandaries and try to figure out how grief and love and consolation work. That the poor man can't really understand why he hurts so much and struggles to wrap his head around what the maiden says — and he fails, like we all do — and how beautiful, detailed, crafted, complex, lace-like poetry is our human way of bringing form and sense and some consolation to an often painful and ugly world. You know now that I actually have a young daughter myself I can't read certain parts of that poem in front of others, as I found my face covered in tears in a coffee shop the other day… Though I think crying in public over poetry makes you a real professor, *ikke sant*?

From the seeds sown in my seminar on Visions and Madness two years ago I have reaped a master's student advisee writing on an awesome medieval topic he proposed: how death doesn't work in *Sir Gawain, The Vision of Tnugdale,* and a few *Canterbury Tales*. He is working the uncanny Freudian angle but I still need some leads on zombie theory. Speaking of theory, Jack (aka Judith) Halberstam gave a lecture here in the spring at the *Litteraturhuset*, a kind of public space for cultural and literary events, that also has a bookstore and café and (amazing) restaurant. I encouraged my MA students who read Halberstam on female masculinities to come along, and many of them did. The talk was engaging and thought-provoking though I didn't agree with all of it. Most of all just being there I felt a real sense of intellectual community and curiosity.

Last week I ran a trail race that went from the Hardanger fjord up to the Folgefonna glacier—from 50 to 1450 meters (4757 ft)—11 kilometers. Running from one climate to another, from a soft ferny forest covered in moss and occasional sheep, past blueberry bushes and low shrubs, to cold sharp boulders where only lichen lives, across snow that never melts. It was hard and spectacularly fun, especially the last half hour running through fierce winds past clear glacial lakes with blue ice gleaming through and the horizon bringing together the looming depthless white glacier and very low clouds. As we raced higher and higher, "nature resumed an aspect ruder and ruder, or rather seemed the bones of the world waiting to be clothed with every thing necessary to give life and beauty. Still it was sublime" (dear Mary! 76). The *mål* or finish was at a little *kjempe koselig hytte* called Fonnabu where they gave us hot fruit soup (it was gross). Fortunately I roped three other *modige* women into running it with me: smart, kind, tough, adventurous women. Mostly it was a feminist activist move on my part as we almost doubled the number of female finishers from last year. Only 36 people ran in total.

So things are going well. I miss squirrels and swiss chard; friendly strangers; playing in dry leaves in the fall; talking about my research in the hallway; students spontaneously stopping by to chat about Chaucer, etc. (*not* part of the culture here—can I change that?). I don't miss guns; being afraid to walk alone at night; getting sunburned (takes some effort); the tenure clock; bigotry and super huge egos (also here, but less obvious). I am not lonely at work. Lovely colleagues, even if they can't give me easy answers to hard questions that I must wrestle with alone in my office—in front of my sun lamp and ~~dying~~ dead orchids.

Still, still, I agree with Mary: "The country still wore a face of joy—and my soul was alive to its charms" (119)—still we give Norway a chance, and I become more of a missionary medievalist every day.

When will you visit?

xoL

Being a Medievalist in an A-medieval Country and in a Region Overcrowded with Medievality: Two Stories from Brasil and the Western Balkans

Ardian Muhaj, Qendra e Studimeve Albanologjike

Being a medievalist in the Western Balkans, a place overcrowded with medieval documents and monuments (and competing modern explanations of such documents and monuments), can lead a scholar to feel trapped in the midst of plenty. The feeling of isolation this causes is somewhat like the social isolation and loneliness many people experience in modern cities. The feeling is only heightened by the political determinism and interference that medievalists experience in places like the Western Balkans, where almost every site and monument of medieval significance is reclaimed from different countries. The medievalist often faces a politically imposed isolation or alienation, wherein even historians of neighboring countries try to avoid cooperation. How does this politically-imposed isolation compare to the geographically imposed isolation of a place like Brasil? In other words, how does a socio-politically created "lone" medievalist compare to the experience of a medievalist in a place far removed from the historical context she studies?

I have conducted a short interview with Cybele C. Almeida, a medievalist from the Federal University of Rio Grande do Sul in Brasil. I follow the remarks of my Brasilian colleague with a brief explanation of my experience from the Western Balkans.

I began by asking about some of the positive and negative aspects of being a medievalist in Brasil. According to Almeida:

> The first point of the list is, paradoxically, positive and negative at the same time: the fact that there are few teachers/ medieval history researchers in Brasil means that we have to deal with a very wide reality, in the spatial and temporal point of view. So, although most of us have an area of expertise — in my case the late Middle Ages and the urban environment — nearly all of us are required to keep updated and teach about Byzantium, Islam, and the European middle ages, or the 5th to the 15th centuries. That, on the one hand, hinders specialization — which is the tendency of our and other disciplines — but then offers a comprehensive vision and the ability to understand and make connections between these different realities.
>
> Another major difficulty is access to specialized literature. Despite recent initiatives that are making that access easier, such as the portal of periodicals CAPES, this is even more difficult in Brasil than abroad. It is especially clear to me now, coming back from my postdoc in Germany, that the problem of access is particularly acute here. Another big problem is the difficulty in funding for research in a broad sense and, in particular, monies for conferences and other events, especially outside Brasil. This complicates the exchange of ideas and academic upgrading and makes our production something that often repeats itself, with little chance of deepening and diversification.
>
> One positive, I think, is that our research, like the formation of our country itself, represents a pluralistic tradition. Despite the predominance of French historiography, we also

have contact with, and openness to, German, American, Iberian, and other constructions of history.

Almeida describes a situation where the medievalist is "lonely" due to not being surrounded by fellow medievalists. Now, if we compare the positive and negative sides of both situations, I personally think that the Brasilian case has many advantages over the Western Balkans. One of the positives in the former situation is that a much greater possibility exists for a medievalist to broaden his or her perspective through the cultural contacts that Almeida describes. Another extremely significant advantage is that freedom of expression compensates for the lack of immediately accessible resources. This situation, obviously, is only improving with the advent of digital technologies that make possible greater collaboration with fellow medievalists in other institutions or countries. The simple fact that my conversation with my Brasilian fellow "lone medievalist" was conducted through the internet shows that a "lone medievalist" in the 21st century can be much less lonely than even a well-placed and well-connected medievalist before the internet era. This is even true in small Western Balkan countries such as Albania, Kosovo, or Macedonia, but collective isolation, or "group loneliness," is tangible also in Serbia or Croatia.

A recent example of the overreaction of political actors to a simple view expressed from the head of the Serbian Academy of Sciences and Arts, Vladimir Kostić, may illustrate the pressure that such academics are still under even if they need to say things that seem to them to be obvious or offer facts proceeding from their research and knowledge. Kostić, in a radio interview, simply said that we must accept that Kosovo is not actually under Serbian control. After Kostić's declaration the President of Serbia, Tomislav Nikolić, urged his dismissal, while the local media launched a campaign against Kostić because he allegedly had broken a taboo. Meanwhile over a hundred prominent public Serbian figures, including intellectuals, university professors, representatives of civil society, and journalists, have expressed their support for Kostić and the freedom to be able to publicly declare one's opinions.

Why it is so hard to accept and express something obvious? According to Olivera Milosavljević, Albanians are today unquestionably considered the greatest "enemies" of the Serbs. Contemporary writings about the Albanians commonly include racial stereotypes, repeated over and over again during the past one hundred years: that the Albanian people do not constitute a nation and that their lack of civil behavior precludes Albanians from establishing an independent state. It is accepted within Serbian public discourse that these sentiments, along with the opinions of non-historians, are valued highly in shaping historical perceptions. This is especially true in the case of conservative members of the Orthodox Church and the political class.[1]

On the other hand, in Albania the most important voices in shaping public perceptions of history in recent years have been a novelist and a literary critic. In other words, it is not the case that the medievalist is alone; rather, he or she is surrounded by an academic environment where the last word in historiography is dictated by "intellectuals" who are not actually (or primarily) historians, but are instead known as politicians and novelists. The historical description of a region with a structure as diverse as that of the Balkans is not an easy task for historians, but surprisingly proves very easy for novelists, politicians and clerics.

In Albania, as in many other countries in southeastern Europe, the textbooks of the Communist period dedicated to teaching history were highly political. History was, among the standard school subjects, almost certainly the most extensively politically-manipulated in Communist-era schools. Historians, during the fifty years of Communist rule, were kept isolated from the historiography taking place in the non-socialist world and from exposure to a range of different approaches to his-

---

[1] Olivera Milosavljević, "U tradiciji nacionalizma: ili stereotipi srpskih intelektualaca XX veka o 'nama' i 'drugima'," *Ogledi* 1 (2002): 218–31. It is worth mentioning that the author is a member of the project "Dialogue between Serbian and Croatian Historians," based in Pecs, Hungary.

torical events. They became accustomed to being restricted to historical sources from eastern European countries only when undertaking the writing of new history textbooks. The content departed notably from the previously dominant Marxist-Leninist interpretation of history, but not from contemporary nationalist views, many of which remain still unchallenged and unchanged in the present day.

Democratic developments in the field of history teaching had their impact, however: in the design of the new history curriculum, in new history textbooks based on standards issued by the Council of Europe and other European organizations, and through changes to the training of history teachers. The philosophy upon which the design of the Albanian history curriculum is based calls for the building of bridges between peoples, nations, and those of differing cultural backgrounds, to the end of eliminating misunderstanding and prejudices between peoples.

The competing historical narratives are very often seen as a major problem in the mutual perception of people that share a difficult past. Yet there are bilateral projects and mixed committees between Turkey and Kosovo, between Greece and Albania, etc., set up by governments with the goal of revising the way these neighbors are seen.[2] These bilateral committees mainly deal with two important periods: the medieval pre-Ottoman period and the post-Ottoman period.[3]

These initiatives (particularly one organized between the Ministry of Education and Sport in Albania and the Ministry of Education in Greece) and their focus on the revision of history textbooks for the eradication of prejudices with respect to nationality, religion, etc., has given rise to a public debate, in which historians, politicians, history teachers, education specialists,

---

2   However, over a hundred Albanian intellectuals, among them the Albanian writer Ismail Kadare, signed a "Petition against the review of history under the supervision of Turkish state authorities" in March 2013.

3   For a snapshot on these initiatives see Fatmiroshe Xhemalaj, "The Situation of History Teaching in Albania," *Albanian-language textbooks* (blog) (2 April 2014), https://albanianlanguagetextbooks.wordpress.com/2014/04/02/fatmiroshe-xhemalaj-the-situation-of-history-teaching-in-albania/.

and laypeople have been involved. Greek participants in this debate, principally parliamentarians in this instance, have called for the reestablishment of the Albanian/Greek Committee, which was set up in 2004 to revise the history textbooks of both countries. Many Albanian historians, however, reject the idea of shaping history in accordance with the wishes of politicians in both countries as well as the politicization of history textbooks. They argue that the revision of history textbooks should happen only as a result of bringing to light new historical sources.

I totally agree with Almeida that her situation makes participation in conferences, particularly international conferences, much more difficult and considerably more expensive than in Europe. But in the case of the Western Balkans, conferences and other academic gatherings are not meant to involve historians from neighboring countries. Generally, if we hear about some conference or research project that includes historians from different countries of the region, it is almost always due to European initiatives about fostering the dialogue between peoples of the region. Their impact, therefore, like their origin, is much less tangible in the academic climate than would have been similar projects originating from the countries' academic representatives themselves.

To conclude, I think that although it seems strange, a lone medievalist might be less lonely in a country like Brasil that lacks a European medieval past than in countries where the lone medievalist is expected to have a certain view shaped from and conforming to his or her society's modern viewpoints. These views, mainly nationalist in origin and nature, confine the historian, leaving no space for new ideas and approaches. As a medievalist you simply need to find new ways to stress the same old views, or new approaches to reinforce the same ideas, or new methods to reach the same conclusions repeated over and over for decades. Even the era of the internet has yet to soften this harsh academic environment, while in the case of Brasil access to technologies seems to be working every day to better ease the "loneliness" of the medievalist.

Is the Academic Medievalist Alone?

Kouky J. Fianu, University of Ottawa

The trend towards a "shrinking past"[1] is undoubtedly a reality that those of us working in American and Canadian universities have known for many years now. Humanities disciplines, devoted more than others to the study of the past, have suffered inordinately from this situation. The result, one that we as medievalists know all too well, is that we end up being the sole departmental expert on the entire pre-1700 (mostly European) world. The reasons for this historiographical downsizing are complex: administrative proclamations of declining interest in the humanities in general are but one piece of the historical puzzle. There is no need to enter into this debate here, though; what matters is the result. Where there used to be two, three or more medievalists, there is now barely one: a single soul who is often asked to also teach outside the period on more "relevant" issues. So, one it is. But does that make this sole specialist a lonely researcher? And is this a novelty?

When presenting oneself as a "medievalist," one automatically associates with all of the disciplinary specialists (literature,

---

[1] Terms used by "The Kritika Index: The Shrinking Past," *Kritika: Explorations in Russian and Eurasian History* 3, no. 4 (2002): 575–76.

history, philosophy, music, etc.) working with a unique goal, that being the study of the Middle Ages. This association-by-time-period has translated into the many university, regional, national, and international medievalist associations that have flourished in North America since the early 20th century. The situation can be very different elsewhere. The French, for example, still maintain strict disciplinary divisions among medievalists: the "Société des historiens médiévistes de l'enseignement supérieur public" (SHMESP) only brings together historians. There is no "Société française des médiévistes," like there is a Medieval Academy of America. The point is that, in North America, academics working in a medieval field see discussion, participation, and collegiality outside their discipline (more or less, depending on the individuals) as a real and significant option. As such, a medievalist-historian might be alone in his or her Department of History, but can still have links, or even work collaboratively, with a medievalist from, say, the Department of English or the Department of Philosophy. Multi/pluri-disciplinarity in North American medieval studies has been encouraged for a long time, just like it has been in Classical studies.[2] Taking advantage of this trend can help the medievalist to feel less lonely than some other colleagues in the same disciplinary Department who do not have such opportunities.

Moreover, because the Middle Ages span a one-thousand-year period (more or less), the medievalist is used to thinking across large time frames and in terms of both continuity and change. Exchanging ideas with colleagues who study other periods might therefore be easier than one might expect; doing so helps to mitigate what can be perceived as solitude in the field. The recent development of "medievalism" in academia — i.e., the use (and sometimes abuse) of medieval life, history, and culture from the early-modern period to today — provides a significant opportunity for medievalists to critically analyze the reception

---

[2] Hence, we see in grant agencies the existence of committees for "History," "Philosophy," or "Literature" in addition to those evaluating research in "Medieval studies" or "Classical studies."

of their object of study in other/foreign contexts, and to reflect on their practices. The medievalist can thus engage in a fruitful dialogue with colleagues, either through teaching, research, or public interventions. Medievalists can be alone among their kind in an academic unit, but they can take part in more networks than many of their colleagues: the academic medievalist does not have to be lonely even when working alone.

The other aspect of the question concerns novelty. Academics in the humanities tend to work alone, at best with a team of students. The research model used in the natural sciences, with teams of numerous members, multi-authored publications, and large laboratories, is not the one developed over generations by researchers in the humanities or social sciences. A science based on physical experiences requires huge amounts of human and material resources compared to a science based on digging, reading, and thinking. Understandably, the former relies on groups of researchers while the latter relies on individual time. Needless to say, medieval studies falls into the second category, with medievalists looking for their material in libraries and archives, isolating themselves to think, read, and write. This century-old practice is still the prevalent one. No better or worse than others, it is (for now) the most appropriate way to research and reach sound results. Digital tools like electronic editions or digitized manuscripts, which require collaboration between disciplines and which medievalists have been prone to develop, are still less efficient in terms of the amount of time taken to produce knowledge than are the traditional methods of research in our field. So, yes, medievalists, like many of their colleagues in similar disciplines of the humanities and social sciences, tend to work alone because it is still the best method to answer their research questions.

This is not to say that academic medievalists are shy and reluctant to share their findings. On the contrary, professional associations with their annual congress, their web sites, their bulletins, their blogs, and even their bibliographical tools witness the extremely lively milieu in and through which medievalists contribute to and build networks around themselves. As just one example, look at the *Regesta Imperii* bibliographic database[3]: what other field or discipline has free access to such rich, multilingual international material? Colleagues in other, narrower fields envy this fantastic tool.

To conclude, medievalists might not exist in great numbers on particular campuses, and their methods of work make them work individually rather than in teams, but their object — the study of the Middle Ages — opens them to other disciplines and other periods. For years, medievalists have met regularly, travelled from one library to another, and exchanged ideas inside and outside their field. Academic medievalists may be alone, but they are certainly not lonely. Or at least they shouldn't be.

---

3 *Regesta Imperii,* http://opac.regesta-imperii.de/lang_en/.

A Philosopher's Approach to Being a Lone Medievalist

Pilar Herráiz Oliva, University of Murcia (Spain)

First of all, I should say that I am a philosopher. If medievalists have a bad reputation anywhere, that is in philosophy. At least, that is how I felt in the beginning. That is how I have been feeling up to this point. The problem lies mostly with people's conceptions regarding the Middle Ages: a sort of dark, historical parentheses whose content remains mostly unknown. No surprises here. Anyway, my intention here is not to complain about other people's thoughts, but most importantly to share my own. Thus, I will start by what it was or what it is to be a medievalist within my academic environment, that is, in my experience, but I will also try to briefly provide our field with some constructive ideas in order to face the "I am a lone medievalist" issue.

When I told my colleagues in Spain that I would focus my research on medieval philosophy, their questions made me feel I had to justify my choice. It was already hard enough to explain to the world that I had decided to study philosophy, but it was even harder to find obstacles from people who should have been more open, since they called themselves philosophers, the lovers of wisdom. Not of every kind of wisdom, it seems. Furthermore, as medieval philosophy was not a widely-studied area — as you may imagine by now — the materials at the university library were close to non-existent. So I was left, not only with nearly no one to discuss my research with, but also with very few, if any, materials. For years, my best friend in academia was a very old but excellent Latin dictionary.

When it comes to philosophy, the prejudice against the Middle Ages came from an aversion towards religion. Most philosophers think of the medieval period as completely linked to religion, and, therefore, they assume that there is no proper philosophy as such within this epoch, since it cannot be considered as completely "rational" — remember, everything is a matter of faith, or so they presume. I believe in this way they show how irrational they are because their judgment is based on nothing but ignorance, while they claim to make an appeal to reason. Sadly, I have found a lot of this during my academic career.

Things were not better within our research seminars at the philosophy department, where Antiquity was far more "interesting." However, I have to admit I was allowed to present the influence that the texts we were discussing had in the Middle Ages. I did not have as much feedback as my colleagues while talking about my work, but I was prepared for that. There was only one exception, when they could not believe that Thomas Aquinas had said that the earth was round in his *Summa Theologiae*.[1] Didn't they think that the earth was flat in the Middle Ages?

In any case, my purpose here is to be as helpful as possible, and it is about time to try to be so. We, medievalists, often forget that we have a tool that not every field can count on, and that is solidarity among peers. We usually share our work and discoveries; we do not mind asking for help when we need it; and we are happy to help other medievalists — be it with materials or translations — because we are well aware of the difficulties all of

---

[1] "The astronomer and the natural philosopher both conclude that the earth is round, but the astronomer does this through a mathematical middle that is abstracted from matter, whereas the natural philosopher considers a middle lodged in matter. Thus there is nothing to prevent another science from treating in the light of divine revelation what the philosophical disciplines treat as knowable in the light of human reason" (Thomas Aquinas, *Summa Theologiae*, I^a q. 1 a. 1 ad 2).

us face. We may not be physically in touch, but we are a strong ongoing community. Another thing we can benefit from is the multidisciplinarity of medieval studies, which opens paths both for intellectual exchange and when applying for positions: history, philosophy, literature, religious studies, etc., converge in the study of the Middle Ages. Thus, when it comes to intellectual exchange, people from disciplines different from ours can give us great ideas. At the same time, we can apply for positions we might not have thought of in the beginning. A philosopher, for instance, can apply for a position that may seem to be for an historian of literature, and certainly all of us can — or should be able to, in my opinion — work with Latin to some extent, which is a great asset for many positions. We have to be more multifaceted and versatile than many other scholars, that is true, but I think we in fact are, even though we tend to forget that.

Another thing we should take advantage of is the increasing development of Digital Humanities. This should be done not only by being in touch with other scholars, but also by properly placing ourselves within the academic sphere. We are sometimes our own worst enemies and we tend to think that people do not really care about what we do. That is exactly how I felt when I was starting my research, and I promised myself not to feel that way ever again. Humanities have been questioned for a long time already, and we are not doing things well if we do not stand up for ourselves in this regard by being more visible, more present. Collaborative blogs, online journals, Facebook groups… we have a world of possibilities ahead and we should make the most of it. It is time to stop questioning or justifying the value of what we do and show it to the world.

These are, of course, very personal reflections on the subject, but if any of my contributions can help or encourage other medievalists in any way, I will feel truly satisfied. I hope we grow stronger as a community in which sharing our research is an everyday task, rather than questioning the impact of what we do. That day will come, and, then, those who are lone medievalists will no longer feel lonely.

A Lone Medievalist on the Island

Christine E. Kozikowski, The College of the Bahamas

Discovering a medieval French cloister in the Bahamas was one of the most surprising moments of my first semester of working at The College of the Bahamas (COB), where I thought I cornered the market on the Middle Ages. This fourteenth-century re-formed cloister and the talk given by William Whobrey from Yale was a reminder that the medievalist world is not so small. This closeness was also reminder of my scholarly identity in the midst of the complete and utter difference of my new situation at a college where I am the first and only medievalist. Transitioning from a large R1 university with active medieval programs in history, literature, Spanish, and French to a college whose programs focus on postcolonial Caribbean development was, while not unexpected, still a bit of a shock to my senses. My employment at COB has provided not only a number of unique experiences as faculty but it has also given me a new perspective on teaching medieval literature, as well as opportunities for research and development that would have never arisen if I weren't a lone medievalist.

Perhaps best known in the United States for its reputation as a vacation destination, The Bahamas is part of the British Commonwealth, becoming independent in 1973. Its history is similar to many Caribbean nations, although it has the distinction of being the location where Columbus first landed; it was settled by a variety of European imperial forces, Native Americans, freemen, and slaves, deeded to the British in 1717, and approximately 85% of the current population is descended from those first settlers. This historical past informs so much of the Bahamas' present, not in the least because Bahamian independence from Britain was so recent, but also because of Bahamians' desire to affirm their unique identity by distancing themselves from British rule and culture even as they see themselves as products of it — a traditional postcolonial dialectic.

It is with the past and present in mind that my perspective on teaching medieval literature has been most influenced. Although I was hired as a generalist, one of my main responsibilities is to teach the Early British Literature survey, a requirement for English and Education majors. I teach the usual suspects out of the *Norton Anthology of English Literature,* which is the required text, with its predominantly white and male focus as subjects and authors. My students are eager and their knowledge of the Middle Ages comes mainly from what little bit they see on TV or in movies; like so many undergraduates, they are surprised to learn that medieval people did not think the earth was flat and unnerved by the imagery of Jesus as mother. In our class discussions, my students talked about race, class, and imperialism with an openness that my American students had been unable to achieve. Through their conversations with each other and with me about these topics, I began to wonder about the continued imperialism which occurs through labeling British literature "foundational" and my role in that as a medievalist.

Recent analyses of the study of the Middle Ages have seen rising trends in inclusivity and an emphasis on making the Middle Ages accessible and significant for any audience. But the question is how to do that when a month in my class and about a week in Western Civ are the only exposure to medieval literature, history, and culture most COB students will ever get. And how to make sure that my class isn't just the literature of the conqueror, or of the expat teaching them, which becomes a challenge with a required anthology.

For my efforts, I worked to incorporate more lectures, readings, and discussions of topics that are of interest to my Bahamian students: colonialism, race, religion, population migration, slavery. Like most students, they want to connect to the literature they read and they want to picture characters in their minds that are similar to them. Therefore, conversations about Anglo-Saxon literature become conversations about race, migration, and slavery; *Gawain and the Green Knight* is now about female desire and gender stereotypes; Margery and Julian connect to Obeah and other Caribbean religious practices. Because of these adjustments, my students have enjoyed that the Middle Ages others the British, changing them from imperial colonizers into something different, something similar to their own historical identity. This critique of a shared European Middle Ages provides Bahamian students with a new way of understanding their own past as well as rooting them in that history. Moreover, it helps them understand their present differently since much of modern Bahamian society incorporates recognizable elements of the British medieval past.

In addition to teaching, I do all that I can demonstrate the importance of studying the Middle Ages. I recommend medievalists to invite for lectures; I apply for funding to research medieval topics; and I incorporate Caribbean culture into my research interests in order to provide a more critical connection between the past and the present. As the lone medievalist, it is my job to make sure that the Middle Ages doesn't become lost in the shuffle among disciplines. Because there is no medieval minor, program, or club (although I live in hope that there will be enough interest one day), I help with other programs because the more I get involved, the more potential I have to remind people that studying the Middle Ages is relevant.

In academia, we hold high the tenure-track job regardless of the recent arguments against it. Graduate students and faculty compete on the market for a shrinking number of opportunities and a growing number of temporary positions amidst fears of impermanence. Opportunities for working abroad may be scary to some, but I would recommend that those who are willing to explore something new, to do something bold, that you take a chance. Living and teaching outside of one's home country has unquestionable value, and it is a critical reminder of the importance of the diversity, acceptance, and challenge that being a lone medievalist entails.

Contributors

Sarah Barott has her BS in History and MA in English. She focuses on women in medieval Germanic literature and their ties to the ritual surrounding the warband. She has been working on outreach and the online portion of The Lone Medievalist.

Peter Burkholder is professor of History at Fairleigh Dickinson University, where he is also Founding Chair of the Faculty Teaching Development Program. He has won Teacher of the Year and Distinguished Faculty Awards at Fairleigh Dickinson, as well as the American Historical Association's Gilbert Award for the best article on teaching history. His research interests include faculty development, history pedagogy, history and film, and medieval warfare.

Diane Cady is an English Professor at Mills College in Oakland, California where she teaches and writes about the links among medieval literature, contemporary culture, and literary theory. Her current project, *Gender, Value and Economy in Late Medieval England,* explores the role gender ideology plays in the formation of fears and fantasies about money and value in the late Middle Ages, and is forthcoming from Palgrave.

Jane Chance is Andrew W. Mellon Distinguished Professor Emerita of English at Rice University and published her twenty-fifth book, *Tolkien, Self and Other: "This Queer Creature,"* in Palgrave-Macmillan's New Middle Ages Series in 2016. Recipient of NEH and Guggenheim Fellowships, membership in the Institute for Advanced Study-Princeton, a Rockefeller Bellagio Residency, numerous best book and article awards, and editor of three book series, including the Library of Medieval Women, she has recently returned to her first love, poetry-writing, and has published a book, *Only Begetter,* eight medievalist poems in Oz Hardwick's anthology of *New Crops From Old Fields: Eight Medievalist Poets,* and has a contract for a second book, *The Middle Ages.*

Carolyn Coulson is associate professor of Theatre at Shenandoah University in Virginia, where she teaches both academic and acting courses and directs theatre productions. In addition to writing on early drama, she is featured on several original-pronunciation recordings of medieval drama. She is currently writing a play and working on a project which applies modern physical acting techniques to early drama.

Michael David Elam is assistant professor of English and Communications Arts at Regent University in Virginia Beach. Although his primary scholarly interests are in Middle English literature, primarily the poems of the *Pearl* Manuscript, his teaching is mainly focused on Western and early British literature surveys, and first-year composition. His conference presentations and publications in recent years have focused on Great Books pedagogy, Tolkien and popular culture, and C.S. Lewis's view of the medieval world.

Geoffrey B. Elliott is a long-time resident of the Texas Hill Country and has been a lone medievalist more than once. He is also the Vice President (USA) for the World Fantasy Award-nominated Tales after Tolkien Society.

Kouky Fianu is associate professor in Medieval History at the University of Ottawa (Canada). Her research concentrates on the production, conservation, and social use of the written word in late Medieval France. After first studying book craftsmen in Paris and then forgers of documents, she turned her attention towards French notaries in the 15th century. Her most recent work focuses on the register of a notary in Orléans (France). The edited source has been published in paper and electronic version by the École Nationale des chartes (Paris): http://elec.enc.sorbonne.fr/christofle/index.html.

Danielle Girard is currently a PhD student at Lancaster University in the United Kingdom where she is studying gender and queer theory in regards to Star Trek and the evolution of fan and media culture. She received her MA from the University of Reading (also in England) and her Bachelor's in English Studies from Fitchburg State University.

Natalie Grinnell is professor of English at Wofford College in Spartanburg, SC. She received her MA and PhD from SUNY at Buffalo. Her areas of research and teaching interest include Old French and Middle English romance and contemporary medievalism, as well as the works of Geoffrey Chaucer and John Gower. Her most recent publication is on the use of digital storytelling to teach *The Cloud of Unknowing* to undergraduates.

Amber Handy is assistant professor of History at Mississippi University for Women, where she is also the founding director of the Kossen Center for Teaching & Learning. She holds a PhD in History with a doctoral minor in Gender Studies from the University of Notre Dame. Her research focuses include the cultural history of gender, youth, and education in early medieval Ireland as well as methods for innovative teaching in contemporary university settings.

Sarah Harlan-Haughey is assistant professor of English and Honors at the University of Maine. She researches landscape and animality in Old Norse, Old English, and Middle English literature. Her first book, *The Ecology of the English Outlaw in Medieval Literature: From Fen to Greenwood* (2016), is available through Routledge.

M. Wendy Hennequin is associate professor of English at Tennessee State University, where she teaches everything from medieval English literature to technical writing. Her research includes work on Beowulf, medieval women warriors, pedagogy, and the medieval roots of *Harry Potter*. Dr. Hennequin especially enjoys giving community lectures about medieval and Renaissance literature in order to keep from becoming a lonely medievalist.

Nikolas O. Hoel is instructor of History at Northeastern Illinois University. His research and teaching interests include the religious history of the Early Middle Ages and Byzantium.

Sarah Huff recently finished studying for her MA in Creative Writing at Bath Spa University in Bath, England. She received her Bachelor's in Professional Writing with a minor in History from Fitchburg State University.

Timothy R.W. Jordan is a part-time English faculty member at Ohio University-Zanesville and Zane State College. He is also the site manager of Flint Ridge Ancient Quarries and Nature Preserve and the Historic Site Group Lead at the Newark Earthworks. His medieval research centers around the reception of Geoffrey Chaucer and John Lydgate.

Robert Kellerman is associate professor of English at the University of Maine at Augusta. He teaches composition, a wide range of courses in medieval and Renaissance English literature, and history of the English language.

Christine Kozikowski is assistant professor at the University of The Bahamas, where she teaches early courses on early British literature, the novel, and first-year writing. Her research focuses primarily on Middle English literature, particularly Middle English romances, Chaucer, and the Gawain-poet.

Justine Marsella is currently a graduate student at Fitchburg State University in Massachusetts where she is pursuing a MS in School Guidance Counseling. She received her Bachelor's from Fitchburg State University in Psychological Science, with a minor in History.

Ann M. Martinez is assistant professor of English at Kent State University at Stark, where she teaches classes on Old and Middle English literature, the Arthurian legend, depictions of women in medieval and early modern literature, and Shakespeare. She received her PhD from the University of Kansas with a dissertation on the depictions of environmental awareness in medieval literature.

Aubri Anne McVey has taught extensively at Indiana University-Bloomington, Butler University, and Wabash College. She received her PhD from Indiana University-Bloomington in 2013. Her research and teaching interests are interdisciplinary. Her medieval research includes: textual studies; representations of the body and gender in medieval French literature; and vestiges and transpositions of the topoi of French medieval lyric poetry in Wagner, the twentieth century novel, and the artwork of Pablo Picasso.

Laura Saetveit Miles is associate professor (førsteamanuensis) of English literature in the Department of Foreign Languages at the University of Bergen, Norway. Previously she was a fellow of the Michigan Society of Fellows, and received her PhD in English and MPhil in Medieval Studies from Yale University, following an MPhil at the University of Cambridge. Her research interests include medieval women's writing, visionary literature, Marian studies, manuscripts, the Birgittine Order, and feminist theory.

Ardian Muhaj is a faculty member of the Institute of History, Center for Albanological Studies, Tirana, Albania. He is a member of the Portuguese Academy of History, Lisbon, Portugal. He has a PhD in Medieval History from the University of Lisbon, specializing on the economic impact of the Hundred Years War on the economic landscape of Europe in the later Middle Ages.

Rachel Munson is part of The Lone Medievalist staff. She is a 2015 graduate from Bemidji State University where she received a Bachelor's in History and the Humanities as well as an English minor. She studies Medieval Scandinavia and Iceland, Old Norse and Viking Cultures, and is now living in Bemidji working professionally in marketing and outreach.

Andrew Pfrenger is the Honors Program Coordinator at Kent State University-Salem and co-host of the *Saga Thing* podcast. His research interests include Old Norse and Anglo-Saxon literature.

Alicia Protze recently finished studying her MA in Arts and Cultural Management at King's College London. She received her Bachelor's in History from Fitchburg State University.

Abbie Rosen is currently studying at Suffolk University Law School, working towards her J.D. She received her Bachelor's in English Studies with a minor in History from Fitchburg State University.

Courtney E. Rydel is assistant professor of English at Washington College. She holds a PhD in English from the University of Pennsylvania, and her current book project traces the reception of women saints in vernacular translations of the *Golden Legend*.

Michelle M. Sauer is professor of English and Gender Studies at the University of North Dakota (Grand Forks, ND). Her latest book is *Gender in Medieval Culture* (Bloomsbury, 2015). Sauer specializes in Middle English language and literature, especially women's devotional literature and monastic texts, and publishes regularly on anchoritism, mysticism, asceticism, hagiography, queer/gender theory, monasticism, and Church history. Of course, being a Lone Medievalist, she also researches and teaches almost everything in the period.

John P. Sexton is co-founder of The Lone Medievalist. He is associate professor of English at Bridgewater State University and co-host of the *Saga Thing* podcast. His research interests include Old Norse literature and culture, Anglo-Saxon literature and culture, and medieval disability studies.

Alicia Spencer-Hall is a Junior Research Fellow at the Institute of Advanced Studies at University College London. She is currently working on a project investigating depictions of chronic pain in medieval texts, considered in conjunction with modern theories of disability, illness, and queer temporality. Her book *Medieval Saints and Modern Screens: Divine Visions as Cinematic Experience* is forthcoming from Amsterdam University Press.

Robert Stauffer is assistant professor of English, specializing in medieval and Renaissance literature, at Dominican College of Blauvelt in Orangeburg, New York. He has co-edited a volume for Brill's Companion series focusing on Marguerite Porete due out in March 2017. His chapter in the Companion focuses on the Middle English translations of Marguerite's *Mirror of Simple Souls*. He is proud of the opportunity to bring medieval literature to a new audience at a school that requires at least one medieval class as part of the General Education curriculum.

Jackilyn Teague is a writer and actress currently working on both a novel and graphic novel. She received her Bachelor's from Fitchburg State University in English Studies.

Lee Templeton is associate professor of English at North Carolina Wesleyan College. His research focuses on issues of gender, grief, and chivalric identity in medieval romance. His work has appeared in *Medieval Perspectives, Preternature,* and the *Sixteenth Century Journal.*

Kisha G. Tracy is co-founder of The Lone Medievalist. She is associate professor of English Studies and Co-Coordinator of the Center for Teaching and Learning at Fitchburg State University in Massachusetts. Her main research interests include medieval memory and confession, medieval disability, and higher education pedagogy.

Misty Urban is the author of *Monstrous Women in Middle English Romance* and co-editor of *Melusine's Footprint: Tracing the Legacy of a Medieval Myth,* part of Brill's Explorations in Medieval Culture series. She teaches and runs the writing center at Muscatine Community College in Muscatine, IA.

Holly M. Wendt is assistant professor of English at Lebanon Valley College, where she teaches medieval literature and creative writing. She has been the recipient of writing fellowships from the Jentel Foundation and the American Antiquarian Society, and her writing, scholarly and creative, has appeared in *The CEA Critic, Barrelhouse, Memorious,* and elsewhere.

Tiffany A. Ziegler is assistant professor at Midwestern State University. She received a BA from Hastings College in Hastings, Nebraska, a MA from Texas Tech University in Lubbock, Texas, and a PhD from the University Missouri in Columbia, Missouri. Dr. Ziegler's expertise include Medieval history, the Crusades, Greece and Rome, the Mediterranean world, Renaissance and Reformation Europe, and World history, while her research interests include Saint John hospital — the subject of her manuscript — urban society, medieval health care, and the history of charity.

www.ingramcontent.com/pod-product-compliance
Lightning Source LLC
Chambersburg PA
CBHW071733150426
43191CB00010B/1561